Learning
for
Teachers

Edward Arthur Townsend

Associate Professor

Paul J. Burke

Associate Professor

School of Education, City College
of the City University of New York

The Macmillan Company   *New York*

Macmillan New York, London

A Division of the Crowell-Collier Publishing Company

© The Macmillan Company 1962

Second Printing

Library of Congress catalog card number: 62-16964

The Macmillan Company, New York
Macmillan New York, London
Brett-Macmillan Ltd., Galt, Ontario

Printed in the United States of America

contents

contents

foreword

THE PURPOSE OF THIS TEXT, as indicated by its title, is to present the established facts about human learning to those who have chosen teaching as a profession.

Good teachers are those who succeed in promoting greater development and better understanding in their pupils. Books or courses, in themselves, will not produce superior teachers, but they can upgrade the performance of those who are motivated to learn more about the dual processes of learning and teaching. Those who understand the principles of psychology and of methodology are likely to be better equipped for their role as educators.

Theorists have generally paid only passing attention to the problems of translating their findings to the classroom situation. On the other hand, methodologists usually focus on the "how-to" aspects of teaching.

This book is intended to bridge the gap between the general principles of psychology and the courses in methods of teaching. The concentration here is on the behavior underlying teaching and learning. It is hoped that the explanations of concepts and phenomena will highlight the rationale of various teaching procedures and produce a general understanding which can be readily transferred from one set of circumstances to another.

There are several questions facing every teacher:

(1) How can I best encourage the desire to learn?
This theme is developed in the chapters devoted to motivation, readiness, the climate for learning, managing the classroom, and level of aspiration.

(2) What conditions and procedures in my classroom will be likely to foster learning and which ones will tend to hamper it?

These considerations are discussed under the headings of conditions for learning, remembering and forgetting, reinforcement, cognition, and communication.

(3) How can learning be broadly useful to help my pupils meet the changing demands of life?
This development of wider applicability is indicated in the chapters on generalization, discrimination, and transfer.

(4) How must general principles be adapted according to various types of learning activity?
These points are developed in the sections on motor learning, serial learning, and problem solving.

(5) How can I judge the effectiveness of my teaching?
This is the content of the concluding chapter on the measurement and evaluation of learning.

For each major principle, pertinent studies are cited; where these are extensive, they are set aside from the rest of the text by a distinctive type-style. This permits the reader to move at will from general reading to deeper coverage of selected topics.

The principles and procedures suggested here are the distillation of years of teaching experience by the authors in elementary and secondary schools and in college. It is the authors' hope that following these recommendations will help the teacher to be more effective.

It is impossible to acknowledge the contributions of all those who have influenced the content of this book. We are greatly indebted to Harold H. Abelson, Dean, and to Arthur Mallon, Assistant Dean, of the School of Education of The City College of New York, for their continual assistance and guidance. Without the constant help and encouragement of our wives, the work would not have been completed at all. To these, and to many others who have aided us, we extend our heartfelt thanks.

EDWARD ARTHUR TOWNSEND
PAUL J. BURKE

1

introduction

aS CHILDREN AND ADOLESCENTS grow and develop, parents, teachers, and friends try to assist them. These adults may not understand how to help most effectively, nor give much thought to their role in relation to needs of young people, but their intention is clear—to help make life easier. They do not want the children "to go through what we went through."

Efforts to guide learning vary within two extremes. On the one hand are those who "throw the person in to sink or swim," or "let him learn the hard way." On the other hand, some persons provide too much help, standing by at every step of the way with excessive guidance. In fact, overdirection probably serves more to meet the needs of the director rather than the needs of those directed. The most desirable procedure consists of nurturing individual development to fruition through a series of graded tasks, each of which requires (and also allows) the person to venture beyond his present skill and understanding. While it is true that people often learn from their bruises and that the best fruit comes from the tree that is pruned, it is equally true that some never recover from the damage of certain experiences. The net result is that, whether the approach is close to one extreme or the other, efforts to guide learning may be too rough or too protective for maximum development. Most efforts fall well within the extremes and rely more on the capacity of the individual to deal with the world about him than upon the ability of others to guide him.

Most persons are hesitant about directing the behavior of others because they are aware of the great variation in the capacity of different individuals to cope with problems. Such people hesitate to intrude on self-direction chiefly because they distrust their own knowledge and understanding. There are, however, a number of basic considerations in teaching and learning, and it is these underlying factors which are the core of this book, with the following reservations:

(1) There is nothing to be gained by attempting to integrate the principles into a system, nor do the principles support any particular methodology to the exclusion of any other. When the basic factors are considered as a whole, they are often somewhat contradictory.

(2) The elements of teaching and learning are highly individual, that is, they apply to one person in a given situation. Efforts to generalize for several people or several situations often lead to contradictions.

(3) The basic factors in teaching and learning are confused by the notions of adjustment and conformity, and by the idea that everything worthwhile contributes to a smoother, more comfortable adjustment. If comfortable adjustment is the objective, then the guidance of learning becomes a series of techniques for avoiding annoyances and disturbances. Individual differences alone, however, without considering the content and the situation, are sufficient to demonstrate that both the comfortable and the abrasive situations can contribute to satisfactory development.

Adjustment, Individuality, Conformity, and Contradiction

The elements of teaching and learning are sometimes unsystematic and antagonistic, always individual, and always intimately related to personal development and acculturation. The adjustment and conformity (or lack of conformity) of each individual are the focus of attention. Since many people talk and write about adjustment, conformity, and individuality, there is a need for a workable description of the frame of reference for individual development in the social situation of the school.

Persons learn to further their individual development by performing in ways which satisfy their own needs while meeting the requirements of society. They need to appear adequate, and their feelings of adequacy develop from meeting the demands which are made of them. People always attempt to meet the demands both of society and self-realization: there is the crux of their struggle as social beings. The demands of the society in which they live are not always compatible with emerging self-development, and they cannot afford to relinquish either self-development or society. Consequently, people learn to perform for others and for themselves in ways which will give the appearance of adequacy while promoting feelings of self-satisfaction.

Learning and Personal Development

Everyone seeks adequacy. Children, adolescents, and adults all feel the need to appear adequate. They will change their performance for anyone who helps them to deal effectively with real or imagined inadequacies. They will cooperate with anyone who helps them to feel more sure of themselves, and will do almost anything to acquire and retain a sense of security. If a person is asked to add numbers, or to read a history book, or to clean the car, he will gladly attempt the tasks if he thinks they bring approval, provided that others do not receive more approval for doing something else. He will read history for approval if his peers read history for approval. If others are gratified because they keep the car clean, he will be likely to keep the car clean. However, if he thinks that others are not required to do these tasks, he considers the demands made of him to be unreasonable. If other homes do not require arithmetic, history, and car cleaning for approval, he resists the inconsistency. With greater maturity, self-approval will direct changes in performance; but until this happens the environments of the home, the school, the work-group, and the play-group direct what is done for approbation. Anyone will change his behavior for approval if the demands seem reasonable.

Feelings of Inadequacy Develop from Learning Situations

Although learning situations are intended to help us become more adequate, specific and obvious deficiencies are always coming to light. Such shortcomings aggravate feelings of inadequacy in any learner. A few mature individuals cover their annoyance with an admission of complete inability, e.g., "I'm not at all mathematical," or "I'm no good at science." These admissions serve as a self-excuse (i.e., a rationalization), although the admission cannot be considered as accurate. For those who do not resort to this kind of rationalization, limitations in a particular area of work or play serve only to emphasize the inadequacies. For instance, spelling deficiencies may mar all one's work and help to emphasize other errors in English usage, sentence structure, and punctuation. Poor reading ability limits self-expression in many situations. Deficiencies in subjects build resentments toward anyone who makes the defect more obvious. Conversely, anyone who provides help in overcoming real or imagined inadequacies greatly encourages personal development.

The Individual in a Democratic Society

Personal development, the need for adequacy, and the struggle against feelings of inadequacy are framed by society. Not only do people have to handle their own self-development but they also have to meet the demands of a democratic society while pursuing the goal of self-realization.

Democratic Responsibility. In a democracy, individual freedom, self-control, and a sense of adequacy are fostered by self-esteem which operates to further the interests of oneself and others. Respect for the image of oneself arises from a realistic self-appraisal, not to be confused with pride or conceit, both of which tend to be rigid attitudes. By comparison, self-esteem is expressed in drive—the free energy which stimulates the personality and which can manifest itself in forms either constructive or destructive to society. For instance, some psychologists believe that the drive for power is a compensation for the feeling that one is weak, contemptible, and unloved.

When a person's self-description does not coincide closely with an objective description of him or when his personal adjustment is inadequate, the phenomenon is called perceptual defense. This means that either the individual does not allow himself to become aware of what is threatening his stability or his adjustment, or he perceives inaccurately the facts about himself or his environment. Thus the adequacy of personal adjustment is inversely proportional to the degree to which experiences are denied awareness [77, 83, 85, 324].

Self-Realization. Self-realization fosters self-esteem and the acceptance of responsibility. Self-realization in a social being is an orderly process which takes account of his inherent characteristics, level of development, and the task he faces at a given moment. Self-realization means efficient perception of reality and comfortable relations with it; acceptance of the self, of others and of nature; spontaneity; problem-centered rather than ego-centered behavior; a capacity for detachment and a need for privacy; some autonomy from the influence of the culture and the environment; a continued freshness of appreciation; feelings for mankind; and deep interpersonal relations [262]. There is no need to quibble over whether anyone ever reaches such a state of being. It is important to point out that these characteristics facilitate personal development, to the degree that they are present.

The process of self-development must be orderly because such development permits the most efficient use of energy. When a person cannot come to terms with a task because of its nature or because of his own personality, a state of disorder develops. This is annoying to all who are touched by it and usually disturbs self-realization in quite obvious ways. Yet to encourage the fullest self-realization, individualism must be recognized and cherished [129]. Although the culture demands conformity of the individual to its mores, albeit with some degree of variation around a norm, the highest level of achievement is the creative fulfillment of individual potentiality.

Conformity and Acculturation

In the process of becoming, the individual is impelled to identification, a process which imposes the barrier of conformity [225]. To attack the conformity can lead to punishment from others and sometimes self-punishment. To conform or to attack those who are unlike brings the approval of those with similar standards, although this is dangerous if those to whom one does not conform are powerful and close. Thus no matter how one compensates, there is the possibility of being hurt. One way to avoid the anxiety regarding such choices is to adopt an inflexible position and take the consequences of defending that point of view. But most persons compensate by adhering to some identifications while being flexible about others. This position lessens anxiety by reducing uncertainty and inconsistency. As an illustration, consider the relationship of laughter and compensation. A person may laugh at the conformity which his identifications impose, but the laughter is the echo of his anguish (58). He has lessened his anxiety about the world by conforming, but does not want to be found out, so he appears to laugh at the conformity.

Acculturation leaves people no choice except to conform in most circumstances, but they struggle with themselves and the world to preserve some individuality. School, as an agent of acculturation, deals with and encourages these steps toward independence and freedom of action. Then, when children feel that the school offers assistance instead of requiring the submission of conformity, they feel free to enjoy their teachers and the curriculum, and to achieve the purpose of learning, that is, their development as persons.

The cultural role of the school is midway between the primary groups, such as the family and playmates, and the secondary groups, such as social and industrial organizations. The school aids the acculturation process by providing training and knowledge appropriate to the society. It offers a wealth of material with which the child can identify, and supplies him with persons who support rather than protect and dominate him. During the school years, the child must learn to live for himself, so that those who try to protect him often meet with unexpected opposition. Sooner or later, the child must break away from his would-be protectors and learn to use only their support.

The learning process includes a large amount of assimilation of the cultural heritage. The transmission of the knowledge, skills and attitudes of one generation to the next generation is accomplished through many agencies: the family, the church, the neighborhood gang, the school. The function of those helping the learner is to verify the quality of his assimilation. The experimentalist insists that mere borrowing from the culture has little value because it is not personally experienced. It is true that direct experience produces the greatest change in one's personal organization, but persons have neither the time nor the ability to learn everything firsthand. They must depend on the findings of others for a shortcut in order to have time to pursue their own inclinations and to seek their own truths. The teacher's role is to verify effectively the quality of the assimilation, whether experienced directly or vicariously.

In learning to conform to the culture, people do not give up their individuality without a struggle. Consequently, all statements about learning must include the adjustment of the individual to the demands of the social situation, but it is difficult, if not impossible, to predict the adjustment of any person at a given moment. The result is that there are no easy rules and generalizations to cover the learner and the situation. It follows that statements regarding how people learn and how others help them to learn are broad principles rather than specific prescriptions.

The Basic Contradiction

Children must learn how to be receptive to learning. Others can guide them and influence them by approval and disapproval, but each one must actually learn for himself. No amount of patient, careful direction, even from persons whom the child loves and admires, enables him to learn unless he makes the effort to do so. He learns the attitudes, meanings, and expectations which shape overt responses. As he learns, his overt behavior changes with the situation, that is, with the field of external forces and his internal state of tension. Lest anyone introduce the notion of a mechanical model, it is well to remember that attitudes, meanings, and expectations are covert and unobservable. Others guide one's performance as part of the field of external forces, and, as a person is able to combine the directions with his needs, he learns how to be receptive to learning.

Learning how to learn takes two directions: learning for oneself and learning for others. A person learns to perform in ways which satisfy others because this recognition bolsters self-confidence and self-acceptance. But more important to the self than performance for others is the personal organization of knowledge and information which contributes to each performance. This personal organization evolves from the effort one puts into it. Although a person performs for others, he also needs to satisfy the self. The most effective learning takes place through the mastery of these two processes.

Learning for the self and learning for others are basically incompatible, because we rarely meet the demands of others and gratify our own desires in the same action. Usually we suit ourselves to some degree or we pursue activities which we think will bring approval from others. Because both are combined differently in each situation, and because self-learning and the situation are different with the content of each subject of study, the essentials of teaching and learning are not integrated into a system or method. Whenever one attempts to organize the basic factors into a method, he emphasizes the contradictions—contradictions which evaporate if one considers the dual aspect of self-learning, the differences in each situation, and the differences in the content of each subject. There may be systems and methods, but even these may produce more confusion than enlightenment.

Education

In the light of what has been said of individual development and democratic society, teaching to educate requires emphasis on what the pupil can be encouraged to say, think, do, and feel, rather than on what the teacher says, thinks, and does [380]. If this emphasis on the pupil's reactions is coupled with the fact that individuals behave according to the way things seem to them and that the most important ideas are those which individuals acquire about themselves, we have the essential context for education [84]. The emphasis is not on teaching but on learning, not on the teacher but on the pupil and how things seem to him.

Learning is acquiring new information, new or changed ways of responding, new understanding. Teachers help individuals in this development, and this is true whether teachers are encouraging study, understanding, thinking, skill development, or evaluation. Naturally, it is more difficult to assist individuals in groups, particularly large groups, but the same emphasis is required. The teacher supports individuals, enjoys their successes with them, and helps them with their shortcomings. Self-development is like rowing upstream; lack of struggle is like drifting downstream. As the teacher acquires the ability to see the world from the pupil's viewpoint, the individual struggle for self-development, the struggle to learn, becomes a joint effort.

2

motivation

hUMAN MOTIVATION IS COMPLEX. We react to various experiences, and each new one is affected by the accumulation of previous events. For instance, a person may become angry at a snub, impatient with the slowness of others or his own ineffectual activity, hungry for affection and approval, or distracted by thoughts of a family crisis when he should be concentrating on a school problem. Often, a person functions under tension while unaware of its presence.

Since internal motivating conditions change from moment to moment, although the external situation remains relatively constant, behavior is highly variable. The observer who seeks to interpret another's actions may often be misled or puzzled because of his inability to detect the motivating factors. Theories of learning attempt to incorporate internal influences, but the factors involved are numerous and intertwined. Here are a few examples:

Interests lead to the acquisition of knowledge, understanding, and skill.
That which appears to be *useful* and *practical* enlists great effort.
Confidence stems from personal control of people, objects or events.
Knowledge of progress toward mastery and achievement directs behavior.
The *uses of talents* and the *development of potentialities* are satisfying.
Curiosity stimulates search.
Love and affection inspire effort.
A sense of belonging or exclusion forces some choices.
Praise and approval make some activities attractive.
Blame and criticism discourage other activities.
Rivalry is a spur to achievement.
Cooperation enlists support.
Special privileges may corrupt us.
Sympathy and empathy entrap one subtly.
The search for security or *the threat of insecurity* influences decisions.
Motivation is the condition that incites action in any given situation and determines the direction of that action.

Thirty students enter an English class in high school one Monday morning. They will each spend forty-five minutes in that room—but how? Some will daydream, some will surreptitiously work on a neglected assignment for another subject, some will read another book hidden behind the text, one may worry about a family problem that arose over the weekend, and others will listen to the teacher's earnest words about *Silas Marner* and find them meaningful.

From the teacher's point of view, only that last group of pupils is "motivated," but in fact all thirty are reacting to their individual needs. The daydreamers are preoccupied because daydreaming is more satisfying than the lesson. Those stealthily at work on their geometry homework may be motivated by a fear of the consequences of not preparing the assignment. At any given moment, a person does (or does not do) a particular thing because of his existing motivations.

Teachers frequently have goals in mind which are not shared by many of their pupils. The goal-objects that the teacher believes desirable are often matters of indifference or even repugnance to the child. Appreciating a symphony rather than popular songs, reading a biography instead of a comic book, becoming a good citizen instead of a juvenile delinquent —these may be what the teacher is trying to inculcate during the school year. The child's goal of establishing his status with the gang may lead him to conform to the gang's standards and reject the teacher's suggestions entirely.

When a teacher "motivates a lesson" or "motivates his pupils," he is actually attempting to demonstrate some relationship between his goals and those of the students. When the pupils' community of interest exists within the school curriculum, the teacher's task is greatly simplified. The instructor in the automotive shop, who can show his pupils how to convert an old car into a hot rod, has no problem of motivation (or of discipline). He offers something that the students want. The same boys may be bored and hostile when the Social Studies teacher discusses the causes of World War I, because no relationship has been established between the war and these boys' lives.

Basic Factors in Motivation

Motivation and Adjustment

If the teacher depended on transitory interest, motivation would be a spur-of-the-moment diversion of energy. The long-term pervading interests would be a less precarious guide, but the general adjustment of the learner is a much more basic motivation [19, 148]. The constant need to adjust to the changing demands of life is the source of movement toward objectives. While there is life, adjustment is never complete; thus the basic motivating forces are always at hand, in spite of momentary diversions or long-term prevailing interests.

No matter what theoretical explanation of adjustment one constructs [296], it is still general ability which enables a person to cope with the changing demands of life. Adjustment is a broad term, and its interactions have been described by many authors (for an interpretation, see Murphy [283]). The description given here is concerned only with the effects of adjustment in facilitating or limiting one's motivation.

Satisfactory adjustment in relation to motivation is exemplified by the ability to deal with the events of the day. Coping with these daily tasks requires one to participate, to reach a conclusion, and to proceed to the next event. One does not participate at all by avoiding a task (although such avoidance may sometimes be quite realistic and desirable). One participates by directing himself or being directed to the task, and a conclusion may then be attained according to one's abilities. During this process, the abilities themselves are developed and expanded. This is an expression of life energy.

Adjustment is not healthy when a person is unable to contend, that is, when participation is too limited, and when tasks cannot be completed before proceeding to the next item.

When a task leaves an unresolved problem, energy is required to look after this remainder. As the unresolved residue accumulates, more and more energy is diverted, and even persons of high vitality eventually reach a point at which there is not enough energy to deal with the daily activities in addition to the backlog.

Sometimes there is no harm in leaving a task unfinished, but persons often feel the need to explain away their failure. These rationalizations further divert the available energy, and other items are overlooked while one is busy with explanations to himself and to others. The situation is aggravated by increased feelings of inadequacy, and the result is an uneven struggle to adjust to the demands of life.

To avoid this cumulative effect, one needs sufficient energy to exclude himself realistically from some tasks and to include himself in others. He may be able to manage these adjustments of inclusion and exclusion by himself, but often he needs help. Parents, friends, and teachers are the first line of aid, reinforced by the psychotherapist for more complex situations.

To give help, these people need two different sets of information: on the one hand, the demands being made upon the child and the resources available to him; while on the other hand, the demands as the child sees them and the resources which he perceives as available to him. Adjustment requires the balancing of the demands and the resources, and a realistic perception of the two. Helping others with the management of these factors is the highest level of human interaction, and the teacher is one of those privileged to undertake a share in this process.

This is not a recipe or a prescription, but the process of teaching, focused on the learner and his adjustment.

Drives, Motives and Incentives

Drives, motives and incentives may be considered as three aspects of motivation. While there are many possible interpretations of the relationship of these three, the following ordering is operational—it can be used by the teacher. Drives are aimed by motives and put in motion and kept in motion by incentives. Drives are the basic biological needs such as hunger, thirst, and sex, and are also basic acquired needs such as the need for affection and security. Drives are aimed and directed by motives—the major goals. Incentives are the subgoals within motives: the short-term, hour-by-hour objectives of our energy distribution.

Motivation stems from the lack of balance, the ceaseless adaptation of the organism. Hunger for food is typical of the struggle. The instability of the basic hunger drive is represented in all parts of life. For example, acquired psychological hungers such as the need for affection and security are frequently manifested by physiological hunger for food, resulting in excessive eating. Basic biological drives like hunger, thirst, and sex are present in many acquired behaviors, but whether the behaviors are innate or acquired, the drives are expressed as instability and constant adjustment.

Drives are directed toward goals. Hunger is directed toward food; thirst, toward drink. As a product of the living process, hungers and thirsts develop into tastes and appetites which are directed toward goals (motives).

The basic biological drives are shaped by a person's reactions to the environment, so that descriptions of behavior refer to a lifestyle and a life-pattern—the customary reactions of each person.

Consciously and unconsciously, events and objects develop as motives, as events which channel and direct energy.

Incentives are subgoals within motives, subgoals that are achieved before reaching the goals. If the goal is graduation from high school, the incentives include the daily and weekly subgoals which are reached and exceeded before graduation. If the goal is self-realization, the incentives are the minor triumphs and successes which occur each day. On a short-term basis, incentives work to provide directed energy for each hour of each day. The incentives often control all the movements necessary for development.

Intrinsic and Extrinsic Incentives

Incentives, like motives and drives, may be considered as either intrinsic or extrinsic. Extrinsic incentives such as rewards and punishments are external—they come from others and increase one's effort temporarily. Intrinsic incentives, such as prolonged effort, a knowledge of results, and the economy which is caused by an increase in skill and the correct interpretation of cues, are internal— they come from the self and are more permanent, not only because the individual manages them, but because they operate by maintaining efficiency rather than by intensifying effort [29].

Internal or intrinsic incentives involve the "total" person and provide continued comfortable relationships between the self and its surroundings. Internal incentives are deeper subgoals that are part of the value system and basic purposes of the individual [29]. They are the wellsprings from which cultural standards arise. Internal incentives touch more of the true self, as opposed to the self that behaves for others. These incentives enable learning to persist under very low or almost no drive.

From one point of view, however, all motivations are intrinsic. Let us consider the case of the high school student who wishes to play on the varsity basketball team. If he does not maintain passing grades in all his subjects, he will be ineligible, so he studies his mathematics and history although he finds no value in them. The common statement is that he is motivated extrinsically by the fear of failing a course, rather than intrinsically by finding an interest in the material to be learned. But in a very real sense he is motivated intrinsically by his desire to play basketball. That is his goal; that is what moves him to action; therefore, that is his motivation. It may cause him to study, to eat certain foods, do body-building exercises, avoid late hours—all in the hope of reaching his goal of making the team. These are merely means to an end.

One might probe deeper and ask *why* this boy wants to be on the varsity. This leads to the analysis of the needs which are feeding this particular drive—a need for status or peer approval, a desire to emulate his father's ability in sports, etc. It is often difficult for persons to determine their own reasons for behaving as they do, and it is more difficult for outsiders (teachers, parents, guidance workers, psychologists) to discover these roots of motivation.

Over the years, teachers have shown considerable ingenuity in inventing ways to stimulate the laggard and in attempting to plant the roots of school-motivation. These are some of the punishments that have been (and are) used in elementary and secondary schools:

> The simple reprimand
> Sarcasm
> Ridicule
> Lowered grades
> Demerits
> Extra assignments
> Increased homework
> Detention
> Suspension
> Expulsion
> Being sent to the principal
> Sending for parents
> Corporal punishment
> Banning extracurricular activities
> Ostracism by classmates
> Standing in the corner
> The dunce cap
> Withholding recommendations for job or college

On the other hand, rewards and promises of rewards are used, as in the following:

Praise
Prizes
Scholarships
Membership in honor societies
Teacher approval
Parental approval
Peer approval
Exemption from homework
Exemption from examinations or quizzes
Material rewards (candy, money, gold stars, etc.)
Extra credit for extra work

Such "sticks and carrots" are employed to induce pupils to pay attention to the content of the curriculum. Using these extrinsic incentives to induce pupils to learn has been compared to towing a car from place to place instead of filling the tank with gasoline. The pupil moves when the teacher pushes or pulls him with various rewards or punishments, but tends to stop when the teacher ceases to push or pull. Fortunately, as the car which is towed may coast a little, the pupil who is pushed may gather some momentum.

The basic incentives that bring about self-development for the young are acceptance and approval. Initially, they are external; that is, acceptance and approval are made known to the young by parents and teachers who reward and punish. Gradually, the standards of others are adopted. The young learn to walk, talk, and think acceptably. As they develop, they follow the standards of those who grant them acceptance and approval. Gradually, year by year, acceptance and approval are internalized; the mature person behaves for himself and for his own acceptance and approval rather than that of others.

The incentives of acceptance and approval work well for the vast majority of people because the desire for love almost always survives as the compelling motive. When acceptance and approval do not become incentives, others are needed. People who are not able to manage cultural internalization must be removed from society to hospitals and prisons. Those who can manage self-development within the accepted societal framework have learned to direct their energies.

Motivation is the condition, stemming from our basic biological drives, which energizes, selects, and directs our learning. All of us learn motives and incentives which channel our energies to self-realization and self-actualization.

Individuality in Motivation

Since the basic incentives are acceptance and approval, ego-involvement and reactions to stress are important to motivation. The roles of ego-involvement and stress in this case are peculiarly individual; this individuality annoys those who wish to follow broad generalizations and delights those who champion nonconformity.

Individual Differences

It is necessary to document the fact that individual differences are not the special province of motivation, ego-involvement, or reactions to stress. Individual differences are present in all behavior to confound our generalizations. Although dealing with specifics, people feel more comfortable when they are able to gather a number of specifics to make a generalization. Present understanding of motivation does not permit many generalizations.

Each person is motivated differently by the same needs. This does not imply a necessity for a new descriptive system for each individual, but rather that descriptions cover the common sources of individual differences. Cronbach defined a list of five needs in general terms. Maslow developed an integrated system of six needs arranged in hierarchical order. Both lists of needs describe common aspects of motivation, but neither list describes the needs of an individual.

To demonstrate the individual nature of needs, Cronbach's list and Maslow's list were rated by three classes of college students: two classes of 23 and 26 Juniors and Seniors, and one class of 15 recent graduates. Cronbach's list of needs consists of affection, approval from authority figures, approval from peers, independence, and self-respect, [90, pp. 99-112]. The 64 students were instructed to rate the most important need as five, and number the other four needs in order of preference as four, three, two, one. With these ratings, each student could assign 15 points; therefore 15 multiplied by the number of students in each class yielded the total for that class. The sum of the ratings given to each need is expressed as a percentage of the total for the class. Figure I (p. 20) shows the way these students listed their preferences.

Maslow's list comprises physiological needs, safety needs, love and belonging needs, esteem needs (achievement and recognition), self-actualization needs, and desires to know and understand [260, pp. 370-396; 261, pp. 402-416]. Maslow arranged the list in ascending order: the higher-order needs do not develop until the lower-order needs are minimally satisfied.

Using the same technique with the three classes as in rating Cronbach's list, and rating from six to one, since there are six needs, values for each need were derived. By treating the total score for each need as a percentage of the total score for the class, the values assigned by three classes of different sizes are made comparable. Figure II (p. 21) shows the ratings for Maslow's list.

The data from Figures I and II confirm that persons are motivated differently by the same needs. The ratings vary from what might have been expected, particularly in the areas of affection, love and belonging, and approval from peers. To support generalizations regarding the unexpected differences, the design should be extended to provide for several items: an adequate sampling, more than one administration to the groups sampled, systematic variation of the directions, and systematic variation of the word order in the lists, and the lists themselves.

This experimental work with Cronbach's and Maslow's lists of needs directs attention to experimental design, but the two lists of needs require no experimental data to support their validity and their worth. The understanding and intuition of the teacher and the psychologist need not always be verified experimentally to have great value in both thought and action. Data and statistics are important, but they should not be allowed to obscure the value of thoughtful and experienced judgment.

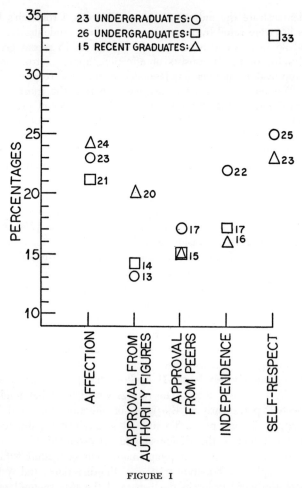

FIGURE I

Reactions of College Students to Cronbach's List of Needs

Ego-involvement

Ego-involvement may be either positive (causing movements toward self-adequacy and self-satisfaction) or negative (posing threats to self-adjustment). Both are motivational factors because they channel and direct behavior. The positive and negative aspects

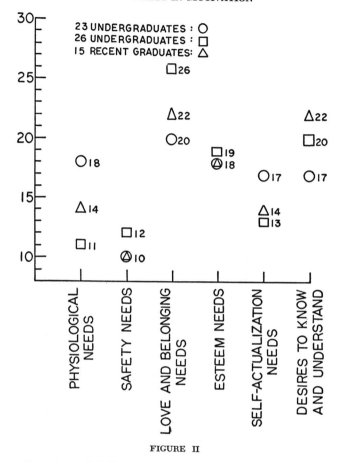

FIGURE II

Reactions of College Students to Maslow's List of Needs

are equally important because people can become just as involved either way. The dual possibilities of success and failure must both be present to involve the ego and cause the use of one's abilities.

Ego-involvement is an individual matter [196]. Whenever objectives are perceived as possible ways to make the self more adequate, energy is channeled toward these goals. Other persons may show us how activities enhance our being, but even while following their explicit directions, the degree of our involvement is individual.

If personal esteem is threatened by a task, attempts are made to avoid or overcome the threat while it is still possible to succeed. The thought of probable failure or self-damage is energizing. It arouses efforts to protect the self from danger.

The full effects of ego-involvement vary greatly from learner to learner. To generalize with respect to which events are positive (esteem-producing) or negative (self-threatening) is impractical. The attempts of teachers to arouse ego-involvement among students must be cautious and tentative, because the effects are so variable and uncontrollable.

Reactions to Stress

Since people make constant efforts to avoid stress or reduce its strength, it is a motivating force. Any situation that thwarts the flow of energy to needs or to the maintenance of self-esteem produces tension.

Stress ranges in nature from a slight pressure to a severe strain which may cause collapse. The events involving stress range from the choice of breakfast food to the selection of a career, or from success in a game of checkers to failure in academic preparation for a profession. The personal qualities that allow development under stress range from timorous approaches to boisterous participation in many damaging events every day. The stress which inhibits development operates through a similar range. The slightest stress causes some persons to withdraw from a situation, while failure, rejection, and disillusionment are insufficient to deter or deflect other persons from achievement and creativity. For example, the continued drive of Edison to discover a suitable filament for the incandescent bulb after testing hundreds of them is the kind of persistence under stress that marks the dedicated man. Stress can be beneficial when the dominant habits are correct; that is, when behavior is generally acceptable in nature and quality, stress can lead to greater productivity.

Stress may result from any event of life. A few typical situations would be: the beginnings of a new task, tasks that become impossible, lack of time to complete a task, deprivations, threats, disparagements, excessive supervision by our superiors, distractions, and failures.

Although it is difficult to fabricate situations that reproduce the stress of life situations, attempts have been made to study its effects experimentally.

For example, Lazarus and Erickson induced stress in college students by requiring an impossible task that was associated with failure through verbal instructions. They tested the hypothesis that performance under stress would be improved for some and unaffected or impaired for others.

The impossible task was an extended version of the Wechsler-Bellevue digit-symbol subtest. Between a first and second trial for the experimental group, verbal instructions were given that related their first performance to failure, e.g., "Many failed to appreciate the importance of this testing to them." By comparing scores on first and second trials for both the control group and the group subjected to the stress of verbal implication of failure, it was found that there was a significant increase in the variability of individual performance in the situation. Speed increased under stress but so did errors. The increase in speed and the increase in errors almost compensated for each other. College students with high academic standing, however, tended to improve their performance under stress, while those with low academic standing did worse and were more variable [229, pp. 101-104].

Those who could contend with the experimentally induced stress of failure responded by doing better for themselves, while those whose performance prior to the stress was characterized by inadequacy and lack of ability responded with another expression of their inability to contend.

Stress assists development, but it also reinforces inadequate and less-consistent behavior [71]. Before using such pressure to channel energy to various tasks, we must accept the facts that the nature of the stress, the nature of the material, and the nature of the individuals may interact either to promote development or, on the contrary, to confirm inadequacy and foster more random behavior.

Samuelson discovered that the stress from a summer session overload produced higher average grades among a group of students than their cumulative averages were prior to the summer session [334].

Possible interpretations of this statement include: the shorter, higher-pressure summer session was a better work period; or cumulative scholastic average is not a good indication of current work ability. What other interpretations are possible?

In a study by Rao, those under psychological stress (combined mental and physical) showed more errors in performance, particularly more persistent errors. This in part explains the influence of rigidity in problem solving [312]. Possible interpretations of this conclusion include: stress makes problem solving more difficult and hampers creativity; stress influences performance but may not cause learning in the desired direction; whenever persevering errors appear in performance, try to find and eliminate the sources of the stress. What other interpretations are possible?

Smock's study concluded that stress results in hurrying to a conclusion (prerecognition hypothesis) in ambiguous tasks. The stress of anxiety results in cognitive and perceptual processes that tend to preserve a familiar perceptual and behavioral field for the individual [362]. Possible interpretations of this statement include: the anxiety of stress obligates us to cling to the known and the familiar; ambiguous tasks do not stimulate our creative, exploratory outlook; to avoid the prerecognition hypothesis, the learner should be prepared for many expectancies so that they are familiar behavior. What other interpretations are possible?

Taking account of the interaction of the three factors—the stress itself, the material, and the individuals—the deliberate use of stress with any degree of assurance about the outcome is impossible. There is consistency in human behavior, but not to a degree that permits easy generalization regarding the attention of the learner. A person directs his energy in order to reduce or avoid stress, but under some conditions with some materials, he may choose to seek stress in order to cope with daily activities. Involvement in pressure situations may lead to self-development but may also lead to self-destruction.

The Role of Motivation

To repeat, motivation is the condition which makes energy available. Such energy is derived from the basic biological drives, then channeled and directed by motives and incentives. The whole process is so individual that generalizations are tenuous. There are some broad statements, however, which are acceptable to psychologists and educators [43, 284]. These are presented here under the following headings: the effect of words on motivation; motivation and learning; motivation, performance, and general educational capacity; the intention to learn; motivation in the classroom.

The Effect of Words on Motivation

The effect of words on motivation has not been fully explored, yet words are used to call forth and marshal people's energies. They are energized by the directions of others, e.g., "Get on with it," and, "Please arrange to be there and bring your records." They are energized by self-directions, e.g., "It is time I had the car greased," and, "I must remember to call home." Experiences that energize or inhibit (that is, which direct energy toward or away from a goal) are begun, kept in operation, and terminated through verbal symbols. People tell themselves how to do something, express feelings in words, manage daily and hourly activities with words. This much is known, even though the mechanism by which words energize or inhibit development is still something of a mystery.

For instance, "SILENCE during FIRE DRILLS" evokes behavior different from the reaction to "Positively NO TALKING," or, "NO NOISE by order of . . ." Verbal symbols energize or inhibit, but in either case they serve to direct feelings and behavior. When helping or hindering others, a person will usually give and receive directions in words. Apart from the semantic distinctions in symbols, which in themselves are a sufficient source of confusion to muddy any clear understanding of the use of verbal symbols (see Chapter 16, Communication, p. 234), not enough is known about how the directions that people give and receive energize and inhibit their behavior and the behavior of others. The directions we give ourselves sometimes inhibit behavior and sometimes evoke it. "I must arrange my schedule for tomorrow" may bring about the necessary arrangement or may only bring us to tomorrow annoyed with our unpreparedness. One cannot determine with certainty whether the directions given to the ten-year-old, the eighteen-year-old, or the forty-year-old will elicit cooperation or opposition. There is a degree of consistency in human behavior, but the ways in which verbal symbols interact with this expected behavior are not yet fully explored. (An analysis of verbal behavior tied to experimental work is found in Skinner [358]; the role of words in behavior is described and illustrated in Hayakawa [174].)

Motivation and Learning

Motivation provides the energy for learning to occur. But it is also necessary to learn how to direct the energy. When the healthy ten-year-old wakes from sleep, he has energy that he will use in a number of activities. At this early age, he has learned to direct his available energy to gratify his needs and to satisfy the demands of his immediate environment, represented by his brothers, sisters, parents, teachers, and peers. By age twenty, this self-direction reflects his personal needs and usually the demands of a broader and deeper immediate living space. He has learned, for his benefit and for society's, to direct the available energies toward a wide range of events and toward many persons. This self-direction is a continuing process. The task of the school is to aid the development of self-direction in desirable ways.

The majority of the young approach life—and school as part of life—with a healthy curiosity that matures in a sex-social drive, and then in the striving for power, position, and prestige arising from the drive for acquisition. When curiosity is encouraged rather than obliterated by boredom and drudgery, it arouses the energy necessary for the first six or seven years of school. By early adolescence, self-direction demands the rejection of many adult standards and some school standards. The new set of rules are established by the group with which the adolescent works and plays, the group which directs him most: his peer group. As long as the peer group is in school and engaged in school activities, there is motivation for school learnings, even though academic prestige is not important to many adolescents at this time. Academic prestige, the desire for "real brains," does not replace the standards of the peer group, but toward the end of high school most adolescents see knowledge and skill as ways to achieve and succeed. As the sex-social drive matures, the desire for approval and for status fosters sufficient motivation for learning. This usually spans the late teens and early twenties.

When a group of children reject the school and its activities as one of their accepted values, the school's teachers and administrators face an extremely difficult problem. Peer approval in such a group is given to the failure, the truant, the disobedient. Reversing such attitudes requires a concerted attack by all the agencies of society dealing with children—social workers, clergy, parents, as well as teachers.

The necessary energy for school-learning is provided by curiosity and allied motives that prevail until the standards of the peer group are more important than those of adults. Since achievement is available through schooling, the desire for more approval, for approval from the boy- or girl-friend, from rewarding adults, and from the self, redirects the energy toward school achievement as a way of life achievement. This is what happens when the maturing adult finds responsibility to himself to be more rewarding than responsibility to the peer group. This redirection of standards from the group to the self occurs earlier in females than in males because the male requires more time to realize how he can succeed. The most difficult time to provoke enough energy for school learnings and other adult standards, is that which is between the waning of curiosity and the arousal of the desire to achieve. The desire for approval and status, centered in the peer group and the self but sensitive to approval by adults, provides the energy necessary for achievement.

Motivation, Performance and General Educational Capacity

When one has learned to perform well, he obligates himself to even higher levels. Better performance does not replace general educational capacity. General educational capacity is the result of a combination of influences: intelligence, a background of knowledge and skill, motivation, and school adjustment. It is heavily modified by emotional factors, such as individual adjustment, dominance-submission status, and parental relationships. General educational capacity, the main determinant of success and failure, is one of the results of our adjustment, even while contributing to it [412]. There is, however, a critical level of motivation that supports good performance, namely, sufficient attention directed toward a task. Increased motivation beyond such a level cannot assist further, because it tends to limit attention by closing out or condensing observations so that full awareness is impossible. Enough attention for good performance is all that is required for learning.

The Intention to Learn

Several experimental studies have shown that intentional learners do better than incidental learners. Intentional learners are those who are under specific directions to learn [333]. They are more highly motivated, and they rehearse their learnings. The incidental learner gathers something from mere exposure, without special effort, specific attention, or specific intention to learn. Typically the incidental learner can recall only a small fraction of the material to which he has been exposed. This sounds as though intentional learning is good and incidental learning is bad. Not at all. Both have their place in common experience and in laboratory studies of behavior [24].

One interpretation attributes the measured differences between intentional and incidental learners to three variables, namely, the tests used to measure retention, the nature of the material, and the amount of work done [333].

Measured differences between incidental and intentional learners vary with the nature of the material to be learned; e.g., stimuli of high association value (bread and butter, pen and ink, Washington and D.C.) are retained equally well by both incidental and intentional learners, while stimuli of low association value (ZKB-HFL; NCQ-PVE) are retained better by intentional learners. The association value of an item is its place on a scale of associative strength ranging from the familiar and acceptable to the strange and unacceptable. Weak associations require intention, while items of high associative value may be learned almost equally well by either incidental or intentional contact.

These differences also vary greatly with the amount of work done. With more presentations, intentional learners perform better than incidental learners. In one experiment, Saltzman and Atkinson divided 160 students randomly into two groups of 80 each. An incidental group was read instructions for coding numbers ("Inspect to see how these numbers are set up"), and an intentional group was read instructions which began, "We want to see how fast you can learn numbers; learn as many numbers as you can." The learning material was a list of 14 two-digit numbers selected from a table of random numbers.

The task was essentially the same for all, but the intention varied with "find out the best way to code" and "see how fast you can learn numbers." Differences after two, six, and eight presentations were not statistically reliable. After 16 presentations, however, intentional learners had significantly higher scores than the incidental group [333, pp. 521-522].

Persons need to pay enough attention to a task to perform well, and "enough" attention varies from person to person and from task to task. Good performance will not transcend general educational capacity, but good performance requires sufficient attention for a task. Sufficient attention is the intention to learn, and intentional learners do better.

Motivation in the Classroom

Motivation determines the presence and vigor of activity. It is commonly assumed that motivation is the basic quality in learning —simply motivate the learner and all else follows naturally. If the motivation to acquire particular knowledge and skill is sufficient, learning will take care of itself. This is a misconception. Motivation refers only to the presence and vigor of activity, to the amount of the self which is utilized. Although motivation provides the energy that makes it possible for learning to occur, more is needed for the realization of learning.

Every planned classroom lesson includes a statement of motivational procedures. If the procedures follow the self-direction of the class, it will be easier to direct the pupils' energies toward the objectives of the daily activities and the purposes of the school year. Learning efficiency may be greatly impaired if there is neither explicit nor self-induced intention to learn.

Motivating the class toward an objective requires that attention be directed to the events at hand. The class is always potentially motivated because the pupils have energy to use, even if they are not cognitively aware of all the forces that influence them. In the classroom, enough of their energy is directed to an event if they pay attention to it, i.e., use enough energy for full awareness. When their attention is focused on events by self-direction, sufficient energy is assured to promote learning as long as necessary until mastery is attained. When their attention is directed to classroom events by adult control rather than by self-direction, the situation should be policed to a satisfactory conclusion. Sometimes the class grasps the adult direction as its own, but in most cases where self-direction is not used, the director must start the activity, keep it going, and carefully appraise the conclusion. Pupils motivated through adult direction may acquire some self-direction in the process.

When self-direction is available, teachers use and rely on it. When it does not provide attention in the desired direction in sufficent strength, the teacher should take over and direct, but always exhibit willingness to allow the development of self-direction. Self-direction is essential to promote complete development of the self. The longer teachers direct children, the more they lessen the possibility of this self-development and the more they foster dependency. The pupils follow their own direction, the teacher's direction, and combinations of these two. Teachers guide and direct their development best when they are sensitive to maturing self-direction in the students.

Self-direction in classes of 25, 30 and 35 pupils will develop if the teacher (a person struggling with his own problems) is sensitive to the class feeling and direction, and clearly perceives the objectives of the moment and the purposes of the longer time span (such as a school term). Obviously, less self-direction is available to the immature. The first-grader, the ninth-grader, and the high-school senior enjoy or are plagued by increasing degrees of self-direction. The ways in which they can find and express self-development in groups of 30 and 35 people depend on their readiness, the climate for learning, classroom management, and their level of aspiration. Chapters 3, 4, 5, and 6 consider the learner in these respects.

Summary: Motivation

Motivation is important for an understanding of behavior and learning, because it refers to a continuous psycho-biological condition that makes energy available. The ways in which energy is directed are learned. Learning is never complete, nor is adjustment. We are continuously adjusting and learning how to direct our energies.

Motivation arises from the basic biological drives. Drives are innate, such as hunger, thirst, and sex; and acquired, such as needs for affection and security. Motives aim and direct drives; and within motives are incentives, the subgoals one reaches on the way to the ultimate goal. Incentives, whether extrinsic or intrinsic, direct activities hour by hour and day by day. Incentives channel drives so that motivation is aimed and directed. Motivation provides energy for learning to occur, while motives and incentives direct and channel our drives.

Since the basic incentives are acceptance and approval, it is important that ego-involvement and reactions to stress lead to satisfactory adjustment and acceptable motivations. The sources of motivation are common to all, but are expressed individually. Common and individual sources of action, interest, and decision are present in adjustment to each event. Incentives that affect the adjustment of one person will not influence another; ego-involvement is a variable in the adjustment of each person; the amount of stress that is energy-evoking, but not inhibiting or destructive of drive, is individual. That which will adequately energize one will not be adequate for another. Motivation is often directed by verbal commands from others, but this process is not yet fully understood. The home, school, and community establish tendencies toward certain levels of achievement. When people have learned to use enough energy for good performance, they learn better. Enough, but not too much, attention assures that they are fully aware. Overinvestment does not yield a greater return; instead it narrows perception and awareness, so that incidental and casual learning is overlooked. This is a valid generalization, whether it is applied to the motivation of one person at a time or to the motivation in a classroom of 35 persons. Each person learns to direct enough attention toward each event for fullest self-expression. Enough attention is the intention to learn.

3

readiness

WHEN THE LEARNER IS READY he is more receptive and amenable to change and development. His "readiness" generally refers to the state of preparation, and embraces age, intelligence, level of knowledge, personal adjustment, and attitudes. All these factors must be considered, because no single aspect of behavior is *the* determiner, and because the interactions of the inherent, the learned, and the maturational characteristics are not predictable.

It is possible to refer to the role of each factor in readiness, but it would be rash to presume to describe the multiple interactions of the factors for one person, let alone for a whole class. Instead, there is reliance on the skill of the teacher to estimate readiness. This approach implies that the teacher understands and is sensitive to the demands of the moment.

Consideration of the state of preparation of both the learner and the teacher emphasizes the complexity of adjustment and teachers' limitations in understanding behavior. Timing and pacing draw attention to the appropriateness of activities and to the teachers' skills.

Age

The existence of different readiness levels for persons of the same age poses a continual problem for education. No matter what criterion is adopted for sorting students—measured intelligence, age, reading level, achievement scores of various types, and social maturity—it will be far from ideal. Of these, age is the single factor which is most satisfactory, since there are several factors such as body size, amount of energy, motor skills, and everyday experiences which keep in rough alignment with it. Even so, the variations within this constant are great enough to be a continual source of difficulty.

The Age of the Learner

A group of 30 children entering first grade in September usually range in age from five years, nine months to six years, eight months in age, although school entrance regulations vary from community to community. Among the younger children will be some who are immature socially and emotionally, even for their tender years, and among the older children will be some who are exceptionally mature. As a result, this entering group spans at least three years in development among the "normal" children (omitting extreme cases). It will take months for some of the slowest children to reach the point which the most mature have already reached.

As a consequence of this diversity, it is necessary to teach first-graders in several groups, based upon the likenesses and differences found within chronological age and other aspects of readiness. Two changes occur concurrently with the increase in chronological age: physiological or biological maturation, and opportunities to learn through varied experiences. The differences in physiological maturation are obvious to anyone who has ever looked at a group of children of the same age. The differences in types and amounts of experiences may be overlooked, especially by beginning teachers. One child's parents are patient enough and interested enough to explain things to him, to take him with them to museums, zoos, food and department stores, a concert, a trip to the country or to another city. In another family, both parents work and then, after dinner, collapse before the TV set. Their spare time may not include anything which can broaden the child's background—mother plays bingo two nights a week, and father bowls and plays poker. It is unlikely that these two children will be equally ready for various school subjects at the same age.

It is sometimes assumed that differences between individuals are greatest at the earlier ages and grow less later on. While this happens in some cases, the reverse is the general rule. The range between the extremes—in height, weight, social maturity, emotional development, reading ability, arithmetic skills, and many other characteristics—becomes greater as children grow older. Part of the resulting problem is handled by setting up separate classes for the gifted and the retarded, classes for those with special talents in music or art, remedial reading work for some, and advanced literature classes for others. In some cases children are moved ahead of their age group, although this procedure is no longer generally recommended [40]. No matter how such provisions are made, however, there will still be a substantial range of differences in any class, even in selected classes. Thus it is the task of the teacher to deal with these individual differences within the class by setting up subgroupings, special assignments, and remedial work.

To return to the matter of moving children ahead of their age group, a lively discussion always arises from this adjustment of the school program. The practice is not generally recommended because of the maladjustments which may arise when trying to correct the one imbalance, and because, when these achievers are moved ahead of their age group, they are no longer able to achieve as much as they otherwise might [40]. From your introspection, what personal attributes foster achievement? For what reasons should a child be moved ahead?

In a similar vein, it has been found that environmental factors have their greatest effect before school begins [104]. Whether or not one accepts this generalization (derived from Scottish primary schools), it does draw attention to the environmental factors conducive to achievement. Since the study of under-achievers is increasingly popular, what of the other side of the coin? What environmental factors are most conducive to achievement?

The Age of the Teacher

Statements about a teacher's age in relation to readiness are tenuous because aging occurs at different rates. Not all young teachers are enthusiastic and adaptable, and not all old teachers are dispirited and set in their ways. Generally, the younger have had fewer experiences and less practice in using their knowledge and skill. They usually compensate for their inexperience by their enthusiasm. Young teachers are closer in age and interests to their students and thus tend to sympathize with the students and appreciate (empathize with) how they feel.

The older teachers are experienced in handling school situations and practiced in using their knowledge and skill. They are usually set in their ways, but this, by itself, is not always a handicap to good teaching. When interests are too different from those of the young, however, and when intellectual curiosity has faded, the set mannerisms are likely to grate on the sensitivities of students and fellow teachers. The older teacher can usually excel the younger if he relies on the dignity of his maturity, on his empathy, and the stimulation derived from working with young people.

Although none of the possible generalizations regarding the age of the teacher is supported by acceptable studies, the generalizations stated in the two preceding paragraphs are tenable in the light of observation and judgment.

Intelligence

The term "measured intelligence" is used in this book to refer to tested performance on the intellectual tasks that predominate in school learning. The use of this label avoids a fruitless effort to separate "native intelligence" from "acquired intelligence." There is a second aspect to the term. Teachers work with measured intellect because this is the level at which the person has shown he can perform. Teachers may believe the student's potential to be much higher and they may strive to have this potential realized, but they work only with the student's ability. This present level of ability is the second convenient aspect of the term "measured intelligence."

The Measured Intelligence of the Learner

Measured intellectual level is important in readiness to learn, because a task is easy or difficult according to the learner's ability. Level depends on both quantity and quality. Within any quantitative level there are always quite distinguishable qualitative levels of intellect—as illustrated in the kinds of items from which the quantitative score came. The quality of measured intelligence in an I.Q. of 115 is sufficient in some cases for college work, while in other instances it barely allows satisfactory accomplishments in high school. When sufficient intelligence of good quality is available, the student can contend with each demand made of him.

The Measured Intelligence of the Teacher

There are two points to be emphasized about the intellectual level of the teacher, First, with advancing age, intellectual abilities deteriorate, but the deterioration is least in people who pursue activities closely allied to school learning. Thus teachers are exposed to intellectual stimulation and should experience minimum deterioration. The second point refers to the intellectual level of the teacher as compared with that of his students. In the early grades there is little problem, but in high school and college the student will often be taught by persons who are not as bright as he is. In most cases teachers know more, but are almost certain to have some students who have higher levels of intelligence. Such students are only a problem when the teacher enters into a competition to demonstrate intelligence. The resultant antagonisms destroy the learning situation. It is preferable for the teacher to find pleasure in the superior intellect of a student, profess his superior knowledge, and invite competition to know more than he does.

Individual differences are too great to support statements that are more positive than the two given: (1) Intellect deteriorates with age, but school-learning offers the best possibility of minimum aging; and (2) the student who is brighter than the teacher can be a source of stimulation and gratification rather than threat.

Level of Knowledge

All readiness is based on some prior learning. When the child comes to school, he has already learned much. If he has lived long enough and has learned to manage enough aspects of the world that keeps rushing in on him, he is ready to add to and reorganize what he already knows. At all ages, learning is a process of adding to and reorganizing what is known. The college student builds on what he has learned from living through the elementary school, high school, and the range of family and community influences. The range and depth of influences for the teacher usually embrace all of the above and more (chiefly from giving and directing rather than receiving).

The Knowledge of the Learner

The learner is ready when his level of knowledge is sufficient; the question of how much is sufficient then becomes paramount. Usually enough knowledge is needed to arouse curiosity, although the term curiosity perhaps diverts attention from the level of knowledge because that level is elusive, lying somewhere between ignorance and satiation. As an illustration, consider the sciences. The learner is not ready when he has no knowledge of science, and he is bored when satiated, but between these extremes are levels of knowledge which support the thirst called curiosity. As the learner begins to grasp and command the content of the sciences, his feelings of mastery enable him to extend his grasp and broaden his horizon. His comfortable command of knowledge in the sciences makes him ready for these and related subjects.

In arithmetic also, a certain level of knowledge is essential to readiness. When the pupil has learned addition, subtraction, multiplication, and division, he is ready to learn to manipulate all kinds of fractions. Any deficiencies that the pupil has in these basic number skills are an obvious handicap to the subsequent development of numerical ability, including the manipulation and consequent full comprehension of fractions.

All learning situations are not marked by such obvious stepwise development. Ability with fractions is the product of total development, not just of the instruction in fractions when the learner was ready. All learning situations are similarly dependent, although not as obviously, on the present level of knowledge as a determiner of readiness for learning.

The Knowledge of the Teacher

Age and intelligence predispose the teacher in some degree but not nearly as fully as the level of knowledge. Many persons accept the statement that one never really knows content until he teaches it. This statement only appears to be true. As students, few teachers learned all of everything in a subject. As teachers, they have found that they are responsible for the whole subject, and they take time to learn it all. Whenever a teacher has not disciplined himself in this respect, his incomplete knowledge is bound to embarrass him.

In addition to this thorough preparation, the amount of practice a good teacher receives in rehearsing others raises his own level of knowledge. If people who do not teach would practice as assiduously, they too could master the subject matter.

There is a generalization regarding knowledge and teaching which needs to be laid to rest, namely, that the teacher who learned easily will teach poorly, and conversely, that the teacher who had to "plug" for the content will teach well, presumably because he appreciates the difficulties involved. There is no validity in this generalization. Teaching skill depends on the ability to organize content, to develop a thought model that others can follow, to start at the level of the student, and to progress (by steps or concepts) toward comprehension. This skill is not related to the ease or difficulty of the content for the teacher.

Personal Adjustment

Even though a person, through maturation and potentiality, may be mentally and physically ready for another learning experience, he may be unready because of problems of personal adjustment, that is, inability to match the demands he feels with the responses he can make. For instance, when the learner feels that those close to him possess more speed, accuracy, quality, thought, and feeling than he has at his command, he will address himself to his adjustment and is not likely to be as ready as when he feels that he can cope with those around him.

Adjustment of the Learner

Personal adjustment is satisfactory when the learner feels comfortable. This state usually exists when he has had some success in dealing with the persons and events in his life and is ready to venture a little, to take on something else. If this feeling extends to the point of overconfidence, it limits adjustment, because the overconfident pay insufficient attention to all aspects of a task and situation. If the daily striving with life up to that time has not developed a fairly comfortable feeling, one is hesitant and prefers to cling to what he has rather than venture a little. Success at coping with life builds confidence; confidence contributes to personal adjustment; adjustment enables one to attempt more tasks without the limitations either of overconfidence or of unduly hesitant approaches. Adjustment is adequate whenever one is able to meet each demand that society makes of him with energy to spare for the next event.

Adjustment of the Teacher

In addition to what was said of the adjustment of the learner, the adjustment of the teacher is also a function of age, intelligence, and level of knowledge, and is expressed in his relationships with his students.

Comfortable adjustment permits the close contact essential for sympathy, empathy, and understanding. Whenever the teacher's personal problems intrude, he retreats from contact. If he must limit his role because of his adjustment, either because of life-problems or the conditions of the moment, he is less aware of the feelings and needs of his students.

Attitudes

Attitudes toward a task are even more important to readiness than intellect, level of knowledge, and general adjustment. Attitudes are more culturally determined than the other aspects. They have uniquely human properties which habits seem to lack [224].

The Learner and Attitudes

Nearly every child in our culture expects to begin to learn the three R's when he enters school. His attitude is one of readiness even if his maturation in other respects may not be up to the tasks. Because nearly all girls play with dolls and nearly all boys play with bats and balls, an attitude of masculine rejection of the former activity and acceptance of the latter is developed in our society. Those who try to teach 13- and 14-year-old boys the kinds of things which girls of that age enjoy, such as choral singing, may find themselves engaged in a wearisome struggle. This does not mean that attitudes cannot be modified, that cultural patterns do not change, but it does mean that the present attitude of the learner determines whether he is ready to learn calculus or folk dancing, or to do something else.

The Teacher and Attitudes

The attitudes of teachers are the product of their understanding of what teaching is all about [224]. Age, intelligence, knowledge, and adjustment find expression in attitudes, but these factors are secondary in importance to the teacher's perception of his role. The following roles may be identified:

> The parent-substitute.
> The director.
> The person in control.
> The source of information.
> The judge, critic and evaluator.
> The source of stimulation and encouragement.
> The friend.

As parent-substitute, he is responsible for the welfare of his students.

As the director, he selects the content and supervises the work of each student.

As the person in control, he manages the behavior of the group and mediates the disputes that arise.

As the source of information, he interprets the content and directs attention to all the other sources of information.

As the judge, critic, and evaluator, he appraises the correctness and the quality of the work.

As the source of stimulation and encouragement, he pushes the laggards and supports the inadequate, while urging the studious to do even better. It follows from his role as director that he points to new horizons for conquest.

As a friend, he is ready to help in any appropriate way.

Many more roles could be named in preference to, or in addition to, these roles. Further, elaborate efforts to weigh the effect of each role could be pursued, but these would add nothing to our understanding of the teacher with a class of individuals. A good teacher combines his roles, and each class (although not every student) will sense the teacher's attitude toward them, toward the subject matter, and toward teaching. As individuals in a class, they feel acceptance and appreciation, familiarity with the subject, and willingness to explain and participate. They are also sensitive to rejection and disapproval, ignorance and confusion, and boredom with teaching, explanation, and the task at hand.

Timing and Pacing

There is a best moment for doing anything, and no other time can match it. The comment, "Boy, what timing!" carries the connotation. When the timing is good, an aura of appropriateness surrounds the choice of events, the people included, and the circumstances.

Pacing carries a similar connotation and at times is used synonymously. Such use is not quite correct [see Ref. 180, p. 239]. Pacing is a broader, more generic term. It refers to matching the demands made with the resources available. If the demands exceed capabilities, development is not fostered—rather it is upset and sometimes reversed; if the demands are less than possible, development that might take place does not occur.

Good timing boosts morale so much and is so infectious, that all persons are apt to overestimate the quality of the participants and the work done. The success of a teacher in a class when his timing is right can make poor technique look good and make good technique look even better. Good timing generates the feeling that the teacher can teach anything to anybody at any time. It is obvious that such a fiction is misleading. The elation of good timing diverts attention from the need for thorough preparation and from careful consideration of all aspects of personal development. There is nothing intrinsically wrong with good timing, except when it leads the teacher to neglect other fundamentals of teaching technique.

Good pacing, while not as buoyant and dramatic as good timing, makes demands of individuals and groups in keeping with their resources. Pacing is a high ideal which a clever coach might manage for one person at a time. Pacing, as such, is quite beyond the skill of any teacher with a class of thirty or more students. Even if the teacher has the energy to work with the class in three groups —a fast, a middle, and a slow group—and moves students from group to group as they accelerate or retard, there will only be a few students for whom the demand is exactly matched to the resources available. For the rest, the demands are either too heavy or too light.

Teachers frequently manage to display their skill in good timing; pacing is usually only a goal to aim at, rather than one which the teacher can expect to reach.

Summary: Readiness

Readiness (preparatory adjustment) is the product of the combined abilities of the individual and is expressed in his willingness to explore and discover, to learn to follow and be directed, yet still inquisitively develop his own way as he works with the assistance of others. Such readiness is an expression of how long the person has lived, the quantity and quality of intellect, the level of knowledge, how easily he contends with tasks and people, and his attitudes. The appropriateness of good timing is apt to divert attention from the necessity of readiness for learning. Good pacing accounts for more of the variables but is not as dramatic as good timing. When the teacher correctly estimates readiness, the learner's development is smoother, and it is easier for others to aid in the learner's development.

4

the climate for learning

ACQUISITION

COMPETITION AND COOPERATION

LEADERSHIP AND SELF-DEVELOPMENT

The Integrity of the Individual
Support
The Emotional Tone

SUMMARY: THE CLIMATE FOR LEARNING

CLIMATOLOGISTS POINT OUT that man's functioning varies according to the general climatic conditions in his area—the temperature, the height above sea level, the amount of rainfall—each having a contributory effect. In the same way, the psychological climate of the classroom has much to do with the behavior of the pupils.

Teachers are concerned with the classroom atmosphere because it is basic to the teaching-learning situation and to the general development of the learner, and because it is largely a product of the teacher's leadership.

The desired climate is one in which the acquisition of learning is accepted as a worthwhile goal by the student, as his own possession, like *his* football, *his* car.

Creating such a point of view in the student requires that the subtleties of individual development be nurtured in the social situation of the classroom. This is difficult. A teacher may understand an individual student, but such understanding of one or two persons is not enough when the interests of 30 or 35 students must be satisfied in a 45-minute period. The necessary group approach must include: (1) respect for the integrity of individual development, (2) support for the individuals and the groups in the classroom, (3) a sensitivity to the emotional tone. Leadership which provides these climatic conditions will encourage the development of the desired responses by the pupils.

Acquisition

The proper climate for learning is one of acquisition. The learner is ready to acquire when he is old enough, is bright enough, knows enough, and believes that he can learn. Under these circumstances, he makes knowledge and skill his own. Acquisition is the storing, the saving, and the preparation for the next day, which is found in each of us. As each individual develops, he learns to acquire, whether it is *his* toys, *his* clothes or *his* understandings.

Since most learning occurs in company with others, and since the learner usually needs the assistance of others, acquisition is customarily social. The learner acquires knowledge and skill with and from other people. He performs simple tasks more rapidly when spectators are present than when he is alone [138]. The presence of a co-working but noncompetitive group increases the quantity of the work done but not its quality [10]. The quality of group results does not surpass the individual results of every member of the group, and generally the top individual comes out better than the group as a whole [258]. The greatest advantage comes when the amount of background work is so great that one individual cannot possibly accomplish it.

Several studies have been done on group vs. individual problem solving to determine whether it is true that group processes far exceed the skill of an individual [425, 258, 242, 243]. The Yuker study specifies four conditions under which some superiority for the group over the individual will be evident [425].

(1) For group participation, the task must be one on which several people can work simultaneously without getting into each other's way. An additive task is required, one that can be built piecemeal rather than by a complete, sudden, and insightful solution. (2) The pieces need to be

independent of each other, otherwise the member participation will disrupt the line of thought, the line of dependence. (3) The size of the group is important because in larger groups there is less member participation. (4) The group atmosphere needs to be one of cohesiveness of feelings about the group. If the group does not embrace interrelationships, there will be little group process.

Using 40 groups of four persons each, Yuker induced a cooperative atmosphere with "see how well you work together" and a competitive atmosphere with "see how well you can compete." Democratic instructions were used, such as, "select a person to act as coordinator," and authoritarian instructions, such as, "select a person who is in complete charge."

Each group was read a story which they (1) recalled as individuals, (2) recalled in a group in the induced atmosphere of either cooperation or competition, or following democratic or authoritarian leadership, and (3) individual recall was measured again. It was anticipated that individuals would do noticeably better after group participation, but they did not. Group recall was superior under the induced condition of cooperation, to group recall in a competitive atmosphere. The expected differences in favor of democratic leadership over authoritarian leadership did not appear [425, pp. 21-22].

The other studies also found some superiority for group learning and group processes, but again under carefully specified conditions [258, 242, 253]. Although acquisition is often social, individual development does not succumb to group processes in any broad general sense. (The average classroom teacher can verify this generalization many times daily, either through observation or through establishing a simple experimental situation following the conditions of the Yuker study.)

Competition and Cooperation

The climate for acquisition is one of cooperation and competition with fellow-acquirers. There are those who insist that competition is wholly unjustified, but this is most unrealistic, since even cooperation involves competition to be more cooperative [47]. In such societies as ours, competition cannot be eliminated in favor of cooperation. As the learner develops, he cooperates to receive benefits from others, while sometimes excelling and defeating them and at other times being excelled and defeated by them.

Both competitive and cooperative tendencies can be developed for the benefit of the individual and the general welfare. In team sports, such as baseball and football, there is intense rivalry to excel individually, and this is good for the team as long as it does not interfere with the cooperation needed for smooth functioning. The five vice-presidents of a corporation vie with each other to be chosen president, but they must at the same time cooperate if the company is not to be torn apart. Thus, individual and group interests in both competitive and cooperative atmospheres are to be fostered to provide a proper climate of acquisition.

When the teacher attempts to foster this competitive-cooperative climate, he faces a dilemma. Apart from the mutually exclusive nature of competition and cooperation, individual and group interests also conflict. Add to this the teacher's inability to estimate accurately an individual's readiness and his perception of the demands made of him and then multiply this by the 30 individuals in a class. Under these circumstances, the chances of managing the situation in a way that does not violate some principles of individual and group development are remote. The extent of the resolution of the dilemma depends on the leadership techniques of the teacher.

Leadership and Self-Development

Education cannot be made easy if it is to provide for intellectual and school-subject development, and to a lesser degree the physical, social, and emotional development. The school is not alone in the process of education because the home and the community are also responsible for such development (with different emphases in each case), but spreading the responsibility does not make the task easier. No one can take over the task for the learner, much as loving parents and sympathetic teachers may desire to be helpful.

Teachers are most likely to succeed in the classroom if they respect the integrity of individual development, support the learner, and establish an emotional tone of mild approach and mild approval.

The Integrity of the Individual

It is generally admitted that the internal processes experienced by the learner, the unobservable ones, are those which are most significant for the achievement of many important educational goals [23]. Subject matter is a means to an end, leading to integrated understanding and development. Since teachers, with their best skill, cannot be fully cognizant of the internal processes for one person, let alone the group, respect for the integrity of individual development is essential. Without it, teachers smother the development of which each learner is capable.

This respect for the individual's integrity transcends all methods of leadership. To illustrate, lecture and discussion methods, and all shades and combinations of the two, can make provision for self-development, or they can be instruments of domination, depending on how the leader interprets his role. If he feels that he has to direct in order to lead, no method is safe from his imposed leadership. If he feels that he is offering his assistance to those under his control, any method will suffice to promote self-development. In the college lecture, the contrast is between "I know, listen to me" and "this is what is known." In discussion, the contrast is between "talk about this" and discussion arising naturally when those present want to talk and exchange information. In the elementary school, the difference in the leader's role is evident in learning something like rules for spelling certain words, namely, "teacher knows the right answer" and "this is the way the spelling rule goes." Respect for the integrity of the individual does not imply that there are changes in the truth or falsity of what is known, or that there is less work to be done, or that the leader has no clear perception of what he wants. It simply arranges the learning process to allow maximum self-development in the learner.

Few persons who promote self-development through the quality of their leadership feel that they fully understand the individual's readiness and his perception of the demands of society, let alone the confusion of a group. Rather than choosing to direct individuals in groups, the better leaders respect the integrity of the individual and so leave each person free to follow his own development. The leader is available to assist and, where necessary, to adjudicate differences, but otherwise he promotes the climate of competitive-cooperative acquisition by not imposing his ways on people he does not fully understand. Even if the leader could fully comprehend the feelings and perceptions of another, he would deliberately hesitate to impose his will and thought standards. Those who do most to promote self-development are aware of their own shortcomings and so rely on the slow process of self-development rather than imposing themselves on individuals and groups.

Support

The teacher supports individuality in the learner in much the same way that a wife supports a husband. A wife helps her husband to adjust to the changing demands which are made of him. She stands by him through failures, acts as a sounding board for his ideas, and helps him to formulate his ambitions and desires. She does not need to understand his business or to compete with him on an intellectual level or on any other level—not that she cannot, it is just not necessary. She does not do these things for him in any way, but it is her appreciation of his fears, his plans, and his aims that enables her to foster his development. School learning (as well as all other learning situations) benefits from similar appreciations of the nuances of individual development.

Here is a striking illustration from the gymnasium. A teacher was present when a class of girls began to heckle a girl who never removed the sock from one foot. The teacher stopped the heckling and told the class that the girl in question had something she would like to tell them and show them. The girl removed her sock from a leg without a foot, showed the class the stump that she was born with, and showed them her artificial foot. She explained how the foot worked and how it was regularly adjusted to match her good foot. The child herself explained it to the class. The only role of the teacher was to stage the explanation, and this she did by being present at the moment the heckling began.

There are risks in the illustration. For instance, if the teacher had not correctly estimated the strength of the deformed pupil, the child might have dissolved in tears instead of demonstrating and explaining. If the class had then tagged the child as a cripple instead of accepting her as she was, great damage could have resulted.

Teachers are rarely this fortunate in arranging situations to aid their pupils in self-development. They cannot protect the pupils, cannot do it for them, but can support the children as they do it for themselves.

The Emotional Tone

An emotional tone of mild approach and mild approval with a slight tension to action is most conducive to encouraging the subtleties of individual development. Strong or intense emotions may cause the learner to over-invest or to reject. The effects of over-investment and rejection are similar: personal involvement, feelings of regret and remorse, and lack of attention. Mild rather than strong feeling provides sufficient attention and tension, enough for personal involvement in achievement, and mild feelings do not generate the backlash from regret and remorse. When the learner feels the need to invest all his attention on an objective, he deliberately excludes others that are available to him. Similarly, when he rejects, he forces himself to avoid material which is available.

Here, as in Chapters 2 and 3, we are dealing with conscious cognitive processes because, although forces of which we are not fully aware also direct our attention, we have neither the time nor the skill to work with these in the classroom. Let it be emphasized: the business of school is education, not therapy, but there is no reason to avoid the re-education provided by therapy if we have the necessary time, understanding, and skill.

Strong feelings invade every aspect of self-expression and pre-empt the role of more subtle yet equally valuable feelings. When the strong feeling does not completely displace the more subtle expression, the milder one is covered with an overlay of the stronger, more primitive expression. We do not recognize even our own masked feelings, and others are certainly unaware of the subtle feelings which are masked by primitive expression. Strong feelings thus limit full expression in the sense that mild feelings are either denied expression or are not discernible.

There may be variations in the degrees of feeling which are desirable in school subjects, such as speech, English, science, social studies, mathematics, music, and art. In the appreciation subjects, strong feelings may be more tolerable, but the richest expression usually relies on the nuances of interpretation and technique rather than on the strength of emotions.

It is also necessary to distinguish between the strong feelings that are mature preferences and those that are impulses of the moment. A passion for the music of Brahms or for certain colors and forms may be an adolescent splurge or an adult choice. If they are adolescent, they limit the fullest expression; but mature feelings for music, color, and form have their foundation in the full ap-preciation of all the subtleties of quality. The adult preference is based on a rich background of knowledge and information which should not be confused with the strong feeling which is an impulse, a crush. Such mature enthusiasms may support a rich and develop-mental curiosity.

Allowing for the variability in feeling which is desirable in dif-ferent subjects, and accepting the fact that the strong feelings of mature preferences are desirable, there may be remorse and regret as we retreat from our enthusiasms. Persons rarely have the privilege of indulging in expressions of strong feeling without paying the penalty for self-indulgence. Delight in a good long sleep is short-lived when one realizes how much could have been accomplished during the same period of time. Appetite which is given free rein in rich food is curbed by digestive disturbances or weight increases.

Unfair treatment of one's fellow man is counterbalanced by the need to consider his welfare. When strong feeling is accompanied by guilt it is usually expressed in self-justification and rationalizations, such as, "Don't you agree with me?" or, "Don't you see it this way?" Comments like these may reflect unjustifiable judgments for which the speaker seeks support. The majority of strong expressions of feeling are caught by their own backlash as one retreats from extreme positions. Both the strong feeling and its aftereffect disturb the emotional tone.

Summary: The Climate for Learning

The climate for learning is one of acquisition. It is an atmosphere in which the learner makes knowledge his own.

Acquisition is usually social because learning occurs with and from others, but the needs and interests of the individual do not succumb to those of the group. In school, the individual learns within the social setting, sometimes in helping others and sometimes competing with them. It is this competitive-cooperative dilemma that taxes the teacher's leadership.

Teachers cannot learn for the pupil or even make learning easy for him. Teachers can lead; they can support; they can provide situations that may encourage the subtleties of individual development.

Because the teacher rarely understands even one person fully, let alone a group of persons, respect for the integrity of individual development is essential. The individual can find his way more surely than anyone can do it for him, and the teacher can only provide support. This is the assistance that allows maximum self-development, particularly if the emotional tone is one of mild approach and mild approval with a slight tension toward action. Strong feelings of like, and all degrees of dislike, have the effect of overdirecting attention and masking the more subtle developments. Mild rather than strong feelings provide for breadth in awareness and depth in the subtleties of individual development.

5

managing the classroom

WE HAVE DEALT WITH MOTIVATION, the readiness of the learner and the climate for learning in relation to the development of the individual. Chapter 5 is a description of the teacher's role as a person in charge of the classroom.

The heading "Managing the Classroom" could be stated as "Control, Discipline, Management, and Learning," but this would stress the negative aspects. The emphasis intended is on management for self-expression rather than inhibition, for the purpose of permitting rather than restricting development; nevertheless, control, discipline, and management are essential in an educational program which aims at the maximum development of each child's potential.

Freedom is a matter of degree. Because of the competitive-cooperative social situation, others control us in varying degrees. Thus self-control, rather than other-control, is also a matter of degree. No matter how self-controlled a person is, he is always dependent on others. A permissive atmosphere in the classroom allows each individual freedom to develop, and in this way respects the integrity of personal development. So long as each pupil's activities do not put him in the way of others, self-control can be at a maximum. But the social situation rarely permits such isolation: someone must speak first, someone wants to use the dictionary when another has it; someone must have the last chance to speak on the new topic. Complete self-control by all persons present would allow the teacher to be fully permissive. Because pupils are rarely so mature, they require direction, and the teacher's problem becomes the kind of direction to promote desirable development.

No group exists without many controls, although they may not be obvious. For a group to assemble someone must have set a date, a time, and place; others have provided heat, light, and sanitary conditions; and others have provided safe transportation to the meeting place. Thus all control is a matter of degree—ranging from the completely self-controlled persons to the persons who need constant, close supervision in order to develop.

Control

Control is the direction of others. "Stand up, John, and speak clearly." If John stands and attempts to speak clearly, the teacher is in control. A bell rings to signal 10:25 A. M., time for the change of classes. Did the class move on the bell signal, or before or after the bell, or on a signal from the teacher? Either the bell sound or the teacher may direct the movement. "Pull your car over to the curb and stop." If these directions are followed, the person who gave them is in charge—but there is a need to distinguish between permissive and directive control. Most control operates between these extremes.

The concept of permissiveness has received much unfavorable publicity through the excesses of the extreme exponents of "Progressive Education," especially during the 1930's and 1940's. Much of this reaction stems from a misunderstanding and misuse of the basic concept. A well-known cartoon of the period showed the children of a primary grade saying to the teacher, "Do we have to do what we want to do again today?"

Permissive control is management that allows the learner freedom for individual development. The implied permissiveness of "Would you like to do this?" is nonexistent. If the student really would like to, he would do it without such coercion. If he prefers not to, the teacher is obviously applying pressure. A permissive person can set limits of behavior and leave the individual free to enjoy self-expression within these limits [23]. Let us look in on a beginning class in educational psychology which has compulsory attendance and for which the persons present have read a section of Cronbach [90]. Permissiveness, in this class or group, is extended through free discussion of any and all aspects of the assignment, in any order and at any length. Those who do not attend are disciplined, that is, coerced and penalized, and those who have not read carefully find themselves at a disadvantage compared with those who have (this may lead to some self-discipline). Control is the direction of others, without excluding self-control (a highly refined self-development which, like all self-development, responds to true permissiveness, not mere surface permissiveness).

On the other hand, when directive control is used, the teacher directs behavior—not all, but a part of it. The learner follows the instructions and in return he expects the teacher to accept the responsibility for his welfare in an area. Take the case of a college student. Directive control of his development in a liberal arts curriculum requires that he subject himself to the number and variety of courses offered, in return for which the college assumes a responsibility to give him a broadly educative experience. All control should imply preparation for eventual self-mastery and increased freedom. Directive control, however, implies that we follow where others lead, rather than follow the self-direction of a permissive approach. Proper directive control implies that the leadership of others will produce the self-mastery of self-control after a period of following directions from others.

The majority of control functions somewhere between these extremes of permissiveness and direction, and this is a source of confusion in human relationships. When students are allowed some freedom interspersed with direction from others, the result may be confusion. Whenever the limits of freedom and direction are made clear and are maintained consistently, confusion is avoided and students learn both self-direction and the ability to follow directions.

Control and Domination

An important distinction needs to be made here between maintaining control and dominating. Every person in control dominates, but he may do so for the common good or merely because he enjoys wielding power. This is the difference between being dominant and domineering. The person who is domineering arouses retaliatory feelings—"Just wait until I'm in charge." When the person in control dominates for the benefit of all, a cooperative attitude is developed [35]. "Please walk through the halls." As soon as those who run realize that they may hurt themselves or others, they will walk. This may require some years of domination by those in control before the necessity of walking in the halls is accepted. No matter who penalizes the nonwalkers, and no matter what the nature of the penalties, the object should not be domination but control for the benefit of all.

Limits

Control for mutual benefit is based on a set of limits which applies to everyone at all times [324]. These boundaries are not to be exceeded; we must live within them. For example, "There will be no smoking or eating during the class hour." At the college level this is a realistic limit. The student may attend or not attend; he may read or not read the assignment; he may learn or not learn; he may speak in class or not speak. These choices are entirely up to the student, but if he attends class he may not smoke or eat during the class hour. Even with such slight limitation on behavior, some students will try to smoke or eat. Each time the attempt is made, the student is reprimanded. This assures him that the limit is there and implies that a positive permissiveness is also still in effect. Such limits may be imposed by the person in charge or set through the cooperative action of those present. Regardless of how the limits are established, if they are there and followed, the purpose of the control is not domination, since the person is left free to develop within the limits. Obviously, the fewer the limits, the freer the situation.

Limits and Self-Control

The art of self-control grows out of common consent and a consensus of the best knowledge. Self-control is always a matter of degree because others control us in varying degrees, whether we wish them to or not.

Self-control is the management of one's behavior within the limits of the situation [85]. For example, the college student is required to follow a specified four-year liberal arts curriculum in a given sequence, to register for a minimum number of credits each term, to attend the classes for which he registers, and to complete the work of each class at a given quality level. Within these limits he is free to develop as he wishes, and within these limits he manages self-control. This does not mean that he will not attempt to vary the prescribed sequence of courses, or to avoid the required minimum number of credits each term, or cut classes, or leave work unfinished, or meet requirements with work of poor quality. The self-controlled student may test the limits of any situation for two reasons. First, to assure himself that the limits are there, that there are things which he cannot do, and second, to assure himself that he is free to behave within these stable limits.

To a degree, as in the case of the college student, self-control allows us to direct our own affairs. However, the assurance that one has freedom to develop within the limits is only present when the limits are consistently maintained. If a student is allowed to exceed a limit without a penalty, he is disturbed by the lack of consistency. The absence of punishment for exceeding a limit raises questions with respect to how many more limits he can exceed and as to how free he is to develop within any set of limits. Self-control, a highly refined development, is a matter of degree, within the imposed limits of the situation. Whenever he goes too far, his feelings of assurance are best supported if he is always reminded through the use of penalties and punishments. These may arise from the situation itself (the headache accompanying a hangover, the upset stomach from overeating), or from the dominant person (the ticket for parking improperly, the adverse comment attached to a poorly-written essay).

Teachers frequently are satisfied with controlling the immediate situation instead of building toward self-control. The pupils then learn to be quiet when the teacher is there, but to be noisy and unruly when he is not. They keep the floor clean in Mr. Smith's classroom, but do not acquire a habit of neatness which carries over to other classes or the street or their homes. The driver who stops at a red light only when he sees a policeman nearby or suspects that one may be watching is a menace to everyone. The light is supposed to control the driver's actions because he recognizes this limit to be imposed for the common good. This is self-discipline.

Discipline

Examine these two sentences:

(A) Anyone who hopes to become a great athlete must discipline himself.

(B) The teacher disciplined the pupils by not allowing them to play ball during recess.

There are, unfortunately, two distinct meanings of the word *discipline* in these sentences, and the difference is not merely whether the discipline is administered by oneself or by another person. In (A) the athlete is told to use *self-control*, as in diet, exercise, rest. In (B) the teacher is *punishing* the class. There is an area of overlapping, since the athlete's self-control involves self-punishment and denial, and the teacher's punishment of the class is aimed at control; but the two meanings are still quite distinct. Since both meanings (self-control and punishment) are so common and so applicable to the classroom situation, it is impractical to avoid either one. The reader of educational books must simply be on his guard to study each context carefully enough to be clear about which meaning is intended.

For the benefit of the pupil, some form of punishment is required when he exceeds the prescribed limits. To illustrate, the teacher asks the class to stand and take places in line in order to walk to the assembly hall. Two members of the class do not cooperate. The teacher's control has been flouted and disciplinary measures must now be used to assure these two pupils that the teacher is in control. Or to illustrate from the home, an adolescent and his parents have agreed that a midnight curfew is reasonable for Friday and Saturday night dates. The adolescent arrives home at three A.M. without reasonable explanation. Parental control has been ignored and disciplinary measures are necessary to assure the adolescent that the parent is still in charge.

In this sense, then, to discipline means to penalize, punish, or coerce in order to maintain control. Whoever is in charge must dominate, no matter how permissive he may be. Whenever the control breaks down, he resorts to discipline, to penalties, and coercions in order to maintain control, and preferably to benefit the offender rather than to dominate for the sake of domineering.

The Disciplinary Episode

Each disciplinary episode is a specific occurrence, and we help the offender most if we can treat it as such. The failure of one person to accede to the control of another has a beginning and an end. John did not stop teasing the baby when he was asked to. Those two boys played hookey from school. The girl stole from her mother's purse. In each case where the control was exceeded, penalties were levied and paid, and the offender was returned to good grace. Once the penalty is paid, the offender is as acceptable as any other penalized or nonpenalized person. If we harbor a grudge, are watching for his slightest misdemeanor to penalize him further, he feels the unfairness of the differential treatment. The apparent unfairness makes it harder for him to conform to the control [125]. The preferable situation is one in which each episode is treated as an event; once the penalty is paid, the event is over.

Punishment

The coercion in school depends upon the teacher, the school, the situation, and the offender. Suitable punishment matches the expectation of the offender. When he is aware that he has exceeded the limit and recognizes the extent of his excess, he expects to be punished proportionately. If not punished in keeping with his excess, he is confused with respect to what he can and cannot do. Punishment, such as the rewriting of an essay because it does not meet the prescribed quality standards, is appropriate in most situations, but the assignment of extra class work for fighting in the hall is not appropriate. It is impossible to prescribe a list of penalties which would adequately weigh all the variables involved in each incident. Consider for a moment the control ability of some teachers. They are not harsh and restrictive, yet a look, a sharp word, or a warning is sufficient to penalize offenders. Other teachers require a range of quite vigorous punishments in order to maintain their control.

Disciplinary punishments vary depending on their purpose and the user. The most severe penalties include some in which the controlling person anticipates the consequences for the uninitiated but decides to allow them to occur as the natural consequences of failure to follow directions. For example, he may say, "Avoid poison ivy because of the skin irritation that it creates," and then say and do nothing until the person is painfully infected. This makes the role of the controller one of mere domineering rather than assistance for mutual benefit. Few of us would choose to be this vicious, although permissive people often allow others to get into strongly self-damaging situations. The domination of others inherent in the point of view, "I am the teacher; I am older and wiser; follow me without question," leads to dependence and eventually vigorous struggle for independence rather than progressive self-development and self-control. Saying, "This is my opinion of your work," and giving freedom to accept and act on all, some, or none of the opinion provides for growth and development. The teacher who disciplines to enforce this point of view does so to dominate others. The teacher who disciplines to maintain control may say: "Bill, you are talking out of turn, and that disturbs us all." When Bill persists, the teacher may penalize by refusing him the privilege of conversation and comment for the rest of the class hour. This follows the discipline of natural consequences, talking penalized by not talking, but only for the purpose of reminding the offender that such behavior is detrimental to others. The penalties used, whatever they are, vary in their role depending on the intention of the person who administers them.

The penalties used should never vary in one aspect, namely, the fact that they are inevitable. When the limits of the situation have been exceeded, the fact that a penalty is always levied has great value. The student knows that he should not throw things in class, either because the teacher said so (punishment) or because the student realizes that he might hurt others or be hurt (self-control). If each infraction is penalized by either the teacher or by fellow students, the limit is consistently maintained. Everyone knows that throwing something without experiencing the penalty is not possible. Whenever this is not the case, the person who is not penalized wonders how much more he can get away with and the one penalized resents having to pay for his failure to comply. Whenever the assurance of penalty or of no penalty exists, the definiteness represents a source of stability.

Consistency

The consistency of punishment is no more important than the consistency of approval and satisfaction, or consistency in all relationships. From consistency comes the assurance that society operates this way, that these things are approved and these others are not approved. The Luchins found that diverse standards made for contradictory responses but did not interfere with the execution of tasks[245]. The tasks were to measure objects with different rulers. The eighty children did not know that the rulers were of different lengths, and although their information from measuring was contradictory, they cooperated in the task. The consistency of the situation took precedence over the contradictions. A person might be consistently inconsistent (e.g., he might order different foods in different combinations every day), and this stable variability would support positive expectations. Relationships with others are fostered when we meet their expectations of us and they meet our expectations of them. If our behavior is variable, others have difficulty in building assuring expectations. Consistency in all behavior builds security and is consequently developmental.

The Accepting Teacher

Within the boundaries set by the limits, the good teacher is accepting. Acceptance provides for empathy—the feeling that each understands how the other feels [35, 372]. Pupils need to know that teachers are aware of pupils' reactions and of what pupils are trying to do. The more acceptance teachers can develop within the limits of the situation, the better the climate for learning.

The development of acceptance is dependent upon the adjustment of the teacher and his familiarity with his subject [129]. Few teachers are so well adjusted that they can tolerate close inspection by others, day in and day out. Many teachers can allow others nearby, in an area or two for short periods of time; then they require the relief of greater distance. They need this separation because their knowledge is too shaky and the fear of having their inadequacies discovered is omnipresent. When there is no danger of becoming lost in subject matter, and when personal security is not threatened, it is possible for teachers to be warm and friendly [279].

Teachers can understand and accept others after achieving a degree of self-understanding and self-acceptance. These qualities follow from a sincere desire for them, namely, a willingness to seek help, a problem-solving attitude and a sustained effort to reach one's own conclusions [189]. The more completely teachers have solved their personal and subject-matter problems, the more acceptance, warmth, and understanding they can extend to others.

The Teacher and the Group

Teachers can develop acceptance of an individual with relative ease, but the group situation is taxing. Given the privilege of working with an individual for eight hours a day, it is possible to exchange knowledge, information, and even insults. Because of the adaptability of individuals, acceptance can develop. In a group situation where the perception of individual differences varies from person to person, acceptance is more difficult. Within consistent limits, the more acceptance teachers can develop, the more they can foster growth and development. Consistency and acceptance within the consistency are more difficult in group situations because of the inability of teachers to take account of the full range of individual differences in group management. Group perception as a whole is nonexistent, that is, groups do not perceive people or problems in a concerted way, so that teachers are dealing with pooled individual reactions to what is considered to be accepting behavior [243]. It is taxing to manage a group in ways which appear to the group to be both consistent and accepting.

Theoretical and Practical Considerations

Before concluding the description of the role of limits, consistency, and acceptance in control, there are a number of considerations with respect to the operation of punishment, negative reinforcement, and anxiety which are of interest in understanding control (but the knowledge of which is not essential to control). Many persons control and support development to the level of self-mastery by consistently using a series of techniques without knowing quite why they are able to help and direct others. The following explanation of the theoretical and practical functioning of these processes is not essential to the use of the techniques, but it is of interest to those who wish to understand *why* they are able to control. Others may turn directly to page 74.

Punishment and Negative Reinforcement[1]

Punishment is pain for doing something we should not have done or not doing something we should have done. (The word *punishment* may include annoyances, disturbances, and pain, ranging all the way from mild disapproval to planned tortures.) Negative reinforcement also has two aspects: pain for not doing something required, or no pain for performing as required. To illustrate, if we do not submit the assignment on time, we are scolded or receive a lower grade; if we stop for the red light, there is no pain (no ticket, no fine, no accident). If we do the kinds of things which are required in school, there is approval rather than pain.

[1] The authors recognize that negative reinforcement is introduced here before reinforcement itself. Thorough study of both the material presented here on negative reinforcement and that in Chapter 12 on reinforcement is essential for comprehension.

If we do not conform to the standards of our social group, we do not receive their approval. If we care for our teeth, we enjoy better dental health and suffer fewer painful reinforcements.

Punishment

The first step in negative reinforcement is punishment. An individual learns to do and not to do because he is punished or not punished. The punishment generates anxiety, the effects of which are broad, general, and variable [114]. Add to this the fact that the effects of punishment are varied and complicated by themselves even without the pervasive influence of anxiety. One learns to avoid certain actions in order to avoid pain. However, in spite of its complicated effects, punishment is the first step in negative reinforcement.

The effects of punishment change according to the strength of the response at the time the response is punished. If the punishment is for doing something we are sure is right, we are amazed. Such punishment usually creates an immediate reaction and struggle in us. If the punishment is for something that is not our responsibility, of which we are ignorant, it is easily dismissed and has little effect. To illustrate, if we say, "Five times six is 30," and are punished for this, we voice aggressive complaints about the punisher. The idea of five times six as 30 is a strong response which we will use our energies to defend. By comparison, punishment for not being able to read Spanish, when we have had no opportunity to learn to read Spanish, is easily dismissed. Punishment for strong responses has a great effect, but punishment for weak responses has little influence.

The person who administers the punishment has an important role [114]. If the punishment is from someone who is liked or admired, or who is in control, it is meaningful. Punishment from someone for whom one has no feeling, from someone who is not in control, is easily dismissed. A warning from a policeman in a strange town is treated as a lucky break— "I got away with only a warning." Punishment from a teacher who has control over us because we are in his classes, or whose reputation is formidable, or whom we respect because of his knowledge and skill, may cause us to change our behavior. By comparison, punishment from a teacher who passes us in the hall, who does not know us, whom we do not know, and for whom we have no feelings, has little effect. Punishment changes the rate of responding, the rate of emission, but not the supply of responses to be emitted [359]. (The rate of emission means the number of times per day or week that one will try to make a given response; punishment changes the rate at which he will attempt such behavior.) Each reinforced occurrence of a response adds to the supply of possible responses. Punishment changes the rate at which the punished responses will be made, and this is a source of confusion in punishment, namely, which responses were punished? For example, the look of disapproval which a person's superior flashes at him has specific rather than general antecedents. The person then tries to guess which specific responses have annoyed the superior and tries to avoid making them, at least in the superior's presence. The punishment from the superior changed the rate of emission of specific responses, but were they the responses that annoyed him? If teachers wish to prevent the emission of particular responses, they punish those responses. For example, punishment for profanity in the classroom limits the use of profanity in the classroom. The more clearly teachers identify exactly which responses they wish to prevent, the more effective punishment is. Punishment may keep the response from occurring again immediately, but does not eliminate the response from the repertory of responses. It is difficult, if not impossible, to get rid of a response entirely through punishment. Punishment only changes the rate at which the punished response is made in a given situation.

Punishment may be used to limit behavior for a period of time, as in the following examples [114].

Punishment may be used to "hold down" behavior, to prevent a particular response from occurring now. If behavior is to be limited permanently, periodic punishment is necessary. Some punishments are so vivid that they hold a place in memory for years.

("The burned child dreads the fire.") But in healthy adjustment, the effects of punishment are usually dissipated with the passage of time.

While one uses punishment to inhibit a response, he may reward other responses in the hope that they will replace the punished response. This may be effective control over behavior if the alternative responses are strong.

Severe or traumatic punishment may eliminate all behavior except anxiety [48, 114]. When the struggle to deal with punishment is painful, persons may give up contending with it and spend their time controlling and satisfying the anxiety. Thus, exceptionally harsh punishment usually evokes a disruptive withdrawal to the behavior of self-protection.

Punishment and Control

Punishment is an unsure and awkward way to control behavior, because it is not possible to determine when it will result in behavioral maladjustments, or even when the undesirable behavior will be eliminated. Teachers can neither avoid receiving punishment nor avoid meting it out to their pupils, because our society provides for punishment at every turn, usually in the form of criticism and disapproval. Even when teachers do not choose to, they punish others without being aware of how punishing and how disapproving they appear to be. Add to this the times when they deliberately attempt to punish, and compound each intentional and uinintentional punishment for an individual with the complexity of group interaction, and it is obvious how teachers punish and are punished. The fact that punishment is so common does not justify its use. It may be the only way whereby the young come to know of the approved and disapproved, the acceptable and the unacceptable, but it is an uncertain and hazardous way to control behavior.

John Seward indicates the reason for preferring reward to punishment. When the subject makes responses resembling those of a loved person, he stimulates himself in ways that are themselves satisfying; in other words, imitative responses strengthen themselves through the secondary reinforcement they provide. Such a mechanism does not maintain itself indefinitely. Without further reinforcement, the response will be extinguished.

Punishment may prevent the undesired response, but it is a poor way to produce the desired one. If the effects include the pain of punishment, the child cannot start to imitate without arousing his own fear, thus checking the response before it is well begun. Once the model becomes a fear object, everything he does will tend to arouse the fear and thereby become nonimitable. By using punishment, the parent raises the threshold to imitation and reduces his effectiveness as a model.

Imitating a beneficent parent is doubly reinforced:
1. It leads to further rewards by the model.
2. Acting like the model becomes in itself satisfying [343, pp. 201-210].

In the school, in the home, and in the community, teachers and other adults punish and rely on the working of negative reinforcement. The child throws the chalk eraser across the room. He knows that he is not supposed to do this. The teacher punishes him and relies on the inhibiting influence of negative reinforcement to work as a self-control. The child knows that if he does not throw the eraser he will not be punished. In the home, if one does what is expected of him, he is not punished; in society, following the rules of the road and respecting the property and person of others results in not being punished. The deterring control in every case is the knowledge that punishment follows whenever and wherever one exceeds the limits, the rules. Knowledge of punishment is the result of experience with similar situations where those in control punished misbehavior. Without this experience, the cultural standards will not become internalized. Without the internalization, persons are more unsure of themselves—there is no personal knowledge of the acceptable limits of behavior. The role of punishment and negative reinforcement is to control behavior.

Reasonable punishment and the workings of negative reinforcement as a self-control work well for the majority of people, particularly if the punishment is inevitable and consistent. The inevitability gives assurances that the world is positive, firm, and stable. The consistency supports the belief that the world is the way we understand it to be. The few who are not controlled by punishment and negative reinforcement require much more carefully controlled environments than society-at-large provides, or than the average home and school can supply.

Anxiety

Both negative reinforcement and punishment involve anxiety— a vague feeling of apprehension that has generalized from the specific situation in which it was learned [95]. Anxiety is learned through association by contiguity, that is, it is associated with events because it has occurred with them. There is a feeling of apprehension about throwing things if one has been punished for doing this. Initially, this is related to a specific instance in which throwing things brought punishment. Once there is anxiety about throwing things, it tends to generalize, to take on the role of a need (really a negative need). It becomes an unpleasantness to be shunned. The avoidance of the anxiety becomes a secondary drive, a need to be met, that is, anxiety reduction functions as drive reduction does [349, 370]. If a person does not throw things, he need not be anxious about throwing. If he obeys every traffic signal, he avoids the customary anxiety associated with the policeman flagging him down. The reduction of anxiety, through doing required things and not doing forbidden things, functions as a broad secondary drive to control behavior. Need reduction is satisfying, and it is gratifying to avoid the vague general apprehension that anxiety creates.

Blau classifies anxiety as the primary emotion of displeasure. Secondary emotions of displeasure are rage, fear, and depression, which are associated respectively with reactions of aggression, evasion, and submission. Tertiary emotions of displeasure are exemplified by guilt, shame, and disgust [48].

The effects of anxiety are sufficiently varied to prevent easy generalization. Usually it absorbs part of our energy; therefore the anxious person can pay less attention to life around him. Anxiety leads to a decline in performance by causing responses that do not relate to the task [335]. Low-anxiety groups perform significantly better than high-anxiety groups [370]. Whenever anxiety is stronger than the drive toward the goal, the goal behavior is suppressed in favor of attending to the anxiety. When anxiety is aroused over achievement, the person will show more rigidity and authoritarianism [337]. Anxiety causes individuals to cling to the definite, the known, and the established usage in order to control and lessen their apprehension. When they are reasonably secure about their achievement, they may be permissive; but, when anxious, they become directive to themselves and others. Task difficulty often prevents the usual anxiety-avoidance in learning relationships, that is, although people usually attempt to avoid anxiety, they sometimes find themselves caught in a task so that anxiety is involved no matter whether they continue or quit [228]. They sometimes embark on a task without realizing how difficult it is, or cannot avoid the task even if they know how difficult it is. For instance, the college student who enters a field such as chemistry or mathematics because of the academic respectability of these subjects often finds that he has involved himself in unavoidable anxiety. To change his objective to an easier subject requires admission of defeat and thus leads to anxiety; to continue with work beyond his level of ability involves anxiety. In this way, task difficulty often confuses the usual anxiety-avoidance pattern.

In practice, while we cannot generalize broadly about the effects of anxiety, two conclusions are permissible: anxiety is functionally autonomous, and it is generalized.

Saying that anxiety is functionally autonomous means that it perpetuates itself once it is established. It provides its own energy and reinforces itself. This is evidenced in the way in which people carry their anxiety with them. Each one has a ready supply that he can marshal at any time for almost any event, and he activates it through his use of words. He can summon anxiety to prevent him from doing what he does not want to do. When he transgresses a taboo and nothing happens, it appears as though he has managed to get away with something, but there is a residue of guilt and anxiety.

When misfortune befalls, one can always recall things he did which he should not have done (even though they happened long before and do not have any real connection with the present difficulty). Persons always have stored, through verbal symbols, reasons for their present disturbances. Note how many mothers of defective children blame themselves for the child's affliction. Verbal symbols, and other symbols communicated through verbal ability, enable persons to generalize anxiety from the specific instances which caused it, to store it in memory, and to recall it. This sounds like a push-button process under cognitive control, and part of it is, but human behavior is not usually at the push-button level. Equally helpful or devastating, depending on whose point of view is considered, is the generalized anxiety aroused in us by processes over which we do not have cognitive control. For example, few people have much control over their fears, loves, and strong likes and dislikes. In many instances they approve highly without knowing why and without being able to avoid these processes or prevent their arousal. Whether under cognitive control or not, anxiety is always available. One is never without apprehension over something. The anxiety may be mild, but its pervasive, self-perpetuating stress is always present.

Because anxiety is generalized rather than specific, a full range of events is easily and completely influenced by a single stimulus. One event may arouse anxiety ranging through the full repertory of human behavior. For example, a failing grade in one subject at school may upset all other subjects, the relationships with peers and the family, and long-term vocational planning. Highly developed associative processes, mediated chiefly by verbal symbols, generalize to control behavior, whether for good or ill. Anxiety aroused through punishment in one situation may spread to many areas of behavior. This may control the person beneficially or intrude on his successful development, but it is generalized in nature, rather than specific and self-limiting.

Anxiety and Negative Reinforcement

Negative reinforcement operates through this generalized role of anxiety in behavior. If one does what he is supposed to do (self-control), he avoids punishment. Punishment creates an uneasiness for specific things which are not done. The anxiety generalizes from the specific things and functions as a secondary drive, as a need to be reduced, and is responsible for much more learning than the negative reinforcement itself could produce, e.g., while avoiding one thing a person learns to avoid others paired with it. The child avoids spilling ink on the floor at school and on other floors. The pupil tries to avoid being questioned by the teacher so that his inadequate knowledge will not be revealed. By adopting a blasé or bored attitude, the adolescent avoids showing a strong interest in many things, because he does not want his ignorance uncovered. Parents and teachers who accept this self-protective approach, which operates through the generalized role of anxiety in behavior, enable the adolescent to build his knowledge and skills while not revealing how little he knows. Such adults succeed in helping the adolescent to manage his self-control. Since persons cannot know everything, they must often be able to conceal what they do not know, but the germs of concealment and deception are thus sown deep in personal structure [77, 85]. The need to conceal and not be discovered is as basic as the generalized anxiety —the avoidance of which leads to the operation of negative reinforcement in behavior.

The avoidance of persons and things, i.e., anxiety reduction, is circular in effect. The child avoids doing his homework, so he must avoid the teacher and his questions in class next day, and also needs to avoid being anxious about what he has not done. The satisfactory completion of any task has a similar circular effect in that a completed task prevents disapproval and exposure, and this gratification fosters the acceptance of more tasks to be completed.

When people are busy avoiding a person or situation, they are not helped by being exposed. They are helped by the adequate completion of one task that is independent of previous failures. References to previous inadequacies with a subject, or to the place, or to a particular school, or to a person, such as a teacher who knows what the pupil has not done well in the past, usually prevents current adequacy. That is why a new teacher and the beginning of a new unit of work often enable children to succeed. To be allowed to begin again without the backlog of previous annoyances breaks into the circularity of avoidance, disrupts the cycle of generalized anxiety.

To recapitulate: in spite of the fact that the effects of punishment are complicated and frequently unpredictable, teachers tend to punish and rely on the workings of negative reinforcement. Negatice reinforcement works to control behavior through the generalized role of anxiety. To avoid anxiety, persons do what is expected of them; the more sure they are of the expectation, the more positive their self-control becomes. They are controlled by themselves and others, usually to their benefit, through the combined workings of punishment and negative reinforcement.

Summary: Managing the Classroom

Because each person is under the control of many others, individual freedom is a matter of degree. Permissive control provides more gradual self-development than directive control, but the objective of each is eventual self-control. Such self-discipline within the limits of any situation is the highest possible level of individual development.

Whether the control is permissive or directive, if the objective of the control is the benefit of those controlled rather than their domination, the individual is allowed or required to perform within limits. When he goes too far, penalties are levied to assure him that the boundaries are there and that he is free to develop within them. Whenever he exceeds the limits, his feelings of assurance will be best supported if he is always reminded of the limits through the use of penalties and punishments that are levied for his excesses.

To discipline means to penalize, usually to benefit the offender rather than to dominate. The disciplinary episode is a concrete specific occurrence and, if treated as such, is an assistance and assurance to the offender. The penalty used will depend upon the situation, the offender, and the person who is in control—the person who is maintaining the limits of the situation. However, penalties should never vary in one respect, namely, they should be inevitable if their purpose is to support self-development. The inevitable penalty is a source of strength because of the assurance it provides of a consistent and stable world.

Consistency in maintaining boundaries is of value in all human relationships. When dealing with individuals, it is relatively easy to establish acceptance within the limits. When confronted with groups of 30 or more persons, however, teachers find it difficult to extend the mutual benefits of acceptance to all without the consistency of controls. The more others can rely on the stability of a person's reactions, the more assurance they develop in their relationships with him, even though he controls them.

6
level of aspiration

"Ah, but a man's reach should exceed his grasp,
Or what's a heaven for?"[1]

r OBERT BROWNING probably never heard of such terms as level of aspiration and goal discrepancy, but he expresses the ideas neatly nevertheless.

The space between one's reach (level of aspiration) and one's grasp (level of performance) is called the goal discrepancy. Teachers are

[1] Robert Browning, "Andrea del Sarto," ll. 97-98.

greatly concerned with their pupil's reach, their grasp, and how closely the two are related.

Guidance offices throughout the land spend much of their advisory time on two groups of students: (1) those who have low ability but aspire to high goals, and (2) those with high ability and low goals. In the first category are those who aspire to become engineers although they cannot pass intermediate algebra, those who are determined to pursue a medical career although their scholastic average will not even suffice for college entrance. In the second category are innumerable bright pupils who are apparently content to settle for occupations which will use only a small fraction of their talents.

The classroom teacher, as the first-line guidance person in any school, is also concerned with these problems and with the day-to-day differences in the pupils' abilities, performances, and aspirations in each subject. If these concerns are framed as questions, they may be listed as follows:

How well does the individual wish to perform?
How superior does the individual wish to be?
What goals has the individual set for himself? Is he satisfied with a "C" or a "B" grade?
Does he plan to be an architect or a draftsman?
Is he satisfied to be on the intramural team or will only varsity status do?

If the individual has enough ability for the more difficult choices, his level of aspiration will greatly affect his decision. And the choice is not his alone, because parents and teachers have aspirations for him too—they wish to see him using his abilities to the fullest.

Parents and teachers who want to influence goal-setting and its level must take into account two factors: the way the young person rates his own abilities, and the groups with whom he associates. He may choose to be a big frog in a little pond (his home town or neighborhood) or a little frog in a big pond (trying for the top in whatever he decides to undertake).

Aspiration is the act of wanting and desiring. People who desire more and who feel that they have more ability are willing to expose themselves to the hazards of failure. They are willing to risk competition with others, particularly with those they consider to be somewhat like themselves. Those with a strong need for security in their personal relationships are careful where they venture. Concern with self-exposure directs which relationships they will attempt and which they will avoid. Aspiration and its level are dependent on the degree of security that people require, on the role which they assign to the self, and on the groups with which they choose to associate and compete.

Experimental Work

It is necessary to recognize that experimental work tends to be specific to a particular set of conditions. Further, experiments tend to deal with one variable at a time, while practical interpretations require the consideration of several significant aspects at one time. Sometimes statements that may be true for a particular study do not have general applicability, in fact may be erroneous or unwise when interpreted as applying to other situations. Thus in reporting and interpreting the results of studies, the choices are obvious. Either the author reports the research and leaves the reader to apply it where he can, or the author takes the risk of interpreting and extending the conclusions. The practical application of the findings of research studies is more stimulating although more risky for the writer. While experiments can be interpreted to support opposing points of view, the purpose is not to provoke controversy but to indicate possible and permissible interpretations. While experimental work tends to be specific and limited, the range of interpretations and applications tends to be broad and general.

Experimental work with the level of aspiration has been used to examine *the formation of goals, success and failure, and ways of handling the self in relation to a group* [128, p. 225]. The essential process in promoting self-development in the formation of goals and in our group relationships has direct application to the classroom. For this reason, the experimental model is of interest to both the classroom teacher and the psychologist.

The Experimental Model

The conditions and terminology for examining the level of aspiration are as follows:

The level of aspiration represents the level of future performance in a familiar task which an individual explicitly undertakes to reach [127, 136, 153]. Success and failure are defined in terms of the relationship of performance to aspiration. A success is a performance which exceeds aspiration or a performance which is considered good although it does not reach the level of aspiration. A failure is a poor performance or a performance which does not reach the level of aspiration [3, 113, 327, 339]. The person indicates his level of aspiration numerically after some familiarity with the material, usually through practice trials [128, pp. 218-219].

To recapitulate: to experiment with the level of aspiration we need (1) a task that is familiar to the subject; (2) a task in which the subject becomes involved, that is, he tries again to reach another goal; and (3) a task that can readily be measured to facilitate comparisons of past, present, and future performances. In the sources paraphrased [3, 113, 128, 327, 339—in 128 Frank summarized the literature up to 1941], the materials used to meet the experimental conditions were a series of similar tasks (mazes or peg boards) graded as to complexity, or simple repetitive tasks with an achievement scale of speed or accuracy, e.g., a series of trials on an encoding task.

An encoding problem is a good illustration of a simple repetitive task. From the list in Figure III the subjects are asked to encode as many letters as they can in a 30-second trial.

More letters are provided to encode, per trial, than the fastest worker could do in thirty seconds, even after twenty or twenty-five trials. This is an example of a simple repetitive task which can be used to demonstrate the mechanisms in goal setting.

E	V	R	T	O	H	B	K	C	M
3	∩	L	K	X	Y	D	4	2	8

E	R	V	E	T	V	R	O	T	E	O	V	H	R	O	B

T	K	H	E	B	R	V	H	C	V	B	M	T	K	E	O

M	V	C	R	H	M	T	K	O	E	B	M	V	H	R	C

H	M	T	K	O	E	B	M	V	H	R	C	V	B	M	K

FIGURE III

An Encoding Task

The experimental situation can be diagramatically indicated as follows:

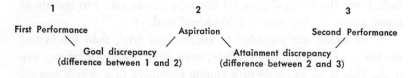

FIGURE IV[2]

The Level-of-Aspiration Paradigm

[2] Adapted from Kurt Lewin et al., "Level of Aspiration," in *Personality and the Behavior Disorders,* edited by J. McV. Hunt, Copyright 1944 The Ronald Press Company.

The difference between the last performance and the aspiration for the next performance is called the goal discrepancy. If the student spelled six words correctly last time, he may aspire to spell more correctly next time. The goal discrepancy shows the extent to which aspiration is running ahead of performance. A negative goal discrepancy would indicate that aspiration was lagging behind performance. This is rare. The difference between the number which he aspires to spell and the number that he actually does spell correctly is the attainment discrepancy. This indicates the extent to which performance is in keeping with his aspiration [233, p. 334].

The experimental model for the level of aspiration is used in the classroom dozens of times a week. To illustrate, let us assume that we are dealing with spelling. The student probably aspires to spell each word correctly, yet he expects to miss some words, so the following example can be cast in the form of the experimental diagram above.

1. The student performs. He tries to spell correctly as many of these words as he can: liquefy, paraffin, embarrass, naphtha, battalion, picnicking, rarefy, kimono, supersede, ukulele.
2. He states his aspiration for his next trial. Based on the fact that he spelled four correctly, he indicates that he will try to spell seven correctly next time, that is, he sets his own goal. It is well to point out that the gamblers may set their goal at 10 after spelling four correctly, while the cautious may only venture to six. (The dynamics of caution and gambling are comprehensible within our knowledge of level of aspiration.)
3. He performs again and compares his second performance with both his aspiration and previous performance.

The extent to which his aspiration for the next trial (2) differs from his past performance (1) is called the goal discrepancy. Usually his aspiration runs a little ahead of his last performance. He aspires to spell seven words correctly after spelling five words correctly. The difference between his second performance (3) and his previously stated aspiration (2) is called the attainment discrepancy. This difference shows how closely his performance is in keeping with his aspiration.

Although aspiration is usually slightly above the most recent attempt, its level is also directly influenced by the student's performance in relation to the middle of the group with which he has chosen to compete. Assume that the mean number of words correctly spelled was five. If he sees that he is inferior to the middle of the group (he spelled less than five words correctly), he aspires to do better and may actually do better. If he sees that he is superior to the middle of the group (he spelled eight words correctly), he may not aspire to advance to a great degree, and his performances may not improve as noticeably as when he feels that he is behind. Persons performing and aspiring above the middle tend to slacken their efforts to improve. The middle of the group with which he has chosen to compete tends to be the fulcrum of the level of aspiration and performance. He strives to keep up with and do better than the middle of his group. (Even in his most ambitious moments, when he chooses to be top man, he is striving in relation to the efforts of other top men.) His last performance in relation to the middle performance of his group is a major determinant of the level of aspiration and performance.

"Real-Life" and Experimental Conditions

It is difficult to create "real-life" involvement in experimental situations, and, in fact, this gap between "real-life" and laboratory measures of aspiration has been confirmed [22]. To illustrate: when we are conscious of the possibility of success or failure in an English course, our egos become involved in the situation; but when an experimenter in the laboratory makes a comment about our performance to attempt to induce involvement, our aspiration is not realistically changed. All of us may change both our aspiration and performance to cooperate with the experimenter; but even if he implies that the experimental work will change our course grade, the ego-involvement is artificial compared with classroom success and failure in English. Despite this discrepancy, experimental work has provided certain checks on our daily observations concerning level of aspiration.

For instance, experiments have substantiated the following conclusion:

The behavior of the level of aspiration is partially determined by such structural properties of the task as the number of steps in the achievement scale, the degree to which individual trials are emphasized, and whether or not the subject is forced to change the height of this level of aspiration after each trial. The apparent difficulty of the material is particularly important. If the task appears much too easy or much too difficult, the dynamics of the situation are entirely different from the task which lies within an intermediate range of difficulty. Moreover, people in a competitive situation tend to overestimate their probable progress when the task is made progressively more difficult without their knowledge, and to underestimate it if the task is made progressively easier [128, p. 220].

For the level of aspiration to be obvious in either real or experimental situations, the conditions referred to above need to be met. The workings of level of aspiration are observable in the classroom provided that tasks are scaled, that is, that they progress from easy to difficult; that individual achievement on each trial is emphasized; that the student is required to indicate what he aspires to do trial by trial; that each trial is a challenge for him, neither too easy nor too hard; that the student is not hoodwinked by changes in requirements of which he is not aware; and that the competitive situation does not cause the student to set an unrealistic goal for himself. If these conditions are met, the classroom-learning situation amply demonstrates that each person strives to achieve at a level slightly above his own last performance and that he may try to keep up with at least the middle performance of some one group within the classroom (each class is made up of several groups, and thus there are usually several middles).

Success, Failure, and Aspiration

To recapitulate, the level of aspiration is the height which a person will attempt to reach in future performances of a familiar task. Success and failure in attempts are defined in terms of the relationship of performance to aspiration. A performance that reaches or exceeds aspiration is defined as success. A performance that does not reach that height, but is judged by the performer or by others to be good, is also defined as success. Conversely, a failure is a poor performance as perceived by our standards or the standards of others, or one which does not reach the level of aspiration. Success and failure are judged in terms of the level of aspiration and the quality of performances in relation to that level.

Success ordinarily leads to the setting of increasingly realistic aspirations [113]. When the student has been successful, he sets his aspiration a little ahead of his own last performance. This realistic judgment of his ability results in good goal-setting, but he must also continue to be aware of the possibility of failure. Each task should be difficult enough to involve the self in possible success or failure but not so difficult that success is impossible or very unlikely.

The complex relationship between the degree of difficulty of a task and success and failure is suggested in a study of threat perception and one's memory for successes and failures.

After a group of college students had selected the degree of threat they perceived, their recall of successful and failed tasks was determined. Ten or 20 pencil and paper tasks could be completed and the other 10 appeared easy to complete but had no solution. After they had performed, students were asked to select the degree of threat they perceived. Three degrees were possible, namely, minimal threat, some threat, and stressful threat. The students read and had read to them three possible situations, one of which they were to identify with. The three situations were the three degrees of threat. The first level was a neutral situation, that is, the solutions to these 20 pencil and paper tasks are an experiment. The second level was evoked by the suggestion that the students' scores would be used to establish norms for others. The third, and the most stressful threat, was evoked by the suggestion that performance on the 20 tasks was an intellectual alertness inventory which would have an influence on their welfare. The students selected the degree of threat they perceived after they had performed. Those who perceived threat recalled more of the successfully completed tasks. The greater the threat, the more college students were apt to forget their failures and remember their successes, but those who perceived minimal threat did not recall a greater number of the tasks in which they failed [139, pp. 359-365].

This study indicated that the college students' perception of threat directed them away from failures and toward successes. All the development of learners appears to be similarly self-protective until we consider how any realistically high aspiration always exposes the learner to the devastation of possible failure. For instance, when spelling ability exceeds that of all persons in the immediate environment, be it school, family, or peer group (by opinion and by test), the learner is exposed to the possibility of being exceeded, whether he wishes to be so exposed or not. The appraisal of ability may be realistic, because the learner can do that well and has done that well. When he is known as the best, he is forced to defend his status, regardless of his need for self-protection. In other situations, however, when a person has a choice, his perception of the degree of difficulty and the chances for success or failure determine what he will attempt. One or two generalizations do not do justice to the complexity of the possible interactions of success, failure, and aspiration.

There would be no purpose in pointing to the complexity of behavior under the influence of success and failure without also indicating what has been learned about this relationship. The level of aspiration is most likely to rise or fall when there is a strong feeling of success or failure, but the effect of failure is more varied than that of success [76]. Severe failure lowers aspiration further than mild failure, while successive failures have a diminishing effect upon the level of aspiration [369].

In one study of 40 college students, undergraduates were assigned to one of two experimental conditions: mild failure and severe failure. The task was the solution of several series of simple arithmetic problems. The students were told that a standard length of time (40 seconds) would be allowed for each trial, but the actual time allotted by the experimenter was varied (presumably without the students' knowledge) in order to control success or failure. Thus, failure was caused by events over which the student had no control, rather than by his own reactions.

Success was measured by the number of problems completed on each trial. After the initial practice trial, each student was required to state a level of aspiration for each subsequent trial. There were 12 trials in all, of which the third, sixth, and ninth involved failure, i.e., nonattainment of the expressed level of aspiration. The third trial involved the same moderate failure for both groups, each student being stopped five to six problems prior to his expressed goal by the announcement that the time was up. The sixth and ninth trials, however, involved different failure for the two groups. The 20 students under mild failure conditions were stopped just one or two problems short of their goals, whereas the 20 students under the severe failure conditions were stopped at a point 10 to 12 problems short of their expressed goals. The students were allowed to reach their level of aspiration on all but these three trials. And on the success trials the students were stopped as soon as the level of aspiration was just reached, so that on all the success trials all 40 students just reached their stated aspiration.

Following each success trial, the experimenter said, "Very good, you made it. How many do you expect to make next time?" After moderate failure, the experimenter said, "I guess you didn't make it. You made (five) problems less than you expected. How many do you expect to make next time?" Following each severe failure, the experimenter said, "That's a very poor showing. You missed by a pretty sad margin. You got only _____ that time. How many do you expect to get next time?" With these comments the experimenter left no doubt in the thinking of the students as to the level of performance in relation to the level of aspiration.

The results confirm those of previous investigations. In general, failure experiences were followed by the lowering of aspiration levels, and more severe failure resulted in a greater drop than mild failure. Objective failure operated in a manner similar to that reported for subjective failure. Interestingly, with successive failures, there was a tendency to disregard the objective degree of failure. The study attributed the diminishing effect of failure on aspiration to the fact that there were successes between these failures. Without intervening successes, the several failures might not have had this lowered effect on the level of aspiration [369, pp. 79-82].[3]

Generally, following success, one attempts a little more, and following failure, performance is extremely variable, ranging from

---

[3] The material from I. M. Steisel and B. D. Cohen is presented with permission of the American Psychological Association.

ridiculous heights to pitiable depths. Following failure, we allow ourselves more unrealistic choices. Reality, unreality, and success and failure in relation to level of aspiration will be discussed in a later section. Not only the experiences of success or failure but their sequence are important determinants of aspiration, confidence, and performance [33]. The findings with respect to the sequence of success and failure are interpreted as showing the continuing effects of prior experience, since changes from success to failure or from failure to success created a lower level of actual aspirations. Aspiration was lowered more when the shift was from failure to success, but with shifts from success to failure, performances became erratic. As we would expect, success produces the most predictable subsequent aspiration and performance. However, children showed preference for the greatest exposure when success was followed by failure [231].

Those persons who habitually fail in school may be helped by enabling them to adjust their aspiration somewhat downward. Regardless of sources of failure, such as motivation, adjustment, and methods of study, children and adolescents who fail habitually have higher goal discrepancies, that is, they aspire to do much more than they accomplish. If their failure is treated in terms of their reactions to failure, it produces the most variable behavior— the level of aspiration is likely to rise or fall sharply. If their failure is treated in terms of its causes, the level of aspiration is lowered slightly [369]. If one gives the person reasons for his failure, he is likely to lower his level of aspiration realistically instead of dropping it to the depths or boosting it abnormally. This reappraisal of performance causes the person to focus attention on successful attempts rather than on feelings of failure.

The findings of Gebhard with respect to experience, expectation, and need, throw further light on the workings of success and failure. In general, experienced and expected success was accompanied by a rise in the attractiveness of the task, while expected failure resulted in lowered attractiveness. Average changes in the attractiveness of the task were significantly greater when both the expectation and the experience were in the same direction. Personal interest was greater and general comments were more favorable when success was experienced or expected. When the subject felt little need for the task, experience and expectation both produced significant variation in the mean preference rankings, but this was not so under strong need. The attractiveness of an activity is thus determined not only by past experiences of success or failure but by expectation of future success and failure as well [138, pp. 387-388].

Apart from all the studies of the rise of aspiration following successes and the variable aspiration following failures, there may be a general personality factor which accounts for reactions to success and failure in relation to performance [376]. The stability found in performance following a wide range of events suggests the development of a broad, stable, personality factor, although no one has yet been able to demonstrate its existence. Explanations of behavior will be easier if future experimental work shows that one's general personality has such an overriding effect.

Aspiration, the Self and the Group

Aspirations are influenced by the groups with which the person chooses to compete, but one refuses to feel frustrated or satisfied by goals which others set. Goal-setting develops in relation to the goals of the groups with whom one identifies and whose standards one accepts. Goal-setting is dependent upon maturing self-awareness and awareness of others [158, 265, 327]. Until self-awareness and the awareness of the self in relation to others matures, goal-setting follows the wishes and desires of those who control us. It usually becomes evident during the third or fourth grade that the student derives most satisfaction from his own aspirations and that these, in turn, are based on the goals of the classroom groups with whom he chooses to identify and whose standards of expectancy he incorporates. As the child moves into adolescence, groups outside the classroom become as important as the classroom groups (or even more so). His standards are oriented from his knowledge of group aspirations. In novel situations, nearly all persons "sit tight" and do nothing, since they do not have the group background to rely on [56]. Aspirations are influenced by the standards of the groups known to the individual and with whom he has chosen to compete. The selection of the groups which influence goal-setting and shifting from group to group depends on the development of self-awareness, awareness of others, and the need-fulfilling functions of the groups. As self-awareness and awareness of the self in relation to others develops, the person recognizes the contributions that others can make to his development. Experimental results suggest that whenever the person knows or feels that group solutions of problems and group action have exceeded his individual efforts, he strives to be at least as good as the middle of the group [347]. When he feels that his individual efforts excel the group action, he either shifts to another group or relies on his individual skill. From his involvement with others, the individual increases his range of knowledge and skills and the scope of his aspiration. As the person develops and matures, he shifts from group to group.

These shifts are usually in keeping with the need-fulfilling functions of each group. When the classroom or community recreation center does not take account of the shifting which occurs with maturation, trouble develops. Development implies instability, variability, and change. As each group in the classroom or elsewhere has contributed as much as the person feels that it can, he shifts to other groups to find the levels of ability and skill which are of interest. If he has fallen behind in his development and achievement, or if he has excelled, he seeks to change to groups more like him.

Judgment and Aspiration

Working from his perception of the previous performance, the learner judges how well he has done and how well he can do, particularly if the knowledge of results includes the range of possible scores [311]. Thus, as a judgment, the level of aspiration is determined by the perceptual anchor-points in reality, the last performance being most influential [74]. From his perception of reality, of what he is really doing as compared with his fantasy, he judges his performances and sets the height of subsequent goals. In play life, where there is very little threat to the self for not reaching aspirations, the goal discrepancies are high, that is, there are great differences between performances and aspirations [153, 339]. In play he is not anchored to reality; and failure to reach levels such as, "Watch me hit the ball a mile," are dismissed with, "I'm only playing," or, "I'm only kidding." When the person can "play" or "kid" and succeed, he capitalizes on his venture, knowing that he can always retreat to a safe excuse. In real life, if the contact with reality is good, judgments advance a little from the last performance. When fantasy and other unreality factors such as failure, "putting up a front" of socio-economic status, frustration, and antagonism, weaken the contacts with reality, the judgments of past performances and subsequent performances are likely to be unrealistic.

Cassel and Saugstad suggest that the significant differences between the sixth and eighth grade students are attributable to changes in the amount of unreality, which undergoes great changes at the time of puberty as a function of psycho-sexual development. They found popularity to be directly related to the unreality dimension of personality at the sixth and eighth grade level.

A sociometric technique was used to determine a popularity score for each child. ("Select the persons with whom you wish to work.") The unreality dimension was scored by averaging the discrepancy between the world as the sixth and eighth graders see it and the world as it is, i.e., as the performance score shows it to be. Eighth graders had higher popularity and higher unreality scores than sixth graders, and adolescents with higher popularity scores had higher unreality scores [69, pp. 321-325].

Socio-Economic Status and Aspiration

Persons constantly compete with groups at varying socio-economic levels. It has been found that persons of lower economic status have higher goal discrepancies [154], that is, the difference between their aspiration and their performance is higher than is the case for those who do not contend with socio-economic problems. Persons of lower socio-economic status have more to strive for, and they consequently tend to set their level of aspiration well ahead of their present achievement. This may be quite realistic, in that they see their potentiality as being well ahead of their present level. They consequently look to move ahead to what they perceive as higher levels. This is the mechanism of "keeping up with the Joneses." The "Joneses" are the group with whom they have chosen to compete. They see themselves as being like the Joneses, or they aspire to be like them. In spite of the cost to the self and others close to them, both economic cost and personal involvement and anxiety, which introduces dimensions of unreality, they try to keep up with the chosen group. As they exceed them, they move on to other groups. As they fall behind, the goal discrepancies become greater and greater until failures with that group, and/or successes with lower groups, change the level of aspiration. The need-fulfilling functions of groups cannot be overlooked [347]. People aspire to work with groups who aid them in reaching this perception of their possible development.

Individual judgments tend to be like the average judgment of one's group. Almost all persons of lower socio-economic status are interested in improving their lot, but they may not have the necessary ability to fulfill their aspiration. It is interesting to note that the occupational-level score is a measure of the status of interest but not a measure of drive, that is, interests as aspirations are expressed wishes and do not represent ability or even the drive to develop ability [27].

Frustration and Aspiration

Another influence that puts pressure on contacts with reality is frustration. The technical term for the amount of frustration a person can endure and still maintain a balance is "frustration tolerance." Thus, frustration is one of the major determiners of the level of aspiration [351]. When an individual is realistic, he sets his level of aspiration near his achievement level and as a result does not subject himself to great frustration. When he is unrealistic, he sets his level of aspiration far above or well below his achievement level. If his self-development has been bruised, he may either avoid further frustration by retreating to low levels of aspiration and performance, *or* he may continue to subject himself to the ravages of frustration. Some people can stand high levels of frustration and still mature and develop. This means that their frustration tolerance is high and that they will risk their composure in an attempt to succeed.

Individual Differences and Aspiration

Obviously the level of aspiration is not the same for all goals. A person aims at those goals he considers desirable. His appraisal of any situation directs his goal-striving for self-satisfaction, and the height of his goals in such areas as the home, the school, and the community, varies greatly from person to person [257]. To illustrate, the level of aspiration for achievement in English, social studies, mathematics, science, and foreign language studies is bound to vary from person to person according to one's subject matter preferences. Within each area, the level of aspiration works to set the height of his goals. Caution is necessary in trying to predict individual performances from group performances. Among the factors to be taken into account are individual variability in performance, the nature of the task to be performed, and the fact that phenomena found in the group do not always show up in the individuals comprising the group. Frequently, performances appear to be the product of group processes which are the work of one or two persons instead of the whole group. Thus if a teacher always calls on those who raise their hands to answer questions, he will get a highly exaggerated notion of the ability of the class. Lorge and others found that written reports from groups tend to underestimate the full productivity of the group, while individuals may overestimate [244]. If there is true group activity, and if we are aware of individual variability, we can cautiously predict individual performances from group performances on some tasks.

Sex also affects the level of aspiration. Sumner and Johnson found that goal and aspiration discrepancies, in every case they studied, were lower for women than for men, although the discrepancies were lower in the top quarter of the class than in the lowest quarter [375]. Now a generalization from this study that women are more realistic than men would be most untenable (particularly to men!). Individual differences are too variable to allow the broad sweep of such a generalization. A pertinent generalization from this study, however, can be drawn from the lower discrepancies found among the better students. Those who were toward the top of the class set their aspirations realistically close to their performances, while those who were in the lowest quarter of the class were more variable and were not as realistic about either their aspiration or their performance. When persons are low as compared with a group, and the group process is functioning (that is, they are involved with the group's goals), the differences between performances and aspirations are greater than when they are above the middle of the group.

High Levels of Aspiration

A high level of aspiration may be a direct expression of a goal, an incentive to better performance, *or* this high level may be a means of protecting the ego [128]. Those with a need for achievement are concerned with success and attaining a maximum, but a high level of aspiration may also be an expression of self-protection [249]. By setting his aspiration well beyond his performance, a person may hope to direct the attention of others from his performance to his desire to achieve. For instance, asthmatic children and their mothers set significantly higher goals than children and the mothers of children not so afflicted [238]. These afflicted people strive for more, not because they can achieve more, but to be accepted for their desire to achieve rather than for their level of performance. However, this illustration raises another question, namely, do these children have asthma because their mothers ask so much of them, and the children try to deliver? The question cannot be answered, but a high level of aspiration may be a protection.

Then there is the antevert, the person who tends to look to the future [384]. High academic achievers are predominantly anteverts insofar as their thoughts and conversations are concerned. Students high in future extension are more optimistic and will set goals well ahead of their present achievement as realistic possibilities. Thus, a high level of aspiration may also be a direct expression of a goal.

Low Levels of Aspiration

A low level of aspiration may be an objective judgment or a means of avoiding the appearance of failure [128]. Low levels of aspiration may be objective judgments, but only those who can either accept themselves as low-level operators or whose self-rejection is basic can set such low goals [81]. All other low levels of aspiration are compensations for real or imagined inadequacies. Persons wishing to compensate set low levels of aspiration to avoid the appearance of inadequacy or failure and to avoid tension. "After all, this is what I wanted to be. Who wants the ulcers of that job, for any amount of money?" A low level of aspiration may be an objective judgment, but it is more likely to be a device to avoid exposing one's inadequacy and a means of avoiding tension.

Security, Antagonism and Aspiration

A need for security causes persons to stay close to reality, because they are concerned with avoiding failure, with the security of being successful. When they wish to be secure, they plan to achieve a minimal level of aspiration, since their security is not disturbed as long as they do not appear to fail. They avoid the appearance of failure and preserve their safety by staying close to what they are sure they can do [217].

In spite of the need for security, people are sometimes caught in the rivalry of antagonism. Such rivalry produces wide and significant discrepancies both in setting goals for our own performance and in estimating the performance of those considered to be rivals [173]. There are discrepancies in levels of aspiration that are attributable to competition, but they are mild compared with those that result from antagonism. Competition usually functions close to reality, but the rivalry of antagonism is most unrealistic (he "lost his head"). The imagined schemes of a rival take one as far from reality as does the hope of exceeding an opponent. Goal discrepancies are high and variable whenever the rivalry of antagonism has disturbed contact with reality. To repeat, every judgment which we make of ourselves and others, and which others make of us, needs to be related to the degrees of ego-involvement. Whenever feelings of security are involved, or when antagonisms arise, each judgment will be more inaccurate than if these feelings are not aroused. Every judgment should be made with care and accepted cautiously, otherwise the discrepancies are widened.

Aspiration in the Classroom

The classroom can be a favorable setting for the development of realistic aspiration. In the classroom the conditions described in the experimental model for performance, aspiration, and subsequent performance, are superior to an experimental situation because they are real. Each day the student sets goals relative to many of his abilities and the abilities of others in his classes. Each day he succeeds and fails and learns to adjust his aspirations on the basis of his performances and the performances of his classmates. Furthermore, realistic aspirations in the classroom are possible with group after group and with many school abilities as he moves to class after class and subject after subject. A few conditions, however, should be emphasized to ensure ideal goal-setting in the classroom: the involvement of the student; graded tasks, from easy to hard; attention to individuals and individual differences; the influence of success and failure; cooperation; and reasonable competition.

Involvement and Development

The level of aspiration influences classroom work as long as the student is involved. If he is so superior that he easily excels everyone, or so inferior that there is no object in contention, the groups within the class do not aid his development. The teacher does best when he can pace the demands made of each subgroup at a level a little above its last performance. Even so, there will be those who fail. Their failure, explained to them in terms of the events which caused the failure, enables them to adjust their level of aspiration downward to a realistic point. Level of aspiration can work within the classroom without the teacher's involvement, but as the teacher becomes part of the group, his levels of skill and achievement provide goals for superior students.

Aspects of the stimulation of superior students through involvement with the skill of the teacher are well described in Fales's essay [117].

A Structure for Development

The same classroom procedures and methodology that promote self-development also promote realistic levels of aspiration. Good teaching, no matter what our philosophy of education, has always involved grading tasks from easy to difficult, attention to individuals and individual differences, consideration of the influence of success and failure, cooperative interaction between the student and the teacher, and reasonable degrees of competition. When teaching takes account of the difficulty of the task, individual differences, success and failure, and the roles of cooperation and competition, then individual and group developments in goal-setting and in personal interrelationships are promoted.

Teachers provide a structure to promote the development of realistic goal-setting when they scale tasks from easy to difficult. Some students start with the easy ones and progress only a short distance, while others will work through the full range of tasks provided. Some students slide through the early stages and are not really involved until the middle or end of the series of graded tasks. In order to manage school-subject materials adequately, it is essential to scale them from easy to difficult. This also contributes best to the individual development of each learner by providing a series of workable steps so that he feels he can succeed. (This planned, step-by-step presentation is the essential element of the "programs" used in automated teaching, see p. 177, Chapter 12.)

Attention to individuals and their differences fosters self-development. Good teaching pays enough attention to each person to make him feel that his unique development is the concern of the teacher, that all of his work every day is of importance, and that he is treated as an individual as well as part of a group. Now, within the energies and available time of any teacher, these are demanding conceptions for good performance and good goal-setting for both the teacher and the student. To the extent that the teacher is able to pay attention to each individual and to individual differences, he does better for himself as a teacher and for his pupils.

Cooperative interaction between teacher and students is essential to promote the development of realistic goal-setting. Feelings of distrust, doubt, and uncertainty destroy any opportunity for the teacher to be aware of developments in the student and for the student to follow willingly the directions of the teacher. Just as in the experimental situation, whenever people were hoodwinked, whenever they were not made aware of changes in the experimental conditions, the expected changes in goal-setting and performance did not occur; so also in the classroom, whenever the teacher does not plainly identify what is to be done and clearly appraise the level of performance, or when the student attempts to conceal what he does not know, the essential cooperative interaction is not possible. When people protect themselves from those who would lead them, they spend their time in protection rather than development. The feeling that the teacher knows and will help the student, *and* that the student will work to exploit his own knowledge and skill as well as the knowledge and skill of the teacher, leads to full development for both.

Competition, particularly to a mild degree, enables each person to rate his own performance as compared with others. The desire to achieve provides enough energy for learning and for gradually raising our levels of aspiration and achievement. Care should be used, however, because competition easily exceeds the mild level most favorable for maximum development.

Whenever competition is too keen, the student is pushed beyond his perception of reality to the point where his feelings of insecurity and antagonism disturb the efficient use of his abilities for learning. Good teachers dilute strong competitive urges to the point where the need to strive is present but not destructive. This is done by making achievement possible for each individual and seeing that there are enough success experiences for everyone, so that destructive competition is not necessary.

Superior individuals, moreover, are not usually motivated merely by competition; they pursue the mastery of knowledge and skill as intrinsic goals. They can compete but find the development of their abilities in their own right to be much more gratifying; and it need not be documented that self-development proceeding from mastery guided by intrinsic worth exceeds all competitive development in quality. Unfortunately, not all superior students find gratification in the pursuit of knowledge for its own sake. These bright but apathetic students, plus those of average and low ability, may be benefited by reasonable amounts of competition, hopefully leading to the establishment of an intrinsic interest.

Summary: Level of Aspiration

Aspiration is the act of desiring; and the levels of desire, as goals, are intimately related to success and failure, self-perception, and group relationships. Aspiration sets the level of striving, and this is a highly individual development.

The individual adjusts his expectancies and sets his goals in terms of his previous performances, especially the most recent. Usually his aspiration runs a little ahead of his last performance, but the performance of others with whom he has chosen to compete influences his decision also.

Level of aspiration is a judgment of the height of future performance. True success leads to the setting of increasingly realistic goals but easy success does not change aspirations appreciably. The individual needs to sense the possibility of failure for success to carry its full gratification, yet failure disrupts his development. Failure produces variations in aspiration and performance, and the variability may be quite extreme.

The group does not influence a person's aspirations until he has developed both self-awareness and an awareness of the self in relation to others. Even then, he may not be sufficiently influenced to change—

his last performance is still the most influential factor in shaping his judgments of his own aspirations and those of others.

The relationship between his judgments and his ability to perform is a measure of his contact with reality.

His socio-economic level may lead him to contend realistically with several groups at various levels, or it may lead to unrealistic aspirations.

Frustration tolerance varies widely from person to person, but in each case is a function of the person's contact with reality and his aspirations.

A high level of aspiration may arise directly from a goal, or may be an incentive to better performance, or it may be a method of protecting the self.

A low level of aspiration may be an objective judgment or a way of avoiding tension and frustration, a way of protecting the self. Goal-setting which is low is always suspect, for few persons realistically develop a self-image of generally low levels of aspiration.

If the classroom provides for a series of tasks graded from easy to hard, attention to individuals and individual differences, consideration of the influence of success and failure, cooperative interaction between the teacher and the student, and reasonable degrees of competition, it is quite likely that the pupil will become interested in his self-development. The conditions for the development of realistic levels of aspiration thus have direct application to classroom teaching.

7

the conditions for learning

aLTHOUGH MOST PERSONS pay little attention to their learning habits, learning success is closely dependent on the conditions for learning. Attitudes expressed in statements like: "This is difficult for me," "I'm not good at this," "I work much better alone," "My best time is the early morning," "I just need to get things organized," sound like excuses for inability to learn rather than valid comments. Such tenuous generalities about learning emphasize how little attention is paid to the conditions for learning. Differences in ability cause differences in performance, but few persons have explored where their abilities are full and where they are limited, chiefly because they ignore whole areas of knowledge and understanding. If someone perchance falls into ways to excel his fellows, he accepts his superiority without question. If he is unsuccessful, he rarely stops to consider wherein he failed to learn.

Learning how to learn comes through experience in learning. An ability is developed to acquire sets, to improve discrimination, to direct attention, and to execute performances of increasingly better quality. Because every principle mastered is fruitful in teaching persons to learn more effectively, the conditions for learning are the conditions for teaching.

Practice

That "practice makes perfect" has long been a cherished maxim among English-speaking peoples, and has its counterpart in other languages. While there is undoubtedly a modicum of truth in the adage, one need only examine his own handwriting to discern an instance where more practice makes imperfect. From any theoretical or practical point of view, however, the case for routine, drab practice is weak. Rote learning is of value in a few special instances for an individual, e.g., idioms in a language or a formula in mathematics or science; and someone can always point to something better than rote for even these special instances. Rather, the learner benefits from practice when the other important learning conditions are operative at the same time. While these conditions were initially stated by Thorndike [387], the interpretation here is in terms of practical classroom applications rather than theory.

To be specific, the learner needs:

practice in all possible sets or contexts;
practice with the demands of the situation clearly identified;
practice of responses he can make, responses that are available to him;
practice where the belongingness is established between what is
   required and the responses available to meet the requirements;
practice with a knowledge of results so that the principle of effect
   can work.

Under these conditions of practice, discrimination improves, efficiency develops, and quality level rises.

Of course practice makes a difference. It strengthens associations and provides the opportunity for new associations to occur [322]. Further, the answers to questions such as how much practice and which practice sessions yield the greatest gain require carefully controlled work with the individual learner, and precise definition of the degree of mastery required. Interesting theoretical presentations of the role of practice are found in Guthrie [161] and Wertheimer [415].

Set or Context

Learners should practice under all possible "sets." "Set" means the way one perceives the situation; other common names for it are "context" and "frame of reference." These terms all refer to a structure of temporarily related elements that determine what one pays attention to in the present situation [417]. Set is a selective and directive mechanism.

People confront each situation with a preparation from prior learning. This set and their awareness of the present situation determine the aspects to which attention is directed [168]. If asked, "Can you wiggle your right ear?" the majority of persons will say no, thinking that the skin of the scalp has to be voluntarily moved to meet the requirement of the task. The question was, "Can you wiggle your right ear?" All that is necessary is to change the set from scalp movement to hand movement. Anyone can wiggle the right ear by raising the right hand to hold the ear and wiggling it. The set of either scalp movement or hand movement is what is meant by the preparation from prior learning combined with present awareness.

Obviously, set is not a constant manner of approach. It is changed in keeping with experience and the perception of the situation. Present awareness includes both personal needs and the demands of the environment. Insensitivity in combining prior experience and present awareness results in a fixity of approach, a fixity of set.

Pemberton found that many people perform inadequately because of an inability to relinquish an incorrect response, to change their set easily, to abandon an organization and re-organize. What is required is a freedom from the gestalt being formed by either the objective stimulus or the mental set adopted by the subject [293, pp. 267-288].

One must learn many sets and develop the ability to change sets as needed, but these abilities are acquired only through exposure to a variety of tasks which are ranked in order of difficulty. However, several variables make it difficult to organize such graded, ordered exposure, namely, task differences, individual differences, and the interaction with total behavior of each new venture in learning. If the teacher organizes his understanding of material into what he considers to be a series of workable steps (a thought model), he imposes his understanding, through the structure he chooses, on those who try to follow his thinking. Apart from the varied ways of developing a series of graded tasks and individual variation in the ability to follow the structures that other persons develop, tasks themselves are highly variable. This task variability stems chiefly from individual preferences for tasks and the fact that some tasks are more of an all-or-nothing nature rather than yielding to logical, step-by-step development.

Individual, organizational, and task difficulties are slight, however, as compared with the integration of a new task with the total existing behavior pattern. Teachers may teach specifics, but the interaction of these specifics with total behavior is highly variable [65]. Complete rejection of the new item by the learner may have disruptive consequences, while full acceptance will integrate the item into the general development pattern. As we grow and develop, the scope of our total behavior mushrooms. The suggestion of "mushroom-like" growth, however, assumes a reasonable degree of adjustment, because behavior disturbances sharply restrict our functioning. Theoretically, the greater the number of areas of knowledge and the more situations involved, the better the opportunity for the teacher to aid the learner in his expanding total development. Practically, the interactions of single or multiple tasks may demand so much of the developing individual as to provoke disturbances in the total behavior, and teachers' skills are not yet sufficient to predict when, where, with what, and with whom. Usually teachers include as much of the life situation as possible in each learning episode, but the student learns specific things, such as three plus four. He then requires a variety of tasks that rely on three plus four, including the obvious four plus three. Such a simple variation in task sequence (four plus three and three plus four) amounts to changing the set; consequently the learner usually profits most from experience in all possible task sequences [290]. Teachers who stress the multiplication table as a set of combinations to be memorized often find pupils counting up or down from some number that they know well to those they are not sure of. Such patterning may be helpful to begin with, as a specific guide to task performance, but such crutches often limit the adaptability of the individual in using his new learning quickly and easily. Teachers try to aid in learning set and changes of set through providing experience with a variety of tasks, but they should expect unevenness in development, particularly until each new technique is integrated into the total behavior.

Identifiability

It is difficult, if not impossible, to hit a target that we cannot identify, yet teachers regularly neglect to make clear what the target is. For instance, the instructor may say, "Your assignment for next Monday is Chapter 3." What is the student to do with the chapter? Skim through it? Read it thoroughly? Make notes on it? Understand the main ideas? Memorize the facts in it? If the student is to guess at the assignment, there is no assurance he will guess correctly.

The good teacher makes certain that each student knows exactly what is required of him. This, however, requires that the teacher clearly perceives the objectives of the moment, the lesson, the unit, and the term.

Even when the teacher knows what he wants, the process of identification is time-consuming. The teacher defines the assignment and answers the questions raised; he may find it necessary to re-explain to the class as a whole, and to explain even further for some individuals. Although this process is time-consuming, it is worthwhile because of the gain to the student which arises from it [406].

Practice with the target clearly identified is realistic, self-assuring, and approaches the level of self-teaching. When the student knows exactly what he is to do, he can appraise realistically the quality of his work. Working with teachers who appreciate the value of identifiability, he is stimulated to question them for help, to criticize his own work, and to expect them to be critical of his work—all this as a direct development from knowing exactly what he is to do.

The criticism that identifiability stifles originality and creativity is not valid. In practice, quite the reverse is found to be the case. When the objective is clearly defined, the pupil can think of novel approaches and actively seek permission from the teacher to complete the work with variations and additions. Sometimes high school English teachers will give an assignment, "Write a 300-word essay on any topic you choose." This is quite often difficult to work on. For nearly everyone, being thrown into a creative field leads to floundering, poor achievement, and less satisfaction in the work, chiefly because there is no structure to struggle with or to differ from.

Practice with identifiability fosters the development of teachers and learners. For the teacher, it leads to clearer perception of the objectives and of the content in terms of the objectives. For the student, it leads to assurance and confidence in both accomplishment and self-appraisal. For teacher and learner, definiteness of targets leads to more knowledge and skill.

Availability

Availability is defined by the question, "Can the learner make the response that the situation requires?" If he cannot, obviously it is quite hopeless to expect performances of good quality. For instance, no teacher would assign readings in Spanish if the student could not read Spanish. Yet many teachers make assignments that are similarly impractical.

To be specific, if the arithmetic problem requires the use of fractions, the assignment is defeated unless each student can skillfully manipulate fractions. If the teacher requires responses that are not available, the pupil is confused and learns to disregard the assignments. Students withdraw from such situations to avoid further rough exposure.

To prevent such withdrawal for self-protection, the teacher must go back in each subject to the student's place. For instance, if the algebra student cannot add, the teacher who wants to help him must teach addition. Algebra teachers are dismayed at the prospect of using time for elementary arithmetic and, reasonably enough, they raise the question regarding how students were allowed to progress to their level without skill in addition. (This is a good question, but the answer lies in the philosophy of education, not here in the psychology of learning.)

Consider the student in relation to teachers who make certain of availability. In an assignment to read three paragraphs and report orally on the three basic ideas expressed, if the student can read, and understands the structure of a paragraph, he searches out the topic sentence in each case. He has the three basic ideas. He was able to succeed because the necessary skill was available. Teachers helped him to be more adequate; students will venture with such teachers even into unknown territories of learning.

It is frequently impossible to find a large repertory of responses available in many students. Sensitive, successful teachers nourish those that they do find, *and,* with the students' positive "I can do it" attitude, venture a little way into what the students cannot do. The complaint by teachers of advanced courses that they do not have time for reteaching and relearning the basic work is indefensible. They must find the time if they are going to teach their subjects at all. All advanced notions are founded in a firm grasp of the basic principles. This implies that all content can be arranged in hierarchical order from simple to complex. While there are exceptions to such organization, every teacher who is concerned with availability returns to what he considers to be the fundamentals of the subject, teaches, reteaches, and reviews, and then moves forward to what he considers to be higher levels of organization and content. Whenever teachers follow this procedure, individual students and classes develop with their teachers.

Belongingness

Belongingness is a function of the structure of things. It is the connection, relationship, and organization between things. The failure of belongingness is illustrated by the boy's comment, "Oh, *that's* what you wanted." He did not put the requirement with the responses he could have made.

In a time sequence, belongingness comes after practice, identifiability, and availability. In Figure V, belongingness appears to be an intermediate step to availability, but this is not so.

FIGURE V

The Function of Belongingness

For belongingness to develop, both identifiability and availability are prerequisites.

Just as the teacher, for the benefit of the student, cannot spend too much time on identifiability, so also it is profitable to spend time on establishing belongingness: "This is what you are to do, and these are some ways you might do it." The teacher is rewarded as the successful director of behavior, and the student gains confidence from accomplishment.

Belongingness is harder to achieve than the other conditions for learning, and for this reason it appears to be more nebulous; but it is just as real, just as practical, and just as indispensable as the other conditions for learning. With the maturity and confidence of late high school and college, superior students do not need belongingness spelled out for them to the same degree, but no one ever outgrows his need for help with identifiability and availability.

Knowledge of Results

As soon as possible after he has performed, the student should know how well he has done. If the teacher tells him how well he has done, the realistic appraisal by the teacher of the behavior he helped to stimulate is good for the teacher and even better for the student [6, 42].

The immediacy, "as soon as possible after the performance," has great value for the student. Just after he has performed, the student is most aware of what he has done, exactly what he is sure of, what he barely achieved, and what he needs help with. If the knowledge of results is delayed a week or two, the student is scarcely aware of what he knew and what he did not know.

The knowledge of results should be given in detail. Pointing specifically to the excellent, good, fair, and poor aspects of performance is of inestimable value for both student and teacher. For the student to be told that his work is good without his knowing why it is good is of very little help. Similarly, for the student to be told that his work is poor without knowing why is only discouraging. To be told that we have done poorly, and shown in detail where we have done poorly, can assist and encourage us to better our next performance. Further, giving such detailed criticism obligates the teacher to sharpen his knowledge of content and his perspective of objectives, of what he wants.

A knowledge of results, given as soon as possible and in detail, nurtures the development of the teacher and the learner. This comes about chiefly through confidence regarding what is good and appropriate in the responses made. The learner is encouraged to modify his inadequacies in the proper direction, and the teacher is rewarded by the improvement which results from his leadership.

Effect

That which happens just after a satisfactory performance somehow seems to work backward to strengthen the connection between the stimulus and the performance. Theorists are not sure how this comes about [Thorndike, 387] [Meehl, 268], but the following statement is verifiable and acceptable as a generalization regarding the workings of effect: a favorable condition following the learning produces an impression which exceeds anything else; an unfavorable condition impresses less than a favorable condition but more than a state in which there is no positive or negative effect.

In terms of the classroom, the teacher who confirms responses with "good" and "yes," and corrects responses with "do it this way" rather than "No! No! Not that way!" impresses what he considers to be desirable and avoids impressing responses which he wants the child to change.

Effect stems directly from the knowledge of results and the manner in which the results are spelled out for the learner. And because the knowledge of results follows from practice in all possible sets or contexts, when the learner can identify what is required of him, *and* has the responses available, *and* when belongingness exists between the demands of the situation and the resources in the individual, each of these four conditions for learning (set, identifiability, availability, and belongingness) influences effect.

When the teacher appreciates the influence of effect, the emphasis is on positive, assuring, confirming help. Corrections and redirections are necessary for everyone; but when the negative aspects of correction and redirection found in "No" and "Don't do it that way" are avoided, attention is turned from the inadequacies themselves, and the mistakes are not overemphasized. "Try that this way" and "Change that from here on" are not indefinite statements. They imply that the teacher knows where the error lies. They emphasize the need to change the behavior. It is not always desirable for the teacher to point out exactly how the learner should change his behavior, but in the early stages of any work it is comforting to receive that much assistance.

Arranging the conditions for learning so that effect can work provides for continued development, as demonstrated by maturing discrimination, efficiency, and quality. The workings of effect follow from practice in all possible sets or contexts, with identifiability, availability, belongingness, and a knowledge of results.

Discrimination

Discrimination is a process of detecting differences, and the purpose of detecting differences is to determine what is necessary and to select appropriate responses from those available. For instance, the use of the correct calculations for the solution of arithmetic problems shows a level of discrimination. One of the marks of increasing maturity is continual improvement in this ability.

A fairly regular improvement in discrimination results from successive practice sessions, particularly from combined mental and physical practice [167]. Even the least self-critical person will try to draw a better circle on the next attempt and will be somewhat aware of the inadequacies in his performance. One may think his way through shorthand-forms or a good game of golf, and this thought is of some value in directing learning, but the improvement that results from thought alone is not comparable to that from the combination of thought and action. Practice of the thought through actions results in the greatest individual development. This is most evident in tasks that are largely psychomotor, because principles of learning apply more similarly to persons, whether they are of high or low ability, when psychomotor tasks are considered [319]. The verbalization of responses makes it easier to learn discriminative motor responses, that is, it helps to fix our actions with words. The human solving a maze has an advantage over a rat because he can say to himself: "Two right turns, then two lefts and a right." It is interesting to speculate on the role of words and individual differences in the use of words in directing discriminative ideational responses. For instance, do people with superior ability with words have superior discriminative abilities? This may be so; the possession of names for stimuli in a learning task enhanced performance on that task, but the implications of the generalization have not been proved [328]. Regardless of the nature of the responses involved—motor, psychomotor, and/or verbal—successive practice sessions produce an improvement in our ability to detect and select appropriate responses.

Teachers can help pupils to improve their discrimination [371]. Practice with relevant instructions regarding the events to be noticed and remembered leads to better performance. But a word of caution should be added, because the improvement of discrimination from practice with relevant instructions is not likely to be a broad or general change in behavior. The repetition provides for opportunity to learn what was missed on the first trial and helps to strengthen associations and relationships once they are formed [323]. Discrimination improves with those specific items that are noticed and practiced, and this limited improvement in discrimination with instruction is evident throughout life. Seventh graders were found to be superior in the word skills which they were taught, but the improvement did not generalize to related abilities like general vocabulary and the rate or comprehension of reading [291].

In another study, data were obtained for tasks which were four, six, eight and 10 units in length, both with and without instruction in the principles underlying the solution of the problems. It was found that when no specific instruction was given, the six-, eight-, and 10-unit problems were of approximately equal difficulty, while a four-unit problem was significantly less difficult. With instruction in the underlying principles, the four-, six-, and eight-unit problems were found to be of approximately equal difficulty, while the 10-unit problem was now relatively more difficult. In addition to the shift in relative difficulty, the detailed instructions were effective in reducing error scores generally, for all these conditions [131, pp. 89-97].

The improvement of discriminative abilities is relatively narrow, limited to the specifics included in the instructions [305]. The implication for education is obvious. For discrimination to improve, there is a need for practice with careful instruction for years, perhaps for a lifetime.

Efficiency and Quality

Efficiency in learning means rapidity and accuracy [126]. The relationship between rapidity and accuracy in intellectual work is apt to be positive, that is, the more rapid, the more accurate, and the more accurate, the more rapid. (This is probably due to the capabilities of the individuals concerned.) In sensorimotor tasks the relationship between accuracy and rapidity is likely to be negative, and in tasks that require both cerebration and sensory-motor skill, little correlation is apparent. Individual differences in ability, tensions, social conditions, attitudes, and other influences serve to confuse these generalizations.

Efficiency in learning also requires the detection and correction of errors. One would think it possible, at least in the case of bright learners, for persons to rely on their understanding and reasoning ability to avoid errors. But being annoyed at one's mistakes does not suffice to bring about corrections; ingenuity is required to devise ways of avoiding errors. This is even more evident with dull and average learners than with the bright; but for all levels of intelligence, it is not reasoning or understanding or personal annoyance which usually leads to correction of errors, but the development of techniques for avoiding the mistakes. This explains why analytic methods of teaching spelling that rely on understanding and comprehension do not work better than conventional methods that emphasize the pattern and phonetic scheme of the spelling words. Ingenuity in devising ways to avoid errors still seems to provide more efficiency in reducing the number of errors.

Besides being efficient, performances should be of high quality. The level of classroom performance is directly related to the kind of demands made. Teachers who require performance of high quality generally receive it. Teachers who will accept performance of poor quality are plagued by that kind of work. If the teacher will accept careless spelling and English usage, these are what he will get. When performances of poor quality are evident, persons close to the student have been lax in their demands. The demands of quality are not related to the degree of difficulty or the level of the work. Quality in the demands made applies to the simplest concrete performance of the slow sixth grader, and to the complex abstract performance of the brilliant college student. Whether for the individual or the class as a whole, the quality of performance is directly related to the quality of the demands made.

The Conditions for Learning and Self-Development

Persons become conscious of themselves and their "selves" as particular kinds of individuals as they perceive the response of others to them, to what they do [212]. Those who teach, whether called teachers, instructors, professors, parents, brothers, sisters, leaders, or friends, help to develop self-attitudes by their reactions to what the learner does, by their reinforcement of behavior. This supervision shapes the "selves" because people act in response to these models. If models are provided with which persons can identify themselves, development is fostered. No one can force the development, but if models of good quality are available during the doing and behaving, actions and reactions will tend to follow those patterns.

Development involves two aspects of self-learning, for the learner himself and for others. Persons learn to perform in ways that satisfy others, as expressed in their positive reinforcements, because this bolsters self-acceptance. More important to the self than performance for others is the personal organization of knowledge and information to support performance. Understanding of oneself develops as a product of the personal organization of what one does. People act for themselves and for others. Learning, as self-development, is the continual improvement of these two aspects of self-learning, namely, self-understanding and self-development in keeping with reinforcement from others.

Summary: The Conditions for Learning

The conditions for learning are the conditions for teaching. In brief, the teacher provides for practice in all possible sets or contexts, making sure that the student can identify what is required, that the student can make the responses, that the belongingness is established between what is required and what the student can do, and that the knowledge of results is immediate and stated in detail. Under these conditions the student receives the maximum benefit from the workings of effect.

As a student rehearses, the teacher confirms the responses he wants and avoids impressing the undesirable and the inadequate. The learner's assurance of prompt confirmation quickens his development. His discrimination of correctness and appropriateness improves. He becomes more efficient, and the excellence known as quality may develop. As the student performs for his teachers and himself, his development is shaped. If those close to the student appreciate the value of positive reinforcement, they will provide models of good quality with which the student can identify.

8

remembering

THE DEVELOPMENT OF ABILITY to remember is essential to human welfare. Even the least academic person relies on memory to find his way home from work and to meet the other ordinary demands of each day. Those who are more concerned with thought, ideas, and creativity, are obviously condemned to a daily struggle with remembering. The ability to remember (and to forget "conveniently") allows a person the privilege of facile expression, contrasted with people's halting and embarrassing behavior when they are not able to remember. Regardless of the nature of the activities in which one engages or how competent he wishes to be, the ability to remember is an essential aspect of each activity and of all levels of competence.

Remembering is an elusive ability which is of great assistance when persons wish to remember and a major source of self-annoyance when they cannot. Frequently, in spite of strong efforts, the very things a person wishes to remember elude him. It is almost as though the need to remember them had made them more elusive. Productive thinking, however, requires remembering together with omissions and contributions from recall and recognition. Most persons do not recognize that skill in recall and recognition is the result of ability to reproduce content. The creative urge pushes people to ignore the shackles of reproduction, but productive efforts are still firmly anchored to that ability.

An Indispensable Function

Remembering, memory, and retention refer to a universal biological function which is indispensable for all consistent behavior [246]. Such consistency is based on experiences which one recalls or recognizes so that today's behavior is like yesterday's, and tomorrow's will probably be similar. That a dog responds to his master's whistle involves memory. That persons think for themselves or enjoy a range of interests involves memory. That people manage any of their daily routines for themselves involves adequate remembrance of behaviors which have been responsible for the present level of development.

Memory has no precise location in man. More memory is controlled by the cerebral cortex of the forebrain than by the rest of the body, but it has not been possible to limit this high-level function to a single area. Former hypotheses, such as neuronal networks and the facilitation of anatomical pathways, have not held up under investigation. At its simplest level, memory seems to depend upon a modifiable molecular structure. Remembering is neither a reflex nor an intellectual construct. It is behavior which is made possible through the electrical and/or chemical functioning of the body. Chemical shock, such as an overdose of insulin, disturbs the chemical balance; electric shock produces a disturbance in the electro-potential; either of these physiological disturbances can produce marked changes in memory and in the thought processes. Even these changes, however, are temporary adjustments for the majority of people, because the patterns of learned behavior are restored by memory, a characteristic of the organism which is as basic and as biological as the colloids which keep the tissues of the body together.

Reproduction and Production

Memory unites the past and the present through the representation of aspects of the past in present contexts. Those which are thus brought up again provide an outline of personality, that is, memory makes the past available, but on a selective basis, in keeping with individuality [255]. Careful scrutiny of what is reproduced and what is inhibited from a series of experiences common to a group of people would provide an outline of individual personality for each member of the group. Pessimistic persons, for example, tend to recall more unfavorable experiences than optimistic persons. Obviously, exposure to common rather than different experiences is essential to the experimental design. If the group is exposed to common experiences, the variables involved are individual reactions to perception of the experiences (and these also involve memory) and the individual functioning of memory in the subsequent reproductions. Since each person comes to each experience with a different background, estimation of the role of present perception and the role of memory in awareness and remembering is difficult, if not impossible; yet the individual personality is often clearly revealed. This evolving function makes some of the past available for present redevelopment.

The most interesting aspect of memory is the productive rather than the reproductive quality [30]. If memory yielded only those materials to which it had been exposed, and then in the same form and organization, it would be mechanical. Instead, memory functions as dynamically as life itself. It yields to training, as most aspects of the self do, but its potential is a variable from the cradle to the grave. Memory receives facts and ideas, combines them with the existing residue, and produces a product which ranges in nature from similarity to originality and from rote reproduction to the full expression of mature personality. There may be a negative effect on productive thinking, in that specific prior experiences may limit perception and make experience less available. Productive thinking is not the process of arriving at a solution through the direct application of previous learning; past experience is instead repatterned and re-established to meet current demands. It is a part of reasoning. Reproductive thinking is characterized by the solution of problems through the existence of equivalencies between situations and meanings in the novel or problem situations and in the previously mastered situations. This is the chief process in the transfer of learning (Chapter 11).

Through the function of memory, past and present are united in productions which range in quality from verbatim quotations to full expressions of creativity. As Bartlett wrote, if we wish to know whether a man remembers anything, we ask him; and we generally take his word for it, even when he can give us but little detail [30]. However, when a person wishes to determine the amount and quality of memory, he resorts to measures of recall and recognition or the determination of the savings method.

Recall is skill in the reproduction of material without external support, e.g., "Name the first four presidents of the United States." Recognition, as the name implies, is skill in selecting from presented materials. For example, "From this list of the names of the presidents, select the first four." The savings method is evidence of memory in that the second learning is easier and quicker than the first. The third learning is even easier and faster, and so on. The amount and quality of what is remembered is determined by various testing procedures (Chapter 18).

Aspects of Remembering

The patterns of remembering reflect the development of each learner. For purposes of convenience and illustration, they are treated as separate; but each aspect of learning and remembering is related to all the other characteristics of full development. Persons develop as complete beings, and emphasis on one aspect at a time should not be interpreted as implying that development is piecemeal. Whenever people wish to help themselves to recall, to recognize, and to remember, they resort to the practices which support remembering. Similarly, when others wish to help in this process, they direct attention to a number of considerations which support the ability to remember. Persons are not permanently condemned to poor memory, and it is not by chance that some have good memories. Teaching and learning to remember are well within the grasp of practically everyone. The degrees of mastery which others require and which persons demand of themselves are the stumbling blocks. Absolute or total recall is an unattainable level of development, an impossible goal. The pursuit of total recall distorts both our own perspective and the judgment of others with respect to this ability; this distortion is most unfortunate, since ability to remember need not be perfect in order to be of great service in both work and play. There are a number of practices which improve memory if time and energy are invested in them.

Attitudes and the Material

The influence of attitudes was discussed in Chapter 3, and reactions to the nature of the material to be remembered are a further expression of readiness. Favorable attitudes predispose people slightly toward retention [135]; unfavorable attitudes can limit the use of sufficient ability for learning and so lessen the possibility of retention. Favorable attitudes are not a substitute for ability or for the necessary practice, but they make it easier to remember.

One's attitudes toward the current material to be learned are themselves a product of memory. Thus the past acts directly on present efforts. When persons deal with the kind of content they have previously been able to learn and remember, they are likely to be favorably disposed toward more work, more learning, and further retention. The familiar is comfortable. On the other hand, materials can become the symbols of struggle and defeat and failure; persons are then less willing to approach them and work with them. Without the effort to remember, retention is less likely.

Laboratory situations are obviously artificial compared with life situations, but the artificiality of laboratory situations is only partially detrimental to learning and remembering. Laboratory situations engender only mild conflicts and defensive attitudes, but these conditions may deter learning and remembering. Materials and situations that engender attitudes of avoidance evoke reactions which make learning and remembering more difficult.

College students who through previous learning had developed defenses against hostile and aggressive feelings, were given a learning problem. The criterion for learning was one perfect recitation of a list of hostile words and a list of neutral words.

The hostile word list was: dark-blown; square-harm; slow-fight; blue-rage; short-hate; white-threat; deep-curse; hard-death.

The neutral word list was: cold-bird; swift-tree; soft-room; high-book; green-cliff; light-road; loud-height; long-stone.

The study found a statistically significant retardation in learning rate for hostile words as compared with neutral words [418, pp. 324-331].

Attitudes make hostile words harder to learn than neutral words. Material which is associated with acceptable personal attitudes, feelings or acts (ego-acceptable or congruent) is learned at a more rapid rate and remembered more easily than material which is unacceptable (ego-alien or incongruent).

When the learning is more difficult, remembering is usually more difficult. Of course, there are always a few vivid or traumatic items which hold a place in memory because of the impression they make. But with an extended task like the hostile and neutral words above, the generalization holds, namely, one is less likely to remember the unfavorable.

To restate the positive position, favorable attitudes predispose persons slightly toward retention. This is not the broad strong statement of the influence of attitudes which most teachers would like, but it is as much as the facts warrant. Other aspects of the learning situation are more important to remembering.

Meaningfulness

When the material to be retained is meaningful, remembering is easier. The meaningfulness which is of most assistance is that related to previous learning, rather than on the interpretations and elaborations of others. If one can perceive meaning in the material, meaning which is a development from prior learning and present process, memory is aided. This does not refer to the differences in ease of memory between nonsense syllables and words with meaning. Rather it concerns the individual meaning for each person. Material which is integrated into personal development is easier to retain. Meaningfulness is individual, so material which is meaningful to the teacher is not necessarily meaningful to the pupil.

Experimental work with learning and remembering uses nonsense syllables because they eliminate uncontrolled variables, particularly the influence of prior learning and present meaning. The memory for nonsense syllables depends only on the work done with them. Underwood, and his coworkers on distributed practice, developed a set of nonsense "syllables" from the nine consonants, C, H, F, K, M, Q, R, T, X, as shown in Figure VI.

A	B	C	D	E	F	G
CRX	HQM	XRK	CQM	FXR	RKX	MRH
HTQ	MCK	CHM	KRX	HMQ	QTH	FQT
RFM	HRF	QMT	XTH	CHX	MXF	RKC
QCK	XCT	FRX	HRF	MTQ	CMT	XHT
MKX	FRK	KFT	QMC	KCT	HQF	FQX
HFT	TXQ	HQC	FTK	RKF	CKR	CMK

FIGURE VI

Nonsense Syllables

[405, p. 40]

Each consonant appears twice in each list for a total of 14 times, all lists considered. If these lists are made 11 items long, the learning task becomes incredibly difficult, and more than 11 items are almost impossible. If the student wishes to verify the difficulty found in learning and remembering nonsense syllables, he can compare his learning and remembering for nonsense syllables like these with that of the word lists found on page 262.

It is important to draw attention to the fact that much material which is supposed to be meaningful to the learner remains at the level of nonsense. For instance, the rules of English grammar are often as meaningless as the nonsense syllables in Figure VI (p. 121), and as a result are very difficult to learn and remember. The content does not have to be nonsense *per se* to invoke all of the difficulties found in remembering nonsense.

The Degree of Organization

The degree of organization of materials influences ability to remember, but this statement overlooks the quality of the organization, the amount of integration, and the system. It is harder to remember material which is unorganized, and it is harder to remember material which is highly organized, with the possible exception of the dynamic organization which produces what amounts to a flash-flood of memory. The degree of organization is an important variable in remembering; between the two extremes, namely, unorganized and highly organized, is a level of organization which supports memory instead of making it more difficult.

Organization aids memory but it is a matter of degree, quality, amount, and complexity of the system, because highly organized materials are difficult to learn and remember. Materials are highly organized when they embrace multiple relationships. To illustrate, memories for unrelated historical facts are relatively easy, but to trace the development of nationalism in a country through the web of interrelated events is relatively difficult. Advanced mathematics is more difficult because of its dependence on a series of prior relationships extending back to addition, subtraction, multiplication, division, and fractions. If the prior arithmetical relationships are available from memory, the ease or difficulty of the present solutions stems from the complexity of the interrelationships. More relationships lead to more difficulty, but there are two kinds of relationships, the inner and the outer. Inner relationships increase difficulty, not only because there are more but because of the dependency of each on the others. If one is forgotten, all the dependent relationships are disturbed. Outer relationships increase difficulty in the same way, that is, because there are more and because of the dependencies. To illustrate, the nonsense syllables on page 121 have little inner and outer relatedness. The nonsense syllables are not dependent upon one another for a place in memory and have no relationships to other material beyond the fact that they are letters of the alphabet. However, there is too little organization in the nonsense syllables to aid memory.

Some organization helps remembering, but more organization becomes a memory in and of itself. This means that one has to remember both the material and its organization. Further, the more relationships embraced, the more highly organized they have to be for learning and remembering because of their relationships and dependencies.

Organized practice, as opposed to random practice, aids memory. Systematic work to include all the basic number combinations and simple calculations resulted in more growth and consolidation in arithmetic than did the haphazard use of practice examples. Furthermore, with organized materials the children's interest and confidence in their work did not suffer a setback [267]. Random preparation could not provide for all number combinations to occur, or for number combinations to be practiced equally, or for number combinations to be practiced in keeping with their degree of difficulty. More damaging than the inadequate rehearsal of materials is the fact that random preparation does not provide an organization to support memory. Also, memory is aided when one knows the method (organization) of measurement to be used. Anticipating the organization of one's productions and reproductions leads to preparatory sets which influence how the materials are structured. Not knowing the organization (in this case, how to recall or recognize the material) is detrimental to learning and remembering. Obviously, as the orientation of both the learning and the measurement of learning is directed to more similar organization, memory is supported. Some organization aids memory because systematic work covers all possibilities and provides a structure to strengthen memory.

Identifiability

Retention is influenced by the degree of identifiability. Anyone will agree that it is difficult, if not impossible, to hit a target if he does not know where to aim. Specificity and intention are needed. To the extent that instructions single out and emphasize aspects of learning that are used to test retention, performance is improved; to the extent that learning, instructions, and efforts to measure retention are not in harmony, performance is impaired [401]. Retention is aided by instructions which identify what is to be learned and remembered. The target area should not be at either extreme. A subject area such as history or science is so broad as to be unmanageable as a target, while singling out one detail after another is too minute. A better area for concentration might be a chapter or two from a physics book, or historical events for a country during a decade. Sizable targets like these include minute details and broad generalizations, but they are manageable because they can be identified for learning, instruction, and retention.

Words and Retention

We learn in words and we remember in words, yet the influence of the richness of word usage and control on memory is still largely unexplored; in the same way, the influence of a varied experience on the development of memory through word usage and control is unexplored. A hint of the possibilities is suggested by Figure VII in which words serve as shorthand.

Spoken word: TEST
                          ↓
Auditory receptors: TEST
                          ↓
Intellectual response: literal meaning: TEST
Emotional response: fear of failure
                         hope of success
                         competitive urge
                         insecurity
                         guilt because of poor preparation

FIGURE VII
Probable Aspects of the Word "Test"

Here the word "test" first strikes the eardrum as a physical stimulus. The mind grasps the simple meaning of the term, and this is followed by one or more responses of an emotional nature, depending on the individual's previous experiences with tests and his expectation of being able to cope with this one. Experiences, attitudes, and desires, some of which are memories and some of which are current events, are handled through the symbolism of words, but the workings and interrelationships of these factors have not been fully explored (see Chapter 17, Communication).

Memorizing

To memorize is "to commit to memory" and "to learn by heart." Thus memorizing is a process, and to memorize is to commit to memory, but these dictionary statements have not said what the process is or how one commits things to memory.

This vagueness of definition raises the question as to whether it is possible to be explicit about the processes involved in memorizing. Certainly the processes are different for each person, but to illustrate the elements of memorizing which are common to most persons, consider the following rhyme.

Thirty days hath September,
April, June, and November,

All the rest have thirty-one
Save February, which has twenty-eight
Except in Leap Year.

This is poor verse but fruitful for most of us in remembering which
months have 30 and 31 days. Usually, whenever we wish to remember the length of a month, we repeat the rhyme from the beginning
until we have recalled the part needed at the moment. The question is, what are the processes which enable us to learn and
repeat the verse? The answer is found in individual ability to read
and to reread, to pay attention to the length of line, to the rhythm
of the words, and to the rhyme. All of these are rehearsed through
self-recitation, recitation for others, and sometimes through writing-
out. The emphasis is on ability to practice the verse in our own
way until such time as we can parrot it for ourselves and others.

The defenders of memorizing may be offended by the idea of
parroting, that is, of memorizing which relies on verbatim repetition without thought or understanding. However, to memorize is
self-teaching, and there are often developments from self-teaching.
For instance, in this case one may soon pick up the fact that there
are four months with 30 days, and that February is a law unto
itself. This is information which developed from the memorized
verse, information which exceeds the bounds of the memorizing
itself. It was not required that one learn there are four months of
30 days and that February is different, but it is almost impossible
to avoid this information as a concomitant to memorizing. Consider
the ability to spell 10 difficult words, such as: *liquefy, paraffin, em-*
barrass, naphtha, battalion, picnicking, rarefy, kimono, supersede,
and *ukulele.* Ability to spell these words correctly is a combination
of memorized information, understanding of the words, the sound
of the words, visual imagery, and writing skills. To attempt to indicate which part of the ability to spell the words is due to memorization, information, understanding, and auditory, visual, and kinesthetic cues is both impossible and fruitless. Ability to memorize
contributes to ability to spell, but attempts to define the size of the

contribution are futile because information develops from the parroting process in spite of avoidance of understanding and reliance on memorizing. To illustrate further, assign yourself the task of remembering any one of the lists of popular names in Figure VIII.

John	Linda	John	Mary
Michael	Mary	William	Dorothy
James	Deborah	James	Helen
Robert	Susan	Robert	Margaret
William	Carol	Charles	Ruth
David	Patricia	George	Betty
Thomas	Catherine	Willie	Elizabeth
Stephen	Margaret	Joseph	Anne
Richard	Barbara	Frank	Mildred
Joseph	Karen	Richard	Frances

FIGURE VIII

Popular Names

Speculation regarding the role of memorizing in acquiring command over one of these lists of 10 names, let alone over all four lists, leads to consideration of the role of memorizing in learning [275].

The Role of Memorizing. Persons acquire information through memorizing and understanding. Memorizing is not a first step to comprehension but strides along with it, i.e., one does not first memorize and then begin to understand. Understanding is a development which matures with time and effort from total functioning. Understanding does not arise at any one time from specific practice, yet all such rehearsal promotes some part of the whole complex. This, again, sounds like the development of first this part and then that, but learning is not so compartmented. Understanding history evolves as students work with history. The teacher directs attention to each historical fact or principle, and promotes total development through his interpretations and integrations of the data, but the understanding of the pupils does not take place until each pupil integrates the material in his own way. He acquires information through both memorizing and understanding.

When there are several subheadings to a topic (such as Measurement, Chapter 18), one's ability to acquire information through memorizing and comprehending may be severely taxed. A person's understanding of measurement may be rich and full, but he still relies on his memory to remind him of what he knows and understands. Some people will avoid the details of such subtopics as *the uses of tests, teacher-made tests,* and *evaluation.* Even if they relegate these subheadings to a level which is unworthy of their interest, they may have to learn them to be able to speak of these subheadings without the benefit of notes to support memory. If faced with the task of producing the pertinent details about subheadings in measurement, they are obligated to use all their abilities. A task of this specificity cannot be accomplished without the benefit of both memorizing and understanding.

Ideas and Facts, Generalizations and Specifics. Memory is better for ideas and generalizations than for facts and specifics. From an idea concerning the uses of tests, one can always call up many memories, but the specific factual information necessary for a detailed description of the uses of tests is apt to try memory severely. Specifics may hold their place in memory because of vividness, their unusual nature, their recency, or their frequent use, but only a few details can be retained in this way. After learning the specifics, one often forgets them and remembers the generalizations derived from them. If only generalizations were learned, they would be treated as specifics and broader generalizations would be developed from them. Effective teachers stress specifics, although they realize that most of them will not be remembered. This is done to sharpen the generalizations produced: the more detail there is available, the less general will be the generalizations. People are better able to remember generalizations, even quite specific ones. They remember also that there are specifics to support the generalizations, and they can relearn them if the need arises. One may, for example, read a series of statements about the 1930's, citing how many persons were on relief, how many bankruptcies were filed, and other specifics of this nature. From these, the conclusion arises that the 1930's was a time of great economic hardship. This generalization remains long after one has forgotten the data on which it was based. Details thus support the development of concepts and general ideas, although they themselves are not usually remembered.

Developing a Residue. A fruitful residue from learning piles up slowly, usually after careful preparation spread over a period of time. Even in situations where there is no apparent learning or even more forgetting than learning, there may be a return on the investment in terms of a fruitful remainder to support relearning. The residue is learning minus forgetting. Of course, all such remainder is a matter of degree. A residue is fruitful if it can support performance. The question is how great an investment in different kinds of content does each person require in order to have such a sufficient remnant. For instance, in the study of English, a person learns specifics and these mature to generalizations in memory. The residue develops slowly through years of patient, careful work with specifics. Memories of some aspects of English, such as tense and punctuation, become almost indelible, while others, such as the definitions of various figures of speech, may slip away despite persistent efforts to remember them.

The erudition of the scholar may be the envy of those who cannot recall much material of good quality, but it is generally agreed that erudition is the product of ability plus years of careful work. For instance, some scholars read selectively at high speeds. This skill does not yield them an advantage unless they soon make use of the selected material [310]. There are those who believe that maturing self-development yields a superior product without such strenuous investment, but the majority opinion is that there is no such royal road to learning. Learning is often a tedious chore, slow and annoying. Only motivation may make the years of work in a subject palatable, particularly if the aim is to go on to the more creative and interesting levels. Teachers make the work as painless and interesting as possible through well-organized materials which progress from easy to difficult. Learners take years to build a residue of material which is susceptible to recall.

Whole and Part. In memorizing and acquiring information, the largest possible whole unit should be learned in order to benefit from the intrinsic logic of a total organization. Simplification rather than fragmentation of whole tasks provides for more efficient training [54]. Divisions make the parts easier, more learnable, and more comfortable, but even the most convenient breaks are as well learned as the material itself. The problem is obvious in the memorization of a sonnet. The intrinsic organization is usually not strong, and the difficulties in recall persist where one has learned the breaks. The initial learning of the fourteen lines as a unit may be difficult, but in the long run it is easier than learning eight lines and six lines, or four-four-four-two, or four-four-three-three. Because the organization of units of work is as well learned as the material itself, it is best to follow the logical organization rather than an artificial and imposed structure. (In some cases there is no choice available. Goldner found that material which is structured obligates the learner to learn by parts; the more structure, the more parts [142].) If pauses are used, they are learned along with the material; so it is desirable to have the pauses fit the organization. Within the limits of his capacity and the logical setup of the material, one should learn the largest possible whole units, rather than a series of smaller units connected by learned breaks.

Form. The form of the material to be learned is a basic determinant in memorizing and acquiring information. The form may facilitate learning, e.g., a succinct one-page outline, or the form may hinder learning, e.g., an unwieldy 27-page description. In many situations, a change of form erases learning, but it is not possible to learn everything in all forms. For instance, one may learn to compute standard deviation from data arranged in three different ways. Presentation of the data in a fourth style may make it impossible to compute the standard deviation, but it is not possible to anticipate all the possible forms. The teacher can aid the pupil to memorize and to acquire information by devising presentations which are most likely to be encountered later. Better yet, the teacher can guide the learner to organize and reorganize material in forms from which he can learn. For instance, the notes taken from a class lecture or from readings may require revamping to be put into the best arrangement. This is learning how to learn. Pupils need to learn how to organize materials in workable form to aid memory.

Mnemonic Devices. In spite of understanding and comprehension, people frequently need devices to help them remember; these are called mnemonics. They range from simple associations to complex schemes. The relationship between a person named White and the color white is a fairly simple association, which makes it easy to recall his name. Then, of course, the associative process sometimes defeats the device by producing another name, such as Black or Snow. Complex devices involve learning codes or keys to cue memory such as ROY G. BIV for the colors of the spectrum: red, orange, yellow, green, blue, indigo, violet. Codes or keys can be nonsense, as in ROY G. BIV, or they can be meaningful in themselves, e.g., the Tropic of Capricorn is in the Southern Hemisphere and corns are on your feet, while the Tropic of Cancer is in the Northern Hemisphere and cancer usually infects the upper parts of the body. However, if a person uses mnemonic devices to remember what he understands and then he forgets the device, memory is less available and more confused than if he had not relied on such a key. Mnemonics assist memory but are not substitutes for work of good quality which promotes the development called understanding.

Rehearsal

Rehearsal includes self-recitation, writing things out, and various sensorimotor performances, such as singing, playing the piano, and swinging a golf club. Rehearsal provides an immediate goal, namely, can you now perform adequately for yourself? If you can, you are gratified. If not, relearning is necessary. Further, the self-examination of rehearsal should provide the essential diagnosis for further work. From self-testing, persons find out what they are sure of and what requires further effort. One also becomes quite economical in expending effort, using just enough for the desired level of performance.

Self-rehearsal is a great help in acquiring information. Self-recitation is much faster for most people than writing things out in longhand or even in shorthand.

The Amount. Retention is directly related to the amount of rehearsal and the amount of material to be learned and retained. Up to the point of satiation, when boredom and annoyance generate strong negative feeling-tone, the more work done with the material, the greater the retention. As the point of satiation approaches, the influence of the work periods is lessened. Study contributes most to retention at the beginning; each relearning contributes less and less to the final retention. Logically, if the material is grasped firmly at an early stage, the subsequent work periods yield only some strengthening of the grasp. Under these circumstances, the level of development desired becomes the critical determiner of the amount of work done. If satiation is reached, the strong, negative feeling-tone which is generated causes avoidance of the material which induces this feeling, and avoidance inhibits retention. However, people rarely cause themselves to work to the point of satiation.

Retention is also related to the amount of material to be learned and retained. The greater the amount, the more difficult retention is and the greater the influence of inhibiting processes, such as reactive, proactive, and retroactive inhibition, simply because there is more material and therefore a wider range for the operation of these inhibitions. The influence of these inhibitions is described on pages 140 to 147. Generally, the greater the amount of material, no matter what its nature may be, the harder the task and the more difficult retention will be.

Distributed Practice. Remembering responds to practice. Distributed practice means the spacing of sessions so that they occur with a time interval between them rather than taking the same total amount of time in one session, i.e., massed practice. Four one-hour sessions represent distributed practice as compared with one four-hour session. The massed practice of a 16-hour workday on one task might be better spent in a distribution of four-hour sessions. The effective length of any work session varies from person to person and from task to task, but some distribution of practice rather than no distribution usually yields a better performance [115]. The effect of distributed practice on the acquisition of knowledge and skills depends upon the arrangement of the practice sessions relative to the material to be learned.

How should practice time be apportioned? For some material, one hour may not be long enough to get started, to be an efficient work session. This would probably be the case in working a complex problem in chemical research. For discrete items, however, such as memorizing a set of formulas, little warmup is needed, so they can be studied in brief sessions—on the bus while traveling to class, and so on. The duration of the practice has the most important effect early in the rehearsal series.

If the material to be practiced is meaningful to the learner, he can stand longer practice sessions at the beginning. If the material does not have meaning, he needs frequent rest sessions and short practice periods. The distribution of practice allows the dissipation of the annoyance with having to work at a task. This annoyance is highest when meaningfulness is low (as when college students printed the inverted alphabet for 20 one-minute trials [211]), and when there is much interference between items to be rehearsed. The ideal distribution of work and rest sessions for effective rehearsal varies from person to person and task to task.

The distribution of practice is a performance-variable rather than a learning-variable, i.e., practice changes the underlying abilities, while rest helps performance [5]. Developed ability is altered by practice, but rest helps performance in a way that leaves ability unchanged [211]. One's performance may not reflect the changes in his abilities because of annoyance, boredom, physical fatigue, and the perseveration of old habits. In one experiment, for instance, over a two-hour test period the number of errors increased in each succeeding half-hour period [348]. No matter what the reasons are for increases in errors under conditions of continued work, rest will probably change the performance in the direction of fewer errors. Rest produces jumps in performance levels but not in the underlying ability. Distributed practice also allows for some forgetting to occur. Upon returning to a task, one can both relearn and develop understanding through a fresh approach to the material. This new start helps to uncover the more subtle developments of understanding which do not usually mature when people are bored, tired, or plagued by incorrect habits. The more times persons work satisfyingly with material, the better they learn. Distributed practice facilitates performance and provides for more satisfying practice.

The usual daily schedule in high school takes adequate account of the benefits to be derived from some distribution over none. Five or six work periods each day give the students a chance to come to each subject refreshed by rest from it so that performance levels can remain high. The only question here is whether a one-hour session is long enough to allow superior and mature students to get into the subject matter deeply enough. Duller and less adequate students benefit greatly from more and shorter work periods. It is possible, however, to shorten the work periods so radically that there is not enough time for even the slow student to get his little bit of work done. The issue is complicated further by the variations arising from personality. In every case it will depend upon the nature of the students and tasks involved, but the high school day does provide generally for the benefits of distributed practice.

Benton Underwood, with others, has published the most exhaustive series of studies of distributed practice. In spite of the fact that these are laboratory rather than classroom studies, the essential aspects of the benefits to be derived from some distribution over none are clearly indicated. See one of his publications such as [405].

Review

Remembering is aided by complete, well-spaced reviews. Some material does not require review because the set in which we learned is easily re-established or because knowledge of it is retained from the first contact. This is implied by the proverb, "The burned child dreads the fire," which indicates that the child does not require a long series of burns to acquire this notion. Some early experiences have a lasting and profound influence on subsequent behavior [284-1959], but if forgetting is likely, review helps. Since most forgetting occurs during the few days following learning, the first review should probably take place within 48 hours. Thereafter, the reviews can be spaced wider and wider apart in time and still efficiently preserve the memories. After the first review, the strategic placement of further review sessions to preserve memory becomes individual. For the most efficient lengthening of the time between reviews, consider both the learner and the nature and amount of material to be retained.

Reviews should be complete as well as periodic. Many students assume that a review of the highlights is better than nothing, but this is not the case. Changing the frame of reference involves relearning. Reviewing only the highlights changes the frame of reference so that relearning assists in the memory of the new structure, but the old structure is pushed further into the background of memory than if no review or relearning had been attempted. To review part of a structure creates a new organization which inhibits the former structure (retroactive inhibition, see pages 143 to 147). However, although memory is aided by complete, well-spaced reviews, a fixity of form and organization limits the adaptability of learning and remembering. The development of higher orders of mastery is inhibited by limiting each relearning to complete reviews of former learning. Yet, for a given situation and a body of content which a person must know, he aids memory when he organizes material into workable units, learns those units as units, and keeps them as units through properly placed reviews of the complete units.

Note that it is the work of these spaced reviews which provides for long term retention. Regardless of the emphasis on the new media, long term retention is the product of carefully spaced work [39].

Summary: Remembering

Much of the productive quality of memory is dependent upon ability to acquire, to retain, and to reproduce information. To aid the learner, teachers should consider the following aspects of remembering: attitudes, meaningfulness, the degree of organization, the identifiability, the use of words in retention, memorizing, rehearsal, and review.

Attitudes may dispose the learner to remember, or they may deter participation so that learning and remembering are limited or impossible.

As meaningfulness develops, learning is easier and memory more lasting.

Organization provides a structure for remembering but must be measured carefully, because the more highly organized the material is, the greater the demands on the learner to remember both the material and its organization.

The more clearly one identifies the material to be learned and remembered, the easier it is to aim at the target. Both the specificity and the intent are needed. With identifiability, there are no doubts as to what is to be remembered.

Persons learn in words and remember in words, yet the richness of word usage and the control of words on remembering is unexplored.

One resorts to memorizing to cope with the demands made, not just to avoid understanding. Memory is better for ideas than for facts, and one remembers generalizations rather than specifics. An effective residue accumulates from continual work with specifics in context against a background of total behavior. Persons accumulate and integrate generalizations which are in keeping with their interpretations of the basic specifics. Within the limits of a person's capacity and the logical organization of material, he learns and remembers units of comfortable size rather than a series of smaller units connected by learned breaks. The form of the material may facilitate or inhibit remembering. Mnemonic devices help if they do not themselves become memory problems.

Everyone responds to practice, but several variables influence its value: the amount of rehearsal, how much material needs to be learned, and how the practice periods are distributed.

Well-spaced, complete reviews maintain memory at a high level.

9

forgetting

THE CHARACTER OF FORGETTING

INHIBITION

   Reactive Inhibition
   Proactive Inhibition
   Retroactive Inhibition
   Associative Inhibition

TEACHING TO DETER FORGETTING

EXTINCTION

SUMMARY: FORGETTING

R EMEMBERING AND FORGETTING are opposing functions in development. Ideally we work to foster remembering, but actually our best efforts to remember often succumb to forgetting. Forgetting may be developmental, however, in that it releases us from the fetters of some facts and specifics. Productive development springs from the combined workings of remembering and forgetting. Sometimes people need to unlearn and forget faulty and hindering content, as in the efforts of the teacher to have correct rather than incorrect number combinations hold their place in memory, or as in psychotherapy, where intensive skilled efforts are made to induce unlearning and relearning. Even the best efforts to remember and to forget suffer from disturbances, but usually in a selective rather than a random fashion. However, selectivity in forgetting seems to be due to selective-learning rather than selective-remembering mechanisms [67]. Both remembering and forgetting can be beneficial or undesirable according to the circumstances. For instance, one does not cherish the memories of catastrophic and devastating events, but the part of them which is not forgotton serves as a guide for further development. If one remembered all of everything to which he has been subjected, he would have a collection of trivia. Both remembering and forgetting are selective and protective. At times the embarrassing lack of recall or recognition seems only to emphasize what one cannot do, yet similar mechanisms in forgetting allow a fresh start each day, with some of the memories from yesterday available. If all of yesterday intruded into today, the struggle to change, to put away, and to begin again in different directions would be more difficult. Both remembering and forgetting work to allow productive development.

The Character of Forgetting

Forgetting is the inability to recall or recognize something which we could once recall or recognize. It is the result of the failure of retention, a decrement rather than an increment in retention. Forgetting is the complement of remembering and, as such, is not nearly as devastating as is usually implied. For instance, parents and teachers are always happy to have the young forget such things as thumbsucking, pencil-chewing, and nail-biting. Illustrations like these introduce the notion of unlearning and forgetting, but the effect of each on behavior is sufficiently similar to justify the avoidance of theoretical differences. Depending on the situation, persons enjoy the benefits of remembering and forgetting and at other times struggle with their inability to recall, to recognize, and to forget.

Forgetting is characterized by a decrement in the amount retained and by qualitative changes in the materials that are remembered, and it is possible to manipulate the decrease in amount and to influence the qualitative changes. The passage of time and the principle of disuse are not sufficient conditions, in and of themselves, to explain forgetting. Instead, forgetting is explained by inhibitions and by systematic changes in the reproductions. Even under the best possible conditions for remembering, decreases in amount and changes in quality occur. As the conditions for remembering are less satisfactory, more material is forgotten, and that which is remembered is less recognizable.

Under the best possible conditions, some forgetting occurs between the learning of material A and its reproduction. A . . . . . . A shows some loss of retention even if the interval is a near vacuum. (On the other hand, learning between A and A may be interpreted as the forgetting of errors. What errors? Right and wrong things are learned equally easily, and if as a result of the period between A and A there appears to be learning rather than forgetting, more incorrect than correct things were forgotten.) Whenever any concept other than A fills the interval, forgetting is more obvious. Sleep approaches a vacuum, although experimental work suggests that learning occurs even during sleep [111, 350]. The sleep-learning experiments are under criticism, however, because it is difficult to prove that the learner is asleep while he is learning, even if he is wired for movement and his lack of movement is recorded as sleep. The systematic changes referred to as learning and the equally systematic changes called forgetting probably both occur during the near-vacuum of sleep. To learn A and to reproduce A, with sleep intervening between A and A, shows both loss and changes in retention.

Any discussion of the loss and changes in retention raises the issue as to whether true forgetting, a decay of associations, does occur, or whether a series of systematic changes occur in the memory traces, and the changes then appear as a loss of retention. From a Gestalt point of view, errors of reproduction reflect development of memory traces in the direction of increasing conformity to the laws of perceptual organization. Reproductions tend to be better figures than the originals and changes in reproductions develop progressively in the direction of greater simplicity and uniformity. Progressive systematic changes can, however, be produced under conditions of associative learning through "building in" learned habits of categorizing and responding [303]. True forgetting (a weakening of the percept or association to make it less available to memory) and systematic changes both occur as memory shows loss and change; and true forgetting occurs even under ideal conditions, namely, during a near vacuum between the learning of A and the reproduction of A. When one interpolates other material between learning A and the reproduction of A, the losses and systematic changes in memory are greater and more varied in nature. Both true forgetting and systematic changes in memory contribute to the inability called forgetting.

Inhibition

The major source of forgetting is inhibition. Three kinds of inhibition—reactive, proactive, and retroactive—unite to make remembering more difficult.

Reactive inhibition is the annoyance generated by a task, so that to stop, to put it away, is gratifying. The longer the task, the more reactive inhibition builds, and the more ready one becomes to put it out of memory.

The other two types arise from the connections established between two items, and they are therefore called associative inhibitions. When the interference is produced by prior learning on present efforts, it is called proactive inhibition. When present learning interferes with previous learning and thus weakens the memory of the earlier learning, the result is called retroactive inhibition.

Reactive inhibition works now against the present task; proactive inhibition works forward, from past to present; and retroactive inhibition works backward, from present to past.

Reactive Inhibition

Reactive inhibition is the reaction against a task because it must be done. Whether the task is required by others or self-imposed, the reaction is one of annoyance. There are those who will insist that the need to act, the desire for satisfactions from activity of the right sort, and the joy of sheer activity are sufficient to overcome reactive inhibition, but all effortful responses produce a tendency to avoid repetition of the response. Reactive inhibition is a negative drive state which is essentially a need to cease action. The goal of reactive inhibition is resting, so that the learner puts the material away, usually both physically and mentally. The reaction against tasks has an inhibiting effect on remembering.

Reactive inhibition varies according to the amount of work required and the conditions of the work. More work produces more reaction. Work which is massed rather than distributed in time produces more reactive inhibition, because massed practice does not provide for rest sessions. With planned rest sessions in the work, reactive inhibition is lessened. The reaction against working decays with resting. Efficient planning provides for resting to avoid the reduced work-output that reactive inhibition generates. This does not require much rest, as long as it is spaced properly, as in distributed practice (pp. 132-134). Work situations in which reactive inhibition is not allowed to develop are more efficient. If practice sessions are distributed through the spacing of 10-minute rest periods, the reaction generated against any task, including quite onerous tasks such as 10 hours of study or 10 hours of filing, is dissipated. College students who rested for more than 10 minutes did not improve their performance over those who rested up to 10 minutes [213]. Rest helps performance and dissipates reactive inhibition, although it does not change ability. Rest allows the annoyance generated by a task to wane, so that persons can work with the task to become more capable at it without becoming more and more annoyed. The effect of reactive inhibition is to cause avoidance and forgetting. This effect can be controlled through limiting the amount of work and distributing the practice to allow the inhibition to dissipate with brief rest sessions.

Proactive Inhibition

Proactive inhibition is the interference from prior learning intruding on present efforts and inhibiting them. Proactive inhibition works forward, from past to present. A, the previous learning, in-

terferes with B, the present learning. To illustrate, a person who has habitually opened the front door of his house by turning the key to the right will find it difficult to change this habit if a lock is installed which requires that the key be turned to the left. Practicing the spelling of *liquefy, paraffin, embarrass, naphtha* and *battalion,* disturbs the practice of the spelling of *picnicking, rarefy, kimono, supersede* and *ukulele.* Previous learning inhibits some of the learning which could occur now, and this leads to more forgetting, to poorer retention.

Proactive inhibition comes from associations and is therefore subject to all of the conditions of learning. For instance, the effects of proactive inhibition are highly transitory [20]. Influences which inhibit behavior today may not be at work tomorrow. Meaningful concepts increase the ability to discriminate in the learning of materials and thereby minimize proactive inhibition [46]. Massed practice does not overcome proactive inhibition [26]. It is necessary to distribute practice sessions carefully to overcome the inhibiting influence of prior associations. The longer an association is left unattended, that is, the longer the retention interval is, the greater the inhibiting influence of the prior learning. A pupil studies B after A. If he returns to the study of B tomorrow, the inhibiting influence of A is not as great as if he leaves B alone for five days. This applies to the learning and relearning of any material, and includes the learning of materials that lead into one another. Of course the question as to whether inhibition devastates fields such as ideas and attitudes is speculative, because ideas and attitudes are rarely fully exposed for examination. In the case of A and B, a person unlearns the associative inhibition by returning to the study of B day by day. The inhibition from A yields to the work with B, so that one is not aware of much influence of A on B. And that leads to the next form of inhibitory pressure: retroactive. While unlearning the associative inhibition from A to B through carefully distributed work with B, the A material is being inhibited by B. The work to overcome associative inhibition acting in one direction produced associative inhibition in the opposite direction.

Retroactive Inhibition

Retroactive inhibition is the action of present learning to inhibit memories from previous learning. Retroactive inhibition works backward, from present to past.

B, the present learning, interferes with *A*, the prior learning. Present practice with the right hand disturbs previous efforts to learn with the left hand. Practicing the spelling of *picnicking, rarefy, kimono, supersede* and *ukulele* disturbs the previously learned spelling of *liquefy, paraffin, embarrass, naphtha* and *battalion*. Present learning inhibits some of the past learning, and this leads to more forgetting, to poorer retention.

Retroactive inhibition is also associative in nature, and as such, it is subject to all of the conditions of learning. Ordinarily, daily activities represent a detriment to retention because they are all *B*'s which the learner pays attention to at the moment, and this inhibits the previous learning. Any of the on-going events of the day can be the *B* which inhibits some or all of *A*. As one works through carefully distributed practice to learn *B*, he is inhibiting his memory of *A*. Equal practice and equal distribution of practice for both *A* and *B* might produce uninhibited memory for both *A* and *B*. This is unlikely, however, because any number of other individual factors intrude to favor *A* or *B* in one's associations. Whichever association is favored produces associative inhibition both forward and backward.

The Associative Inhibition of Proactive and Retroactive Inhibition

Both proactive and retroactive inhibition generate associative inhibition which varies in degree with the nature of the interpolated material and with the disruption of set or context [308]. To avoid confusion, these two factors will be illustrated separately, although they are joint determiners of the degree of associative inhibition (so much so that the combined inhibition from proactive and retroactive factors has been called coactive inhibition [165]).

The amount of associative inhibition generated by proactive and retroactive inhibition varies with the nature of the interpolated material. If a person learns A, rests and reproduces A, there is no interpolated material. However, if he learns A, learns B, and then reproduces A, B is interpolated between A and A,—as in this diagram:

$$A \longleftrightarrow B \longleftrightarrow A$$

With this interpolation of B, proactive inhibition works forward to generate associative inhibition,

$$A \longrightarrow B \longrightarrow A$$

and, at the same time, retroactive inhibition works backward to generate associative inhibition,

$$A \longleftarrow B \longleftarrow A$$

Now, if B is a repetition of A (e.g., another arithmetic problem of exactly the same nature), B reinforces A and facilitates the remembering of A *and* B. Under these circumstances, associative facilitation is at work. If B is completely unrelated to A, something of a different nature entirely (e.g., A is a list of nonsense syllables and B is the practice of broad jumping), the associative interference of proactive and retroactive inhibition are at a minimum. The associative inhibition is at a maximum when the interpolated material is similar but not identical, and the inhibition decreases with less similarity. If A is six nonsense syllables and B is six more nonsense syllables built from the same consonants, the associative inhibition of proactive and retroactive inhibition is at a maximum. Such a task is incredibly difficult to learn and to remember. As B becomes increasingly different from A, the task of learning and remembering both A and B is easier. The degree of associative inhibition generated by learning and remembering A and B varies according to their nature.

Second, the degree of associative inhibition generated by proactive and retroactive inhibition varies with the disruption of the set, context, or frame of reference. Since one can never return to the identical set in which material A was learned, there is some forgetting from the learning of A to the reproduction of A. Suppose A is 12 lines of poetry learned in the 10 o'clock class on Monday. Provided that nothing intervened until Tuesday in the same class with the same fellow students and the same teacher, the learner is rested, the temperature and humidity held constant, the set or context is still slightly changed so that there is forgetting when the student tries to reproduce 12 lines of poetry. If B is now interpolated between learning A and reproducing A, the set of both A and B is disturbed. This disruption of set induces inhibition. If B is the same material as A but in a different context, there are two contexts to remember and each inhibits the other. If A is one way to solve a discount problem in arithmetic and B is a second way to solve the same discount problem, the teacher has introduced a strong likelihood of inhibition by changing set. (Such interference is less likely if the two methods of solution have been thoroughly absorbed and understood; insightful learning strongly resists disruptive influences.) As efforts to maintain the same context for learning and reproduction are successful, the inhibitory effects of change of set are held to a minimum. Each set generates proactive and retroactive inhibition to intrude on each other set.

The disruption of set can be reduced through organization and through instructions which agree with the organization. Ordered and arranged materials have a stronger set than random materials, a set which is easier to identify and therefore easier to re-establish. The organized material produces smaller amounts of inhibitory effect and so allows the easier integration of the material into memory. Multiple sets generate conflict, and conflict has broad and generalized inhibitory influences [124]. When the teacher organizes materials and gives instructions which follow that organization, the set of both the organization and the instructions helps rather than hinders learning. Relevant instructions produce greater amounts of facilitation than irrelevant instructions because they help to re-establish the set and the organization for learning and memory

[251]. Persons respond to directions from others which they can integrate, because such directions facilitate development. Irrelevant instructions and random organization disrupt set *and* disrupt development through the inhibitions which they generate. Teachers help most when they avoid the broad inhibitory effects of the disruption of set by adjusting their instructions to the pupils' level of development.

Even without the crude disruption of set which other persons and events impose on the learner, the learner can never return to the same set or context because set is an expression of growth and development. Growth and development are not static; learning, remembering, and forgetting are not static; set is not static. A fixed frame of reference is not desirable or possible. The dynamics inherent in growth and development do not permit return to any static structure, even if memory were unchanging. Forgetting is an expression of the dynamic change which occurs within structures, but a person's changes are not overnight disruptions and upheavals. They involve a little development in various directions for each day. One can never return to the same set or context because, even if nothing external has altered, the person has changed. He contributes to the set and frame of reference and changes with it. Greater changes are managed when a person can integrate the demands of the environment with his personal development. The dynamic changes in set provide for development in that one is always relearning, redeveloping, and re-integrating. In order to remember, he grows and develops, and his personal inability to return to the same context, to reproduce material, is an expression of growth and development.

Both proactive and retroactive inhibition generate associative inhibition, which varies in degree with the nature of the interpolated material and with the disruption of set. More associative inhibition is generated when the interpolated material is similar but not identical and when the context is disrupted. Associative inhibition is at a minimum when the original material and the interpolated material are quite dissimilar and the set is as close as possible to the original context. All interpolated material disrupts sets to some extent to induce associative inhibition, and our daily lives can be viewed as one interpolated event after another. Ordinarily, daily activities provide for proactive and retroactive inhibition to wreak their havoc with memory.

Forgetting curbs remembering through reactive, proactive, and retroactive inhibition. These inhibitions exist at all times to confuse or defeat memory. This confusion and defeat are systematic rather than random processes, in that personality characteristics temper both remembering and forgetting. There are techniques which provide for better memory and provide for less forgetting. These techniques concern instruction, organization, what is practiced, how much it is practiced, the warmup effect, and the use of reviews.

Teaching to Deter Forgetting

Teachers lessen forgetting when they teach general rules for classifying and ordering material. The learner needs to develop to the point where he realizes what is necessary by way of organization to help memory; but long before he reaches such a level, he has followed the instructions of other people. When he remembers, he brings to bear whatever habits he has in connection with these memory items [303]. When he forgets, instruction and habits have failed to provide an organization to support recall or recognition.

When learning takes place in the contexts in which it is likely to be encountered later, less forgetting occurs. Forgetting is substantial when the conditions for associative inhibition can operate at a maximum, as in continued practice under conditions other than those present at the time of learning. Practicing the classification and ordering items to be learned and practicing the items after they have been ordered and arranged are a deterrent to forgetting. If the material is to be remembered in various combinations and arrangements, more practice is needed.

The material that is practiced can deter forgetting. As the material is alike to the point of being identical, practice facilitates

memory. As the material is slightly dissimilar, it produces most forgetting and requires many rehearsals [287]. As the material is more
and more dissimilar, fewer rehearsals are required to inhibit forgetting. Apart from learning to organize, one also learns to deter
forgetting through the careful selection of the material to be
practiced.

The amount of practice necessary to deter forgetting varies from
task to task, because of the nature of the material and its organization, and from person to person, because of individual differences
in ability and development. Theoretically, it should be possible for
a person to practice any kind of material in any organization to the
point where he would not forget it. Practically, even the strongest
memories sometimes slip away. The amount of practice necessary
to deter forgetting cannot be determined. A person's best efforts
with well-organized and well-selected materials do not always provide him with the memories he feels he needs, thus he has never
completed his learning, and he is always relearning. The amount
of practice for the full development of abilities varies with the task
and with the person.

Forgetting is minimized if five to 10 minutes is used for warmup
[101]. Most performances respond to warmup, particularly the full
range of skills, including widely varying abilities: running and
jumping, playing a musical instrument, and skills like recognition
and recall. It always takes a little relearning to recover the set and
organization, and remembering is thus refreshed by five to 10
minutes warmup rather than a cold start [195]. Sometimes the
warmup precedes performances, e.g., a student may take five to 10
minutes before he goes to class to review the content and organization, but wherever this opportunity is unavailable, forgetting can
still be lessened if time is used for warmup. For instance, whenever
people have not had a prior opportunity, the first five to 10 minutes
of an examination could be provided to get them prepared. This,
however, is very frustrating to those who want to start at once because they have prepared themselves ahead of time. Individual differences require that some start at once and that others be allowed

their warmup. Good teaching always provides for this by using the first five to 10 minutes to introduce the topic and relate the topic to previous learning. Playwrights recognize this by starting their plays with material which is interesting but not crucial to the plot— allowing the audience time to get used to watching the performance. When warmup is used, the annoyance associated with cold starts is avoided, and forgetting is lessened.

Reviews are another aid to memory. Since forgetting is most rapid during the first day or two after learning, the first review should be conveniently arranged within that time interval. Thereafter reviews can be spaced further and further apart and still strengthen memory. Each review needs to be a complete recapitulation of the original organization. If the organization has changed, relearning is necessary, and after the relearning, a complete review of the new structure. If the material is to be known in several organizations, one should be learned well through strategically spaced, complete reviews, and then a second introduced, a third, and as many more as necessary, through comprehension of the principles involved. Such comprehension requires the maturity which comes with time and repeated rehearsals, e.g., the work necessary to use fractions efficiently, or the contribution of Freud's point of view to the understanding of behavior. The facile shifting of the mature learner from organization to organization is a product of the work he did to develop his ability. Such abilities are developed through properly spaced, complete reviews.

Forgetting is substantial whenever the conditions for associative inhibition exist, but it is possible to deter forgetting through a number of techniques. It is not implied that by using these devices a teacher can work a kind of mechanical magic on a developing individual. Instead, these techniques provide for more adequate self-expression because memory is aided. Forgetting is less when persons are able to classify and organize materials into structures for both memory and instruction. Instruction is directed by ordered rather than random materials. Practice of materials organized as one intends to remember and reproduce them facilitates memory.

Further, with organization one can select the materials for practice, and so inhibit forgetting by keeping the interference from similar materials to a minimum. How much practice is needed to deter forgetting depends on the learner's ability and the nature of the material. Reliance on these techniques cannot be too great, because forgetting will remain substantial even in the best of circumstances.

Extinction

Whenever forgetting is deliberately induced, the reduction in responding is called extinction. Although educators and psychologists find extinction to be an odd phenomenon, it is an essential aspect of forgetting and remembering. Usually, the attempt to extinguish behavior through experimental procedures is carried out in a laboratory. The teacher uses extinction also, but does not pursue the activities necessary for extinction with the deliberateness or the planned daily procedures of the experimenter. In the laboratory, extinction is forced forgetting, while in daily life, it is more casual and gradual.

Laboratory extinction as forced forgetting can be readily demonstrated. A pigeon placed on a table tends to turn in a crude circle to the right or the left. For each complete circle to the right, he is fed. Two hours of rehearsal for several days yields a response of turning to the right for food, with some pigeons requiring more learning trials than others. When turning to the right has been established as a stable response in a pigeon, extinction can begin (it can begin before a stable response but the results are not as obvious). To extinguish turning to the right, the experimenter allows the pigeon to turn and does not feed him. On the first day of turning without being fed, the pigeon works long and vigorously, but eventually gives up and stops turning. On the second day, he starts turning as vigorously as ever, but gives up sooner. On succeeding days, the turning is a less vigorous response and lasts for a shorter time. Eventually, again taking account of individual differences, there is no turning to the right for food. The response has been experimentally extinguished. Extinction, however, is no more stable than the original learning (in fact, extinction itself may be considered as a form of learning, as a learned inhibition against acting in a particular way). The response of turning to the right for food may and does reappear at almost any time, particularly if there are changes of which the pigeon is aware, e.g., a second pigeon on the table when the first one has not had company there before. This reappearance of the extinguished response is called spontaneous recovery.

Extinction is more suited to the laboratory than the classroom. In the classroom, teachers reinforce the desired responses and do not reinforce the undesirable ones. Lack of reinforcement has an extinguishing influence on a large number of responses. When the teacher approves of his class as a group, he is approving a wide range of responses rather than specific responses from each individual. When he does not approve (no disapproval is needed, just lack of specific approval), he is withholding comment to partially extinguish a wide range of responses from each individual rather than a specific response. The group situation of the classroom does not provide the necessary control over the specific reinforced and nonreinforced responses for extinction to be an effective technique.

Further descriptions of extinction run to more theoretical than practical considerations, and the classroom teacher may not find it fruitful to become involved in theoretical explanations. Psychologists and some educators have found the elaborations of the specialized problems in extinction to be helpful in the understanding of remembering and forgetting. The description and discussion which follows is presented for those who want such additional help. Those who have no further interest in extinction should turn directly to Chapter 10.

Extinction is the decline and eventual absence of a response following lack of reinforcement. All that seems to be necessary for extinction is awareness of the absence of reinforcement. When a response is not reinforced, it is inhibited by a sort of negative feedback from that response, a conditioned inhibition. Not all extinction is explained by response-induced inhibition [94]. When responses compete for expression, some are displaced, and therefore not all of the possible responses are made. With the withdrawal of reinforcement there is a decline in response strength as measured by the increasing length of time between responses, the rate at which responses are made, and the force with which a response is made, e.g., the vigor of toothbrushing or chewing. The rate of decline is a function of the frustrating omission of reward and the manner in which this omission interacts with the original habit [8].

Spontaneous recovery is the recurrence of a partially extinguished response, a phenomenon which indicates that extinction is as variable and impermanent as positive learning. Closely related to spontaneous recovery is the reoccurrence of a response which takes place because of disinhibition. Disinhibition proper is the reappearance of a response because of the interruption of the context or flow of events, e.g., while a child's response is being extinguished, if a loud noise occurs, or other children appear, or some other event which is not a part of the extinguishing sequence is introduced, disinhibition occurs, and the child makes the partially extinguished response. This is disinhibition rather than spontaneous recovery, since spontaneous recovery is the reappearance of a response without this evidence of interruption.

Any response is part of total behavior and is thus related to many stimuli. The response to each stimulus would have to be extinguished to effect complete extinction. Even under carefully controlled laboratory conditions, when the response to each known stimulus has been extinguished, spontaneous recovery still occurs, arousing a suspicion that the extinction of some stimuli was missed. Extinction of all the stimuli is extremely difficult in the controlled laboratory situation; it is even more unlikely in the uncontrolled circumstances of daily life.

Extinction sounds like mechanical or pushbutton forgetting—a response can be isolated from behavior and extinguished. Spontaneous recovery, however, prevents the acceptance of any such view. If the experimenter could isolate a response and then subject it to continuous extinction, he might prevent its reappearance; but spontaneous recovery is evidence of the extent to which any response is integrated in one's total behavior. Nonreinforcement of a response leads to partial extinction, since the response is gradually made less often.

Acceptable theoretical interpretations of extinction and spontaneous recovery are as follows:

Extinction and spontaneous recovery can be explained through response-induced inhibition, competition, and individual variability within these processes.

A response generates some inhibition to itself—reactive inhibition [95, p. 55]. Like fatigue, this effect accumulates from response to response. The positive effect of reinforcement is needed to overcome this reactive inhibition, otherwise the response may be prevented. Without reinforcement, response-induced inhibition accumulates, but rest dissipates reactive inhibition so that spontaneous recovery is likely to occur.

A second explanation of these phenomena is that responding without reinforcement is annoying; therefore, not responding is need-reducing. Need-reduction is reinforcing, so the organism learns to inhibit the non-reinforced response—conditioned inhibition [95, p. 56]. Spontaneous recovery from conditioned inhibition is the result of the incompleteness of the inhibition. Neither spontaneous recovery nor conditioned inhibition is complete or permanent.

A third explanation is associative interference [95, p. 57]. Learning, in its bare essentials, occurs in one trial, but it takes many movements to make up a goal-defined response. Since only one movement is conditioned per trial, it takes many trials to condition all movements. Competing responses to some stimuli have to be unlearned; faulty movements have to be reconditioned. To eliminate a conditioned response, it is only necessary to cause other movements to occur in the presence of the conditioned stimulus (conditioned inhibition, associative interference, competition). Extinction and conditioning are essentially the same mechanism when competing movements are involved. Spontaneous recovery is not covered by this theory.

Regardless of such theoretical explanations of extinction, deliberate efforts to induce forgetting are only partially successful. In the laboratory, where conditions can be controlled, responses can be more nearly extinguished. In life situations, it is more difficult to approach extinction, because the interrelated stimuli which cue behavior are too complex to succumb to simple lack of reinforcement. Spontaneous recovery, the reappearance of a partially extinguished response, is evidence of this inability to cause permanent forgetting. Forgetting is easier than remembering, but neither remembering nor forgetting can be guaranteed.

Summary: Forgetting

Ideally, persons work to foster remembering, but practically their best efforts to remember often succumb to forgetting. Forgetting is not without its brighter side, however, because it does provide for a fresh start. As a result of forgetting, a person can come to each task with a different approach, different in that he remembers less, and there are qualitative changes in what he remembers.

Forgetting is the result of associative inhibition. Under the best possible conditions, some forgetting occurs; but when one is subjected to the combined effects of reactive, proactive, and retroactive inhibition, the ability to remember withers. The combined effects of a person's present reaction against a task, the associative inhibition of present events on past events, and past events on present events produce the heavy load of inhibition which frequently breaks down the ability to remember.

One can reduce the associative inhibition of forgetting through enough practice, with instruction in the organization and context of the material to be remembered. Warmup and adequately-spaced complete reviews are other means to lessen forgetting.

Extinction is planned forgetting, and spontaneous recovery is the reappearance of the extinguished response. These two phenomena demonstrate how complex remembering and forgetting are. The integrated nature of learning makes it practically impossible to eliminate a response so thoroughly that spontaneous recovery will not occur.

Remembering and forgetting are complementary functions in one's development; and judgments regarding which one is more valuable under given circumstances require careful consideration.

10

generalization and discrimination

I F THE SITUATIONS that are later to face children were entirely predictable, education would be a simple matter of training in the explicit and specific situations which are expected to occur. But situations change, and so does the human organism.

Fortunately, humans are able to apply learning to a wide range of situations. In fact, the chief development desired is the reapplication and reinterpretation of behavior in varied circumstances. The processes which support and allow learning to function in new contexts are generalization and discrimination.

Generalization is the spread of learning from event to event, including the spread from the present situation to others which are perceived as similar and to synchronous events (those appropriate happenings which occur at the same time). Simple contiguity is not sufficient to account for all generalization; sometimes persons contribute through the likenesses they see in two situations. Chance [73] suggests that generalization occurs to a greater extent in situations where persons see two behaviors as leading to the same goal, as compared with situations in which two behaviors are seen as leading to different goals. Generalization is both the process and the result of the process whereby a conception, principle, or inference is used more extensively than in the situation from which it was derived.

Discrimination refers to the selectivity with which likenesses and differences are perceived. If one is seeking generalizations, he puts things together that have some likenesses and some differences. Simply putting like things together makes discrimination difficult, since discrimination depends on the perception of noticeable differences. To discriminate, a person selects responses from his repertory, usually in keeping with his perception of appropriateness at the moment.

Companion Processes

Generalization and discrimination are companion processes in all learning. Each supports the other in ways which are almost inseparable. For instance, when a person has generalized, he has differentiated similarities from a mass or context; some persons will prefer to call this differentiation a discrimination. When knowledge of fractions has generalized to embrace proper, improper, and decimal fractions as essentially the same condition, a person has differentiated these fractions from the mass of numbers. The differentiation is essential to the process of generalization. When one detects which fractional form, i.e., $3\frac{1}{4}$ or $\frac{13}{4}$ or 3.25, is most suitable, he has discriminated the manipulation of numbers and fractions needed for appropriate computation (and there is no need to document what happens when he fails to discriminate which fractions to use). In this illustration, the word "discriminate" is used in a more restrictive sense than "differentiate," yet the distinction is academic when one considers that generalization and discrimination are companion processes in all learning.

Both these processes are learned [318]. Primary generalization occurs when somewhat different stimuli evoke similar responses without previous learning. For instance, babies are born with the generalized (or similar) responses to sweet and sour tastes. As generalizations are learned, that is, as a person begins to perceive certain cues as equivalents, secondary generalization is possible, but secondary generalization also requires an acquired distinctiveness of cues, acquired discrimination. Secondary generalization is the product of learning to respond to different situations which serve equivalent functions. To respond to different situations because they are perceived as equivalent requires the learned discriminations present in selectivity. Awareness of differences and the ability to detect differences are the result of the development of innate capacities through learning, particularly the development of concept formation, concept identification, and discrimination.

Concept identification, for example, is dependent on the ability to discriminate among the items involved. In a study of the discrimination of form, size, and brightness by college students, it was found that, if the differences were noticeable, such as differences between form and size, form and brightness, and brightness and size, discrimination was easier than if the differences in a dimension, such as form, were barely noticeable or subliminal. Special instructions did not increase the overall performance of these students in the discrimination of form, size, and brightness, but did facilitate performance on more complex tasks [16]. A group of four- five-, and six-year-old children learned different names faster than similar names because of the differences in discriminability [100]. Persons learn to generalize and discriminate when they can identify and select equivalent similarities and differences.

The Use of Words

The majority of generalizations arise through symbols which represent concepts, rather than through exposure to the actual physical equivalence such as multiplication in school, multiplication at home, and multiplication on the street corner (or sunbathing on the roof, on the beach, and under a sun lamp). The physical equivalence of geographic conditions in New Jersey, New Hampshire, and Virginia, may be grasped through physical experiences with the geography of the three states; but it is much more likely to be acquired through maps, charts, graphs, and verbal descriptions which portray various aspects of the geography. Even on the maps, charts, and graphs, the customary equivalences are words. Most human discrimination is in words, as indicated by the word "green" and its various shades, such as "pea green," "apple green" and "emerald." Each of these words is a symbol for a color one has experienced. In learning colors, a person first discriminates green from other colors, and then shades of green. Also associated with shades of green and other colors on a map is the notion of altitude. As color concepts mature, words as symbols may convey vicariously a wide range of discriminations between shades of green.

In human learning, the formation, identification, and generalization of concepts through the use of verbal symbols is evident. Verbal symbols obviate the need to perceive physically the actual relationships. Persons can understand symbolically, usually in words. But generalization among symbols requires the correlative process, discrimination.

The Basis of Discrimination

The rapid learning of the mature animal depends upon the slow, difficult, early learning of the infant organism, and this is where and how instruction facilitates discrimination. Instruction from others enables persons to detect differences and be selective at levels beyond their own discrimination. While following the discrimination of others and enjoying the benefits of their superior development, one sharpens his own skill. The more careful and precise the instruction is, the easier the early discriminations are, and the sounder the basis of support for the person's own skill [63]. The years of careful, precise preparation necessary for good reading are a representative example. (We teach something specific; the child adjusts to something specific [65].) Sixth grade pupils given exercises in word discrimination as part of spelling instruction did better than those without this emphasis [263]. If children are well taught through patient, specific, explicit instruction, they learn to handle words well, and that ability, in turn, supports good discrimination in many other developments. The person who does not learn to deal easily with words is permanently relegated to a lower level of development. The early, slow learning is needed for perceptual organization so that the later, rapid insights can occur. Good reading in the fifth grade is the product of four years of careful development in word recognition, phonetics, and comprehension. Good reading leads to good vocabulary development. The precise use of words to discriminate between the fine shades of generalization and discrimination—in fact the fluent use of the complete symbolic system—is dependent on the early work with words, such as "door" to represent "door," "arithmetic" to represent "number combinations and manipulation," and "azimuthal equidistant projection" to represent "a map projection of the surface of the earth, so centered at any given point that a straight line radiating from the center to any other point represents the shortest distance, that is, an arc of a great circle." In three printed lines, the symbolism of words can move from the objects in a room to the high levels of abstraction found in concepts such as "togetherness" or "basic English." However, words cannot serve this function without early, careful training in their precise use. The rapid learning and facile adaptability of the mature person are based on the careful preparation of the young.

The quality of the early preparation is always apparent in later learning, particularly when adjustment is subjected to the tensions of the moment [64]. If the early learning is sound, it will withstand the impact of passing tension and emotional episodes. Sound basic learnings are essential for lifelong development. They are also good for the specifics of the moment. To illustrate, years of careful, good speech in a grammatical pattern enable a person to use language well in all circumstances, no matter how disturbed or excited he becomes at a given moment. An accent or speech pattern learned under tension for a dramatic role often breaks down to one's basic speech pattern. Many persons prepare for the moment, adopt a particular role of behavior for the moment; but if placed under any degree of pressure, their more basic level of preparation, their fundamental adjustment, attitudes, and opinions assert themselves, because they have been better learned. The years of careful, precise preparation necessary for learning and adjustment of good quality cannot be replaced by the training of the moment. Following the direction of others, pupils prepare themselves through 12 to 16 years of formal education and many years of informal education. Parents and other early teachers start the process, and it continues with the development of capacities in keeping with the start they provided. If the foundation is of good quality, the subsequent development can more easily lead to maturity. If the foundation work is omitted or carelessly done, children are doomed to years of compensating for the deficiency while competing with others who are not similarly handicapped. There is no substitute for the year-by-year, careful, specific learning which yields mature, adaptable behavior.

Such behavior is impossible without discrimination of good quality; and such discrimination is only possible when persons have had experience, either directly or vicariously, with knowledge and information, and in dealing selectively with that knowledge and information. Discrimination is the selector mechanism which enables persons to direct their attention and to be selective within this attention. Experience makes it possible for the learner to discriminate in the present situation. Through learning, the discriminability tends to become a consistent mode of behavior, against which patterns stand out clearly, rather than occurring in a variable manner [146]. The ability to discriminate, to employ selectively aspects of the self and the environment, is the result of careful preparation for maturity.

Distance, Generalization, and Discrimination

While everyone is able to manage some generalization and discrimination, the critical point is the range or distance through which they will operate, together and separately.

The idea of distance can be likened to the concept of abstraction. As a generalization, how much does the word "color" include? "Color" can arouse associations as variable as "rainbow," "primary colors," "secondary colors," "shade and tint," "the spectrum," "decoration," "artistry," "dress," and many others. If the possible associations from the word "color" are arranged in any order, some will be further from the stimulus "color" in time and space, and therefore are less likely to be associated at all. This is the idea of distance in generalization, discrimination, and the thought processes. Abstractions which are less likely to be included in a series of associations are at a greater distance than those which are immediate, available, and close.

The notion of likeness ranges from identity to complete dissimilarity, in a continuous scale. This involves the concept of distance, both physical and psychological. The idea of physical distance is easy to accept and does not require explanation. Psychological distance is also a reality and refers to one's perception of closeness or remoteness of events in time or space. To illustrate, through the thought processes persons can bring events together, e.g., they can compare the climate of France with that of Eastern United States, in much the same way that one would compare neighboring states like Minnesota and Wisconsin as banks of the Mississippi River. Similarly, the thought processes can place great distance between events, even though they are almost contiguous in time and/or space. For example, compare A's relationships with two people, B and C, whom he sees one after the other. With B the relationship is close because of intercommunication, while with C there is great distance because there is no exchange of information and ideas, although the similar pleasantries about the weather and health were exchanged with both B and C. Likeness and unlikeness can be physical or psychological, and this involves the notion of the distance between like and unlike.

The distance between two events in time, space, or other dimensions is a function of perception and understanding. The spectrum is viewed by some as a rainbow in the sky with a possible pot of gold, an almost pure but distant fantasy. To others, the spectrum is a phenomenon of light refracted into its components, present and manageable. With careful, explicit, specific experience with events and things, persons can come to a close relationship with them through learned understandings. This does not imply that they comprehend everything, but that those things which they comprehend are close to them; they are not psychologically distant. As understanding deteriorates, the distance tends to increase. Blind spots in perception, such as inability to find an error in addition which is clearly there on the paper, give the appearance of great psychological distance. When the error in addition is pointed out, it reaches a front position in awareness with a crash. What seemed to be a great distance between items is closed quickly. The distance between two events, symbolically or practically, is a function of perception and understanding.

Generalization and discrimination are mediated by the physical and psychological distance found in the range from likeness to dissimilarity. How far can one generalize unlike items, and conversely, how far can one discriminate similar items? If arithmetic problems are perceived as being like those which have been done previously, the child can do them easily. If they are perceived as unlike anything done previously, they will be new and difficult. If the problems are only slightly different experiences, the learner can usually progress the short distance without much difficulty.

If the teacher wishes to encourage discrimination, how similar can he make the items, or how great a distance can be interposed? Distance is needed for discrimination, but too great distance makes generalization impractical, if not impossible. Are the months of June on three successive years too far apart to provide for generalization and discrimination? Both processes involve the notion of psychological distance, and, as companion processes, both are essential for appropriate behavior.

The greater distance through which generalization and discrimination will function, both separately and together, the wider the range of possible development. When a person can generalize, he can bring events close to him and gain a measure of control over them. Similarly, when he can discriminate, he has control because he can arrange the distances between events. Eventual mastery, of both one's self and one's environment, develops from the range of generalization and discrimination.

Gradients of generalization and discrimination are usually of interest to the academic and experimental psychologist, rather than to the person interested chiefly in applying psychology in the classroom.

These gradients are the graphed relationships between generalization and like and unlike, or between discrimination and like and unlike. A gradient is an ascending or descending slope. The more alike events are, the more generalization will occur and the harder discrimination is, not because of generalization but because of likeness. When the situation is alike to the point of being identical, the graphed relationship between generalization and likeness is as high as it can be, and the graphed relationship between discrimination and likeness is as low as it can be. As one moves from like to unlike, the slope showing the relationship with generalization drops to its lowest level and the slope showing the relationship with discrimination rises to its highest point. The more events are unlike, the harder generalization is and the easier discrimination is, not because of discrimination but because of unlikeness.

The concept of goal-gradient can also be integrated with gradients of generalization and discrimination. A good review of the present status of the concept of goal-gradients is to be found in Cohen [80].

Motivation

Intention is a major determinant in the development of discrimination, although being overly motivated does not improve discrimination. Motivation is at its best level if enough attention is used for perception of all aspects of each situation. What kind of discrimination is most fruitful—accuracy or general awareness? Whenever persons concentrate on being accurate in a number of responses, they usually impair their incidental discriminations. Conversely, whenever full awareness includes the casual and incidental in a situation, discrimination cannot be as accurate. Not only are some discriminations harder for some learners, but there are limits to the number and the conditions of stimuli which the learner can discriminate. In striving for accuracy, one tends to miss some perceptions, and in striving for full awareness, one sacrifices some accuracy.

Up to a point, anxious people discriminate better than those who are not contending with anxiety [181]. Hilgard and others found that discrimination was affected by the characteristics of the stimuli, the temporary sets and predispositions in the subject at the time of the attempted discrimination, and the underlying basic structure of the individual. Temporary variability in behavior is part of all learning, but as one learns to discriminate, the underlying basic structure, which is not temporary, asserts itself. To some extent then, the stimulation of anxiety sharpens discrimination, but as anxiety invades the more basic structure, its effect is disruptive instead of leading to the development of better discrimination.

This disruption of discrimination by anxiety has been verified experimentally. The Taylor Anxiety Scale was used to select 20 high-anxiety and 20 low-anxiety college students. The low-anxiety students required fewer trials and had less difficulty in responding to the task. The high-anxiety persons required more trials and were more variable in their performance [370].

While it is accepted that highly variable performance is typical of most learning experiments with adults, the level of anxiety influences the ease of discrimination and variability in learning rate. Differences in high-anxiety performance in this experiment, however, were attributed to the way in which the high-anxiety students had learned to respond to their anxiety. Low-anxiety subjects had less difficulty in responding, but high-anxiety subjects performed in an efficient manner, depending on their past experiences. Anxiety disrupts discrimination in learning, but the anxiety of the moment is not as influential as the long-term, learned adjustment to vague apprehension. Not only are some discriminations harder for learners because of their learned adjustment to date, but the temporary conditions of the moment may disrupt learned discriminations.

Under high motivation and in highly charged emotional situations, even the best of discriminations will break down. When highly excited and emotionally stimulated, people lose the ability to respond precisely; they give generalized and more primitive responses. The broadly disruptive effects of anger destroy the quality of discrimination. ("A blind rage" is an apt phrase.) The young man in love does not respond critically to the behavior of his beloved. Under high motivation, discriminations of good quality are difficult.

Adjustment, Generalization, and Discrimination

Both generalization and discrimination are essential for appropriate behavior. A person's behavior is judged to be appropriate when he makes responses which meet the situation without unduly involving the self in tensions. When generalization fails, he does not make former responses in new situations; his responses do not spread from one situation to the next. When discrimination fails, he takes inappropriate responses from one situation to the next. Mature development enables a person to shift his responses in keeping with the kaleidoscope of events so that he responds appropriately. The failure of either generalization or discrimination leads to behavior which is not in keeping with the situation. Such inappropriateness is well illustrated by what is called the infantile personality. Infantile adjustment is characterized by a lack of generalization, an inability to discriminate cues, and a predominance of substitute gratifications to compensate for the inappropriateness. Infantile persons lack the ability to respond selectively to new situations because of the failure of both generalization and discrimination. Infantile adjustment makes it difficult to transfer knowledge and information from one situation to another. This results in responses which are not in keeping with the situation. When persons feel this lack, they resort to actions (symptoms) to release their tension. Since even those who enjoy mature adjustment regress to contend with tension, it is obvious how those whose adjustment is infantile attempt to contend with the hopelessly uneven struggle. Generalization and discrimination are companion processes in the full development of maturity to provide persons with a repertory of responses, in each situation, from which they can select in order to behave adequately.

Summary: Generalization and Discrimination

Generalization and discrimination are companion processes in all learning, yet all learning is a discrimination from generalization. Persons learn to generalize and to discriminate, at first through actual experiences, and at a gradually increasing rate through the use of symbols—particularly words. As symbols, words short-circuit the need for actual experience, through concept formation, concept identification, and discrimination. Words provide for vicarious experience to promote both generalization and discrimination.

The basis of discrimination is the early, slow, difficult, precise learning of the behavior. Without this adequate background, one never develops the selector mechanism necessary to pick out the important features of the environment. The need to discriminate emphasizes that discrimination requires either a broad awareness or accuracy. Both are not possible, but enough attention for one or the other is all that is needed for good discrimination. Up to a point, tension is helpful to discrimination, but past a basic level for each person, the effects of tension are broadly disruptive. The slow, careful, early learning provides a basis for later discrimination which can withstand the impact of tension and emotion, not in a specific situation, but generally, throughout lifelong development.

Generalization and discrimination involve the concepts of both physical and psychological distance. The more alike events are, the more likely generalization is. The more unlike events are, the easier discrimination is. If one considers likeness as closeness, then unlikeness is distance. Distance can be physical or temporal, and these concepts resolve themselves to distance in relationships. Some events which are near for some are far for others. As understanding develops, the relationships become close and familiar. When comprehension is elusive, the distance between events tends to lengthen. Generalization and discrimination involve converse aspects of distance, but both are essential for mature development.

Adjustment is characterized by both good generalization and discrimination. Nowhere is it more evident than in mature adjustment that persons first need to transfer to the present situation their knowledge and skills from previous situations and then discriminate, detect, and use the knowledge and skills which are appropriate. The adjustment of any human requires the integrated operation of all abilities, including generalization and discrimination.

11

transfer

POSITIVE AND NEGATIVE TRANSFER

MOTIVATION

INTELLECTUAL LEVEL

UNDERSTANDING AND TRANSFER

THE TASKS AND TRANSFER

THE INFLUENCE OF PRACTICE

THE USE OF WORDS

TRANSFER IN HUMAN RELATIONSHIPS

SUMMARY: TRANSFER

THE APPLICATION OF GENERALIZATION and discrimination is most evident in the transfer of learning. To what extent does learning Latin help or hinder the learning of English? This relationship is what is meant by transfer. The advocates of the formal discipline or mental discipline theory contended that training had general transfer value, and that certain kinds of learning were therefore good since they helped with all learning. Experimental work has shown, however, that transfer does not operate so widely, but is explicit and specific.

There are educators and psychologists who feel that the effective range of transfer is much broader than the positive and negative influence of one subject on another subject. They feel that the influence of the degree of mastery of a task, along with thinking and concept formation, will permeate the learner and the learning situation to foster broadly positive transfer. For instance, in the course of a week, a person comes to grips with a wide range of materials and many different persons. The transfer of knowledge and skill throughout his weekly contacts is a function of his integrated development and over-all comprehension of his way of life. All his abilities come into play to induce appropriate behavior in the present situation—behavior which is smoothly integrated with the flow of events. This transfer of training is a function of one's mastery of the situation and other similar situations. Practice prepares persons to behave in their usual appropriate or inappropriate ways, and these rehearsals may be physical or merely verbal or mental runthroughs. There is nothing magical about the social graces, the skills of the discussion leader, or the gratifying contacts with the butcher, the baker, the automobile mechanic. One's behavior in each situation is a function of his full integrated development and experience with situations like these. It would be fine if rehearsal in one or two social situations provided a person with the range of appropriate social skills for each situation. In practice, however, there is insufficient generalization available from one or two practice situations to permit much carryover to new situations unless they are almost identical with the original ones.

Mastery of each situation is the product of development in similar situations. The broader the range of experience has been, and the more complete the integration of each experience with one's full range of behavior, the more positive transfer he is likely to obtain. Limited experiences and disjointed or disconnected experiences are likely to induce no transfer or even have a negative effect. Most positive transfer occurs when persons practice exactly what they intend to do. They can rarely practice something else to aid with the learning of spelling or mathematics. The practice of spelling aids spelling, while the practice of mathematics aids mathematics [199]. There is enough variability within both of these skills to require all one's ability to transfer them from one situation to the next, let alone deal with the broader transfer of skill in these subjects to other subjects. Generalization and discrimination respond to careful, explicit practice, and their transfer is similarly explicit and specific.

Positive and Negative Transfer

The processes in transfer are generalization and discrimination. Learnings like *A*, *B*, and *C* are influenced by learning *A'*, *B'*, and *C'*. However, through generalization there is a spread from *A* to *A'*, and from B to B', and from C to C'; that is, generalization, by itself, leads to both positive (helpful) and negative (hindering) transfer [321]. It is necessary to select, from the responses which a person has available, the ones which fit in new situations. To the extent that he is unable to discriminate what is required, negative transfer or interference will result. When he is able to discriminate from the available responses those which are fruitful, positive transfer takes place. In one study involving college students, transfer was positive when the stimuli employed were distinguished by the same property in both tasks, and negative when the stimuli were distinguished by different properties in the two tasks [223]. Transfer does not move very far. Rather, generalization and discrimination operate as complementary processes to transfer explicit and specific knowledge and skills from situation to situation.

Transfer is at a maximum when a person's perception of the operational situation is most similar to the training situation [95]. The less similar the operational situation is, the more broadly generalization must work, and the more sharply discrimination must occur for transfer to take place. Ability to transfer to remote situations is a high level of development. Present learning is facilitated by some kinds of pretraining, but the pretraining cannot be effective without the broad effects of generalization to establish the likenesses and the sharp delineations of discrimination to select the appropriate responses. Transfer is at a maximum when the pretraining is most like the operational situation, but carefully staged training to match each performance situation is not possible. With development, persons learn to use both generalization and discrimination in order to benefit from the preparation and training, whether it matches the operational situation or not.

Motivation

The desire to apply what is learned to a new situation facilitates transfer. Both correct and incorrect relationships which the subjects chose for themselves showed high positive transfer [230]. The "chosen" attracts more attention and more energy because it carries the feeling of willingness and freedom of choice. Too much enthusiasm is not desirable, however, because it tends to confuse discrimination. Sufficient attention for a task, the amount implied by one's choosing to do, rather than not to do, is all that is needed. Overinvestment narrows the field of perception to limit awareness and hamper discrimination. The desire to apply what one knows to new situations marshals enough energy for transfer.

Intellectual Level

Ability to recognize the general principle embodied in a strange situation is an example of intelligence. Those of higher intellectual level have more of this ability and can thus transfer more of the things they learn because they can generalize and discriminate more. They are aware of more relationships and of more nuances among relationships, so that they transfer their abilities with more skill and greater ease.

Understanding and Transfer

When the learner understands the situation, he has acquired the ability to recognize the general principle.

In a comparison of rote memorization and understanding as related to the ease of original learning, retention, and transfer, it was found that the understanding group took longer to learn initially than the memorizing group, that the overnight retention for both groups was equal, and that the understanding group was more successful in transfer where either simple transposition or problem-solving was involved [182, pp. 288-292].

With understanding, a person easily transposes his thoughts through symbols from one situation to the next. Where more than simple transposition is required, understanding allows him to figure out what the present situation requires. For instance, when a person understands the behavior of the people with whom he works, he can cooperate with them. As with superior intellectual ability, there is no substitute for the quality of understanding. Understanding transcends the barriers of set or context and carries the generalizations great distances, while still providing the sharp discriminations necessary for the adaptable use of the full range of abilities (382, 407).

The Tasks and Transfer

Transfer is influenced by the nature of the task to be learned and the nature of the task to which transfer is desired. This refers especially to lower levels of generalization and discrimination, to the more mechanical aspects of the processes. Transfer increases directly as the task to be learned and the transfer task are more alike [107]. As the abilities to generalize and discriminate mature, the nature of the two tasks can be something less than alike and fruitful transfer is still possible. For instance, writing an article for a journalism course and writing a biology laboratory report both involve the ability to write English, but the material and treatment are different enough so that transfer is far from automatic. If the task learned and the transfer task are unlike, creative generalization and sharp discrimination are essential. Structuring the situation to show likenesses will encourage the use of transfer, although highly developed abilities may transcend the necessity for such arrangements.

The Influence of Practice

Almost all learning responds to rehearsal, and practice in learning a task makes it easier to learn. For example, two groups learned different mazes at different times, and both learned the second maze faster [193]. They remembered how to go about the task, just as those who have done several jigsaw puzzles solve a new one quicker than those who have never done one before. Memory was for the method of approach, not for the sequence of the mazes or the actual jigsaw pieces. The method of approach is the result of the formation of learning sets, and these transfer both positively and negatively. To illustrate, one pattern per concept, repeated 20 times, enabled subjects to make fewer errors. With 20 different patterns per concept, repeated once, performance was poorest. However, the 20-different-pattern group showed the greatest transfer proficiency [61]. They were not fettered by one rehearsed set and consequently shifted to a different context with more ease. Practice may facilitate or inhibit set for transfer, depending on what is practiced and how much it is practiced.

In another study on the effects of practice on transfer, groups who were required to shift concepts frequently on training tasks developed a set to shift, which facilitated performance [341]. However, such shifting can be overdone if insufficient rehearsal is provided for in each set or context. There is no advantage in training for transfer, unless conditions permit the mastery of each kind of training [109]. Stolurow and others found more positive transfer when the first task was practiced to a relatively high level [373].

Sufficient pretraining with relevant instructions promotes positive transfer. The facilitating effect of such pretraining is attributed to decreased generalization and improved discrimination [64]. When a teacher directs his pupils to what he wants and provides for practice of it, both learning and transfer are facilitated. Without relevant instructions, Beach found humans to take as long as animals to solve certain problem boxes [34]. The relevant instructions enabled humans to use reasoning ability rather than blunder along in animal fashion. After humans had solved one problem, they solved a second problem noticeably faster than animals. This faster solution of a similar problem box is attributed to memory for the method of approach, for the set of the task, and to relevant self-instruction following the first problem. Learning the set or context alone, without the thought processes to direct concept formation through generalization and discrimination, is not sufficient to bring about positive transfer. Sufficient pretraining with relevant instructions facilitates the use of abilities through the widest possible range of tasks. Without the relevant instructions and the use of the thought processes in generalization and discrimination, pretraining produces a fixity of set which inhibits transfer.

The Use of Words

Transfer is mediated through the symbolism of words. Persons are aware of the fact that they can prepare verbally for a task and that the actual performance provides verification of the verbal preparation, but the role of words in directing, redirecting, and shifting the actual rehearsal is rarely fully appreciated. Without any physical rehearsal, but practicing only at the symbolic level of thought in words, transfer of knowledge and ideas can occur from situation to situation. To verify whether such transfer supports skillful performance, doing is necessary, but the full range of possible performances can be reviewed through the use of words. This implies good denotation and connotation in the use of words through the workings of broad generalizations and precise discriminations. At the highest level, people control their behavior and the transfer of their behavior through the use of words as symbols [289].

The superiority of a verbal-learning group over a nonverbal-learning group has been demonstrated, even in motor learning [150]. Those persons who achieved discriminative mastery of relevant verbal responses prior to the motor learning performed better than the nonverbally-prepared groups. The amount of transfer from verbal pretraining to motor performance decreases as the motor-task complexity increases, but there is an advantage in verbal preparation for all kinds of learning [32]. Persons do not learn as well or transfer as easily without the actual performance, but a great deal of the preparation for learning and transfer can occur at the level of verbal symbolic practice.

Verbal responses transfer both positively and negatively. The full use of all one's abilities is required in order to benefit from the

facilitation of positive transfer and avoid the interference of negative transfer. Contextual similarities and the relationships found in
synonyms, antonyms, and homonyms require close attention to
prevent interference. The errors which are more similar to the
correct responses are made with greater frequency, e.g., *entomology*
is substituted for *etymology* with greater frequency because of
the homophony of the two words [404]. In order to benefit from the
use of words as symbols, persons must discriminate precisely the
denotation and connotation of each symbol. As discrimination is
faulty in these respects, negative transfer becomes more likely.
When the symbolism is faulty, even the actual experience is likely
to be misinterpreted and lead to further interference. For verbal
responses to transfer positively, years of careful, precise, verified
work with words as symbols is necessary. To illustrate, the word
"will" may be used in the following senses, among others: volition,
free will, intent, purpose, determination, see fit, originate, choice,
disposition, spontaneous. When the word "will" is used, to which of
these meanings does generalization carry you? How sharply does
discrimination operate to select the most appropriate usage for the
context? Neither generalization nor discrimination can operate fully
unless preceded by years of thorough preparation with all meanings
and uses of "will." The transfer of abilities through word symbolism
is a high level of development and is the product of the lifelong
preparation to which the learner has been subjected.

Transfer in Human Relationships

Transfer occurs in relationships with people also. For instance,
consider the transfer from parents to teachers. Children and adolescents transfer their reactions from one controlling adult to another
quite indiscriminately. When they learn to individualize and discriminate these reactions, human relationships improve. This is a
quality of maturity not to be expected too soon in the young.
Teachers, as controlling adults, usually succeed and fail in about
the same way that the parents succeed and fail. The young gener-

ally react to the teacher as they react to any controlling adult. When parent-child relationships are poor, the development of the child's discriminatory abilities needs to be superior in order for him to see the role of the teacher as anything but a dissatisfying parent-symbol. This is well illustrated in the collection of uncomplimentary jokes about both parents and teachers. As maturity develops, persons learn to discriminate among general reactions to people so that better relationships with all people are possible. A child's early relationships with people inevitably are generalized. If he has been fortunate enough to have experienced good relationships, he benefits by this without appreciating why it happens. When his relationships have been poor, he is penalized without knowing why. Eventually most persons free themselves to some degree from the identifications which were provided for them and develop their own reactions to people and things. This is a limited freedom, however, since the bases of generalization and discrimination are learned early and are thoroughly ingrained in the response-structure.

Summary: Transfer

The most obvious application of the full range of generalization and discrimination is the transfer of training. With generalization alone, the transfer is more likely to be negative, instead of positive. When a person is able to generalize and discriminate, he gains positive transfer of his abilities from one situation to the next.

Factors within the learner which help him to achieve positive transfer are intention to transfer, intellectual level, and understanding. The intention to use previous knowledge and skill in a new situation provides enough attention to make transfer more likely to occur. Superior intellectual ability permits more transfer of better quality. The more comprehensive one's understanding, the easier it is to transfer knowledge and skill for fruitful adjustment. Sufficient attention to transfer, sufficient intelligence, and sufficient understanding yield transfer of training.

There are other factors influencing transfer which are, to varying degrees, outside the learner's basic equipment: the nature of the material on which training has been given, the nature of the new situation, the amount and quality of practice, and the use of verbal-symbolic rehearsal.

Transfer from situation A to A' is easy, almost mechanical, while transfer from A to E involves the broad operation of generalization and the sharp operation of discrimination. Practice aids in all development; and practice of the conditions for transfer, namely, practice in generalization and discrimination, promotes more transfer. Words as symbols provide for the transfer of concepts, concept identification, and discrimination, from one situation to the next. Human relationships, with all their complexity and variability, provide for both positive and negative transfer to promote and to interfere with full development of maturity. Transfer is essential for the fruitful use of all one's abilities, but in a specific, explicit manner rather than in a broad general way.

12

reinforcement

REINFORCEMENT IS A BASIC CONCEPT in learning and teaching. As in many other concepts, there is little agreement about an exact definition [314]. For a teacher, however, the term embraces confirmation and reward. There may be important theoretical distinctions between the terms confirmation [Tolman, 394] and reward [Thorndyke, 388, Meehl, 268], but the two terms will be used interchangeably here.

"Yes, do it that way" is confirmation for behavior. Even "uh-huh" has been found to be reinforcing [363]. The teacher gives such confirmation because he wants the student to continue that specific behavior. In practice, the confirmed action is continued to such an extent that most behavior theorists believe reinforcements to be the most important determiners of what people do [300, 326].

Typically, reinforcement is the condition that causes one response instead of another to be associated with a given stimulus. This is a practical and operational definition in that it refers to events which can be observed and measured; theoretical definitions of reinforcement in terms of entities and constructs are unobservable.

The consequence called a reinforcement is the confirmation or denial that follows an event. The teacher says yes or no; he agrees or disagrees; he nods his head and smiles in approval or shakes his head and looks reproachful. Reinforced, positive cues (desirable outcomes) and non-reinforced, negative cues (undesirable outcomes) lead to better subsequent learning, and to better discrimination [121]. The liberal use of reward during the early stages of learning induces a set or frame of reference that encourages identification and imitation; punishment does not encourage this set [343]. Reinforcement thus strengthens habits.

The aspects of reinforcement that most influence learning and teaching are the temporal relationships of the reinforcement in relation to the strength of the response, the number of reinforcements, the amount of reinforcement, intermittent reinforcement, and secondary reinforcement.

Temporal Relationships and Strength

The strength of an association or of a given field organization is more obviously increased if reinforcement occurs in close temporal contiguity to the event. The closer in time the reinforcement is to the occurrence, the greater the effectiveness of the reinforcement. If the teacher checks work as soon as it is completed and confirms or denies the correctness and quality of the job, his reinforcement is most effective. The longer the delay of such confirmation or denial, the less effective it is. Thus there is a gradient of effectiveness of reinforcement related to the time of reinforcement. Maximum habit strength is a function of the absence of delay in administering reward [166]. Reinforcement increases the strength of a response *most* if it follows directly after the event.

Many experiments have been conducted to check on the operation of factors affecting reinforcement. Several of these studies are referred to in this chapter.

The delay of reward in human verbal learning resulted in slower learning and in more errors [331].

Increasing the delay interval between performance and knowledge of results reduced the rate of learning, but a delay of up to 30 seconds was still superior to no information [159]. Subjects were required to draw a three-inch line while blindfolded, and information concerning the accuracy of their drawing was delayed, in varying times up to 30 seconds. While line-drawing, blindfolded, is remote from most learning situations, the experiment confirms the weakening effect of delay on reinforcement.

Even in parapsychology, an immediate knowledge of results helps. The effect of reinforcement on human guesses of coin tosses was to decrease the number of alternations of response; this suggests guessing habits [37]. When people were told of their correct card guesses right after their guess, hits resulted, while if they were not told until 15 minutes later, only chance results occurred [31].

When the subject saw or expected the direction of his error, he performed more accurately than in a comparable series when this knowledge was withheld [247, 248].

The Number of Reinforcements

The number of reinforcements increases the strength of a response. Generally, the greater the number of reinforced occurrences, the stronger the response, although the effects of satiation confuse this generalization at the extreme upper level. Most learners reach a point after many reinforced responses where they are not as keen to continue that activity, but responses and learning do occur even under conditions of satiation [385]. The number of reinforcements necessary to produce satiation varies for different persons and different tasks. Generally, however, the strength of a response is a function of the varying numbers of reinforcements [151].

The Amount of Reinforcement

The amount of reinforcement influences motivation (willingness to perform), but not the rate of learning. The rate of learning depends upon how often the event occurs and is reinforced. The rate at which one learns facts in history depends upon the number of confirmed repetitions of these facts. The amount of confirmation and the amount of satisfaction arising from the confirmation influence the willingness to continue and willingness to return to repetitions and reperformance. A nod of approval provides confirmation just as well as enthusiastic praise, but people are more willing to work for warm praise than for a nod of approval. Appreciation that is sensitive to needs and progress is most suitable.

Advice like the following suggests that there is a sex differential in the need for approval.

Praise women more than men. Women really expect praise in greater quantities than men. Failure to comment favorably is likely to be interpreted as disapproval. Don't correct too harshly. When a woman makes errors, corrections should be low pressure. The sting of a rebuke is hard for her to take.

Bear in mind that women take things personally. Ask a man the question: "Where did you buy this steak?" and he will answer "At Green's Market." Ask his wife the same question, and she will answer: "Why? What's wrong with it?" [392].

Intermittent Reinforcement

Reinforcement that is given periodically establishes and maintains responses of the greatest strength [7, 41, 66]. The acquisition of behavior is more rapid under continuous than periodic reinforcement, but the responses are stronger under partial or periodic reinforcement. Periodic reinforcement may be given at a fixed time (interval reinforcement), that is, "Every Friday I'll check your work;" or it may be at a fixed ratio (ratio reinforcement), namely, "Whenever you have finished a unit of work, I'll check what you have done." Variable-interval reinforcements (aperiodic reinforcements) are also used. A periodic or aperiodic check sets up an expectancy of confirmation or denial in the learner so that he will perform well for several weeks, knowing that reinforcement is coming [236].

The following conclusions were reached in studies of intermittent reinforcement:

Extinction takes place sooner under conditions of alternate reinforcement than under random reinforcement [240]. The irregular nature of the latter sets up a stronger expectancy than that established by a pattern of reinforcement every second time.

Nonreinforcement followed by reinforcement leads to the greatest resistance to extinction [160].

Following partial reinforcement, more correct responses were made than with total reinforcement or no reinforcement [21].

As Skinner and others have pointed out, the principle of random reinforcement is evident in the strength of the gambling urge. The slot machine pays off at irregular intervals; the roulette wheel comes up with the right number occasionally; the dice appear in a winning combination once in a while. The gambler always feels that next time he will hit the jackpot.

The full influence of intermittent as compared with total or no reinforcement can be appreciated when one considers the effect on the child or adolescent of giving-in sometimes. The 15-year-old is to be home by midnight, but occasional exceptions are allowed. This establishes the strongest possible feeling that one can stay out later than 12 and actually defeats the purpose of the rule. Lest anyone be concerned over the arbitrary authority of this illustration, consider the following approaches. Where possible, parents and teachers make rules together with those under their control. These are the rules which are followed. If either party wishes to change the rules, both parties talk it over to reach other agreements. When this kind of cooperation is not possible, arbitrary authority is preferable to a "no-rule" approach. The parent or teacher who gives-in sometimes (just as a reward) establishes an expectancy that is the reverse of the desired ruling. "No candy before dinner" works well so long as there is never candy before dinner; but if the indulgent parent, in-law, or grandparent rewards good behavior by giving-in even once, there is always the hope that such behavior (rather than the no-candy behavior) will again be rewarded.

Intermittent reinforcement requires us to carry some of the burden for our conduct. Someone is not checking us at every turn. We perform, knowing that we will be checked sometimes, but not knowing just when. This expectation requires us to perform each time as though the trial is to be fully reviewed. Whether it is or not, we are more in control of our own behavior than if we know that someone will review every bit of work that we do.

Secondary Reinforcement

Secondary reinforcement, as implied by its name, comes after primary or first-order reinforcement, but its influence in learning is not at all secondary in importance. A reinforcement is any stimulus which can increase the strength of a response when it is presented in close temporal conjunction with the occurrence of that response [95, p. 12]. Secondary reinforcement means those things that occur with an event and that come to have reinforcing and sometimes eliciting value. This acquired reinforcement was called secondary or higher order reinforcement to distinguish it from primary or first order reinforcement [95, p. 22]. Someone said "good" after the child's action, smiled, and seemed to relax and enjoy the situation. The smile and the enjoyment, feelings similar to those implied, and our verbalization (vocal or subvocal) may become reinforcers through repeated association with an action that is reinforced. Anything that the learner associates with the confirmation or denial of responses may acquire secondary reinforcing value. Thus the classroom learning situation, which always lacks control over the possible occurrences of reinforcement, cannot assure the final desired behavior. For instance, teachers do not know what is being reinforced by what kinds of associations in a class of 35 persons. They can rarely have any conviction about what has been reinforced with as large a group as 35.

Most human behavior is subject to the influence of secondary and higher order reinforcement. People verbalize their associations either vocally or subvocally and these words are then used to elicit and to verify or deny the responses made. They do it for themselves and thus provide for the maturity of independence in managing behavior.

Secondary reinforcement is subject to similar principles as primary reinforcement [426]. Its effect is strong if it occurs in close temporal contiguity. There is a gradient of effectiveness—the longer the delay, the less effective the reinforcement. The number of reinforced occurrences influences response strength, and the amount of reinforcement influences motivation more than it influences the rate of learning. Through the use of verbal behavior as a secondary agent, persons achieve independence from the confirmation and denial of others. A recent study by Kanfer and Matarazzo supports the point of view that generalized reinforcement is somewhat more effective than secondary reinforcement in human verbal learning [206]. However, the value of this generalization will depend on the continuing study of the role of verbal abilities in directing human behavior.

The extent to which the quality of a person's self-verification agrees with ours will determine how mature and adequate we consider him to be, and this is a source of major ambivalence. Each person has to learn to be independent while being dependent. He is dependent upon others to verify to him what he feels himself to be. He needs others to confirm or deny his self-verification, yet the less he needs to depend upon others, the more mature he becomes.

From the Laboratory to the Classroom

The control of learning in the laboratory has usually been much more effective than in the classroom. However, apart from the control over the living conditions of the experimental animals, and thus over many variables, there are improvements in control that can be applied directly to the learning-teaching of the classroom.

First, the Law of Effect has been applied through prompt reinforcement of desired behavior. Feeding a hungry pigeon at the right moment directs him to turn, to stretch his neck, or even perform complex acts such as playing games. Both competition and cooperation have been artificially induced.

Second, behavior is maintained more consistently through the use of intermittent reinforcement.

Varying schedules of reinforcement cause varying rates of response. Analyzing the way various subjects react, both animal and human, has helped in the analysis of some serial and coordinate behaviors involved in attention, problem-solving, and self-control. By working through complex interrelations among responses, one may gradually control behavior in the areas of perception, thinking, and personality dynamics.

Unfortunately, education has used little of this new knowledge about learning. For example, arithmetic requires many verbal responses using words, figures, and signs for numbers and processes, and requires responses to many stimuli, as in counting, or recognizing odd and even numbers. This should prepare the child to handle complex arithmetic processes.

Years ago, negative reinforcement in the form of corporal punishment was used to induce pupils to do their arithmetic homework, and occasionally the pupils experienced positive reinforcement through their increased efficiency at the task. Today, without corporal punishment, there is still much aversive instead of positive control. The child works to escape the teacher's displeasure, low marks, and ridicule. Thus, getting the right answer itself is unimportant, lost in anxiety, boredom, and aggressions.

Usually reinforcement comes from the teacher's approval of the work, but this is often delayed for minutes or even days. Since most reinforcement effect is lost with a few seconds delay, it is surprising that classroom reinforcement works at all.

Third, programs lack the carefully planned progressive steps leading to complex behavior. The teacher cannot reinforce each step, and reinforcement which follows only after a series of responses is inadequate.

Even worse, frequency of reinforcement is low. In the first four years, there should be roughly 25,000 to 50,000 contingencies to develop efficient mathematical behavior, whereas only a few thousand are provided. Thus arithmetic is learned badly, accompanied by anxieties and aggressions that cause other problems.

The teaching machine using linear programming avoids many of these pitfalls by providing material in tiny units, carefully programmed, and reinforcing each response immediately. The child progresses at his own rate and is reinforced with correct answers [357, pp. 86-97].

Directed Learning from the Teaching Machine

Directed learning follows from the control over reinforcement. When one reinforces exactly the bit of behavior desired, it is possible to direct what the learner will do next. To this end, teaching machines have been created, but few of the machines provide for precise control.

Skinner claims that his teaching machines are like good tutors because they perform the following functions: sustain activity, insist that a given point be thoroughly understood, present just the material for which the student is ready, help the student to come up with the right answer, and reinforce the student for every correct response [360]. Skinner's emphasis in programming material, as Hively puts it, is on the detailed behavioral analysis of the responses to be acquired, and the programming of stimuli to shape and maintain behavior [183].

While the paraphrase from Skinner is logical and academically sound, the claims for the machines often run beyond fact.

Programmed Instructional Materials

The teaching machine presents a program, but programmed materials are not basically new. Workbooks are programmed materials; so are self-teaching books and correspondence-course manuals. Slides, filmstrips, films and television presentations are all programmed—that is, they are arranged in a carefully planned sequence and in most cases in an ascending scale. In a sense, good teachers have always programmed their instruction. The present emphasis is on the value of the immediate reinforcement of the learner's responses and on two special ways of organizing the learning material —*linear* and *branch* programming.

Linear programming breaks subjects into small bits (frames), and the subject progresses a short distance in each work period. For instance, a frame might be as follows:

(A.) Immediate reinforcement has a greater effect than reinforcement
which is delayed. This statement emphasizes the value of
_____ reinforcement.

immediate   (B.)

The emphasis is on making certain that nearly all answers are given
correctly and on providing immediate reinforcement for these correct answers. The answer "immediate" is exposed only after the
learner has constructed his response. He is fed enough cues to
prompt the right answer—in frame (A) above, the answer is in the
statement. The frame could be written to require the learner to
produce the answer, e.g.,

(A.) Delayed reinforcement is not as effective as _____
reinforcement.

Each bit of behavior is rehearsed a sufficient number of times in the
context in which it will be used, as the cues to appropriate behavior
are gradually withdrawn and the person learns to manage for himself. Sometimes the frames are independent of each other, and sometimes a number of the frames are interrelated. It is assumed that the
mastery of knowledge and possibly of other processes can be arranged in a simple additive progression.

Branch programming, on the other hand, presents longer blocks
of information (a paragraph or so), followed by questions with
multiple choices. If the student chooses correctly, he is rewarded by
referral to an advanced frame (branching off); a wrong choice
sends him to a remedial frame with an explanation of his error. The
branch technique appears to be more adaptable to less definite types
of material, including problem-solving.

In Figure IX, steps (frames) *A, B* and *C* required elaboration.
This development is called "augmentation," and it should be noted

that one can have a choice of frames as in A_1 or A_2, or a single
frame B_2,

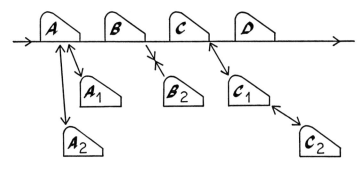

FIGURE IX

or two or more interrelated frames as in C_1 and C_2. In Figure X,
more work on frames A, B and C was necessary and the person was
returned to re-do them.

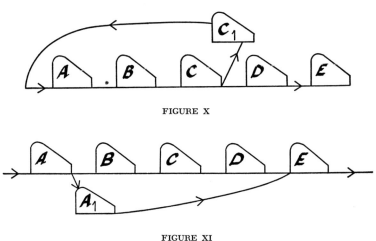

FIGURE X

FIGURE XI

In Figure XI, frames B, C and D had already been accomplished
and the person jumped (leapfrogged) directly to frame E, thus
avoiding unnecessary work and the accompanying boredom.

In Figure XII, there are two linear tracks to the same goal. There could be three

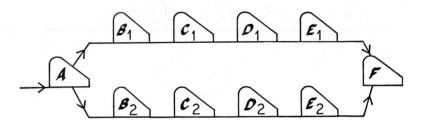

FIGURE XII

or four such tracks, each with the same number of frames, *or* some tracks could take larger steps with fewer frames, *or* some tracks could take smaller steps with more frames. This helps to accommodate different interests and levels of accomplishment.

The mention of individual differences in interest and accomplishment draws attention to special features of programmed instructional materials, particularly to active responses, reinforcement, small steps and self-pacing.

Active responses. Much of the behavior ordinarily classified as reading or study is too passive for the frame-by-frame presentation of a program. Active behavior is required, even if the learner is only to select an answer rather than construct an answer. In a good program, there is enough behavior in each frame to require active participation. If a program is to be of assistance, each learner must sit and work (behave) his way through the entire program.

Reinforcement. Immediate confirmation of the student's performance produces a change in his own environment that aids learning and is in itself gratifying or rewarding. It is preferable, however, to gratify the learner for correct responses and leave those which are incorrect unrewarded. (Few programs do this.)

Small steps. The material is arranged in very small bits. The desired information is arranged in logical sequence so that the learning is a dynamic process building up very gradually from elementary levels to highly complex behavior. There is still a question regarding understanding. Many persons believe that even if the program rehearses the individual in all the appropriate behaviors, understanding will only mature through some additional contribution of the individual to the content.

Self-pacing. Ideally, each student proceeds at his own rate of speed. Allowing progress according to one's own ability is more effective than forcing him along on some predetermined pattern. It has always been the hope of the good teacher to pace content to match individual rates of maturation, learning and interest, but this would practically require individual coaching. Programmed materials offer the next best possibility for such ideal pacing.

Many programs are published in book form. The books are relatively less expensive than machine presentation, less restrictive and more portable than many machines, and more closely aligned with conventional textbook presentations. Turning a page in a book to find an answer is much like moving the machine to the next frame, but the book permits easy "cheating," while machine presentation usually prevents this.

In a book, the answers for each frame may be on the following page *or* directly below the question on the same page *or* scattered (scrambled) throughout the book with page references from the questions to possible answers. In the scrambled presentation the next question usually follows the correct answer. If the subject has selected an incorrect response, he is told of his error and returned to re-do the question and select another choice for an answer.

A recurrent question regarding programming, whether by machine or book presentation, concerns what can be programmed. The answer is simple, although unacceptable to many persons. A program can be constructed for anything which one can specify. In other words, if one can state exactly the behavior (knowledge and skill) he wants, frames of work can be constructed to produce that behavior, *if* the learner will work his way through the entire program.

And that is the crux of programmed instruction. *If* the subject will sit and work his way through the complete program, the following claims may be made:

There is immediate reinforcement (not necessarily for correct responses only).

That which is emitted by the subject and reinforced is impressed.

There is a gradual progression from simple to complex repertoires.

With fading (gradual withdrawal of stimulus support), there is control of the student's observing and echoic behavior, and there is training in quite precise discrimination.

Each subject proceeds at his own pace.

Each subject can stop where he is and go on from there the next day.

This emphasis on directed learning could carry the main burden of instruction in a classroom, or be used for free-time instruction, or serve as a testing and research device. Most persons, however, object to programs as testing devices. They prefer directed learning as a research device and a teaching aid.

As a research device, programming has turned attention to theories of learning, particularly to reinforcement theory [359]. Many persons deplore the lack of emphasis on understanding. At present, understanding is believed to arise from an interaction between the learner and the material, in which the learner makes a contribution of his own to the result, instead of merely assimilating an item. It is not yet clear to what extent the process of programming and the reinforcement from programs can develop understanding or changes in attitudes.

As a device in teacher education, the prospect for programmed instructional materials is almost unlimited. For instance, the careful step-by-step approach emphasized by each program cannot help but contribute to the understanding of classroom technique. If a person constructs a program, he is obligated to arrange content in logical sequence, plan for enough behavior in each step, set up sufficient rehearsal and review of each bit of content, and arrange for the gradual fading of all cues as the desired behavior matures. Work in programming content also emphasizes that programs are not tests, nor do they require merely simple echoic behavior. Furthermore, the difficulty experienced by a person attempting to develop a single good frame for a program is certain to arouse feelings of appreciation for the work of others.

The emphasis on the behavior of the learner, on what he does, and on learning as a change in behavior is sound. Programmed materials also direct attention to content, the behavior necessary to master content, and the teacher's knowledge of content.

It should be emphasized that programmed instructional materials are of great assistance in learning, *if* the motivational problem can be overcome. One's initial experience with a program may be interesting, but the boredom of sitting and working through many programs could be considerable—even if the desire to master the content is great and the programs are interesting.

Summary: Reinforcement

Reinforcement is the confirmation or denial that impresses an act. Its influence is greatest if it follows immediately after the event. The greater the number of reinforced occurrences, the stronger the relationship, excluding boredom and satiation. The amount of reinforcement influences motivation, that is, willingness to perform, more than it influences the strength of the response.

Intermittent reinforcement produces stronger relationships than reinforcement for each occurrence of each event. It is the expectancy that there may be reinforcement that keeps performance levels high and postpones extinction.

Anything associated with the reinforcement a sufficient number of times has reinforcing value. These secondary reinforcements provide for more learning than the primary reinforcement alone. However, they also provide for incidental relationships that may or may not be intended and appropriate.

Directed learning follows from control over reinforcement, and adequate directed learning from the teacher always excels the mechanical and nonspontaneous machine.

Programmed instructional materials emphasize the value of reinforcing the appropriate response immediately, and they direct attention to the behavior of the learner—to what the learner does. In addition, content, the behavior necessary to master content, and the teacher's knowledge of content are highlighted.

13

cognition

COGNITION IS UNDERSTANDING or comprehension. It is the "feeling for the way the thing goes," which is expressed in a pattern, form or configuration. When a person is confronted with a situation that he intends to master, he sees what is required and directs his behavior accordingly.

Cognition is the ability to grasp the essentials of a given structure, to break it into parts, and to isolate and synthesize the parts. It is on the basis of what is sensed as being required, and comprehended as being available to meet that requirement, that cognitions are structured. Levels of cognition thus depend upon the experience, quality, and maturity of the learner. Immature and inexperienced learners blunder through instructive failures to cognitions and to levels of mastery. When sudden, complete, and permanent solutions occur, the background of experience usually includes memories, images, emotional components, and other environmental factors which are combined in acts of perception. When one realizes that multiplication is a way of adding, the sudden solution is not the revival of an old habit. It is a better way of understanding that is the result of prior learning. The flash of understanding from a single trial represents the moment at which previously acquired learning is perceived in a better way—*if* the learner detects the appropriate cue or relationship. And there is the crux of cognition—to prompt, guide, direct, cajole, wheedle, or force the learner to close the gap between his present limited perception and cognition.

The Qualities and Conditions for Mature Cognition

There are several factors involved in mature cognition that separate it markedly from naive blundering: approach (self-control), contact, experiential background, native capacity, and flexibility.

The Approach: Self-Control

The cognitive attitude is a general disposition of personality that guides responses in many varied situations [186]. A person who is actively searching for understanding instead of making random trials is aware of the total situation, including factors that are not present at the moment. He can thus direct his perception by inhibiting some responses while making others. The mature approach thus stifles impulsive reactions, placing a premium on flexibility, the ability to shift readily from one hypothesis to another.

In addition to the widely accepted factors of practice, reward, and punishment (Hilgard), the learning process involves other important elements, among which is the efficient use of repressive mechanisms. Repression is the process by which a mental act capable of becoming conscious is made unconscious and forced back into the unconscious system (Freud). How this process goes on we can only speculate, but the inference is that, while more complex, it is elaborated from the processes of suppression and inhibition observable in animals and men. For the purposes of this discussion the three terms (repression, suppression, and inhibition) are used interchangeably.

The well-adjusted, effective adult appears to be one who represses efficiently his primitive impulses (Northrup) in such a fashion that excessive quantities of energy are not used up in the process, but freed for the expression of the individual's life activity. Life activity is an exchange of energy between the organism and its environment (Herrick). The best expression of energy enables the organism to achieve mastery of its environment. An organism's repression of outpouring energy is of value only if it results in greater mastery of the environment.

Students who learn with difficulty often show patterns of inefficient repressive activity. In a large number of students under treatment, striking improvement in learning and habits of study has followed the expression of anger and resentment toward the parent in the permissive atmosphere provided by the psychiatrist. These students unwittingly transferred feelings of anger and rage from fathers to fatherlike teachers. The resulting rebellion, often revealed only in daydreams and procrastination, was but part of the inefficient repressive activity exerted to stifle the feelings of anger and rage that caused it. Under such conditions, a highly intelligent student may function at a level far below his potential. This form of behavior indicates a serious need for the re-examination of the theory of learning (French) and, in fact, the entire process of education [171, pp. 410-411].

Contact

To be aware of possible hypotheses one needs to work with the task in the ways indicated by self-direction and direction from others. Close contact is necessary to come to grips with the properties of a situation. The roots of cognition are in the implicit skills that support understandings as varied as mathematical facility, language abilities, and physical prowess. Work with the foundations supports a superstructure.

Lest this reference to contact seem vague and limited, consider graduate students who are looking for research studies. Those who are searching tend either to plan a study that will take 30 years or to focus on a single hypothesis. To be aware of hypotheses, they should do much more work with all aspects of their learning situation *and* with others who are cogent, either in their writings or in person. Continued contact with cogent people, good and poor studies, and the foundations of knowledge will foster inquiry and, in most cases, the energy necessary to be in close contact and to stay in close contact for the duration of the work.

Experiential Background

Mature cognition depends on a background of experience. Beginners in any field do not have the range, the depth, nor the sensitivity necessary for full comprehension. They require more time for development, because cognitive learning makes a bigger change in people than the formation of simple associations. The change is chiefly an ordering of experience for ready cognition. This readiness to use experience is also dependent upon a sensitivity to the existing relationships. Such sensitivity is both a process and a product of experience.

Native Capacity

A high degree of native capacity leads to cognition because it provides perceptive capacity sufficient for full awareness of the total situation, memory to contribute to the configuration, the degree of motor control necessary, the drive for sustained effort, and the ability to generalize. When the perceptual field is narrow, or memory is insufficient, or motor control is deficient, or drive is weak, or the discrimination of relations limited, understanding cannot take in as much experience; and, with these limitations, understanding does not have the depth and quality of maturity.

Krech and Calvin found the degree of relationship between culture-laden perceptions and culture-laden intelligence to be significant and high in college students. In applying the Gestalt laws of sensory and perceptual organization (proximity, similarity, etc.,) that tied perception to the structural characteristics of the stimulus situation, Krech and Calvin found perceptual responses to proceed through a hierarchical order of levels of organization, and they found that easy progress through such an order is related to intelligence. Even when the perceptual organization seems to occur immediately without intervening steps, the immediacy of the organization may be more apparent than real, because such a developmental process may run its course within a short timespan (milli-seconds). All of the development of our capacity follows from the nature and quality of our perceptual organization [221, p. 400].

Flexibility

Mature cognition is not something that becomes static when achieved. It is dynamic. The mature learner continually refines his trial results. He can repeat a solution he has previously used or modify it as needed. He can interrupt the flow of events for survey, inspection, attention, and critical solution. But no such fully mature learner exists. Cognition to include all of these capacities at a superior level would be superhuman. The combinations of capacities and qualities give rise to the richness and diversity of human expression.

Cole[1] has summarized the viewpoint of certain learning theorists in these words:

Discovering that their animals react to relations, to larger wholes, some have generalized, asserting that this is the fundamental process, that it is basic, more primitive. Others, finding animals capable of guiding their adjustments by sharply discriminated stimuli, have been inclined to build their learning theories upon specific responses to specific stimuli. Looking at the array of evidence, one is inclined to believe that the degrees of abstraction, the selected aspects, the provisional tries, are most varied in nature. Sensory capacities, native preferences, previously established sets, familiar categories, old modes of grasping, and the layout of the field itself, determine now one type of response, now another.

Some have argued that a reaction to the *whole* field is better, that insightful learning comes when the cognitive map is made to include all of the relationships. Certainly the strip map, where a narrow part of the field is reacted to, can lead to a very stupid behavior. . . . And certainly a mode of grasping the situation can be so persistent, so stubborn, so resistant, that a problem remains insoluble. . . .

Much learning requires that we give up our preferred mode of response for another, or that we break up what has long been an integrated whole, dropping out elements and inserting new ones. Particularly in psychology does the learner have to lay aside the cliches. . . . It is diffi-

[1] From *Human Behavior*, by L. E. Cole, Copyright 1953, World Book Company, presented with permission of Harcourt, Brace & World, Inc.

cult to view the novel situation as truly novel (as it really is). We grasp it by the familiar handles, we stop to observe only long enough to identify, classify, and produce the familiar recipe. Maslow (1948) suggests that this abstracting, classifying tendency is a measure of our laziness, of our anxieties, of our preoccupations with too pressing motivations. Perhaps it is a measure of our *ill* health, our degree of *mal*adaptation. Habits are conservative agents, efficient ways of dealing with (and dismissing) situations too complex or too frightening for contemplative study; but they are by the same sign the forces that freeze the mind, stereotype our learning, block an insightful appreciation of the uniqueness of the present field.

Yet without the handle it is almost impossible to grasp the novel event. . . .

It would appear that we can scarcely escape the abstracting tendency. To a degree we can avoid its unhappy consequences by our awareness of what our cognitive maps are like, by the utilization of multiple abstractions, by the free play of the mind over every possible aspect and relation (when we are blocked), by the realization that our hypotheses *are* hypotheses, and by a return again and again to the event itself. Our ways of classifying the stimulus can operate so as to complicate our task; a category can obscure our vision. To alter a Spanish proverb quoted by Maslow: Recognized, the barriers are cobwebs; unrecognized, they are shutters of steel. (Maslow, p. 29, Habits are at first cobwebs, then cables) [82, pp. 345-346].

Guiding Development to Cognition

Cognitions often emerge gradually from previous associations even though some sudden flashes of understanding occur. The field is more than a mere aggregate of disconnected stimuli. Pupils may see objects in relation to each other, but the teacher cannot cause them to detect what he considers to be the appropriate cues to the relationships. This occurs because the teacher does not control the pupils' motivation and because his perception and background of experience is not like theirs. There are, however, ways to facilitate understanding. Understanding will develop if the teacher will take the necessary time, provide a background of relevant experience, build confidence bit by bit, set models for emulation, encourage activity, and arrange and rearrange the perceptual field.

Take the Necessary Time

The long, slow apprenticeship, during which the uncertain, laborious, and irregular progress toward goals is achieved, is almost always necessary and cannot be rushed. Sensitivity is distorted by pressure, particularly by time pressure. It is reasonable to suppose that the less familiar the situation or task to be performed, the more important slow increment learning becomes [175, p. 115].

Provide a Background of Experience

A background of relevant experience is essential for cognition. This background directly limits the possibilities, since one may not be aware of the perceptions needed for cognition at levels other than his own. Teachers try to develop a panorama of experiences rich enough to support the rapid reorganization of knowledge that takes place when understanding appears. Such transitions are a later phase of learning built on a broad foundation of experience.

Providing a background of experience both aids and hinders learning. Through experience, persons are sensitized to various aspects and relationships of the self and the environment, but these experiences also provide inhibitory sets. Having successfully worked with material in one context, persons find changes to other contexts difficult; when inappropriate and false directions have been built up through experience, facilitation is further inhibited. The risk of inhibiting development is minimized when experiences are graded from easy to difficult.

Build Confidence Increment by Increment

Teachers encourage understanding step by step and stage by stage if they grade tasks by order of difficulty from easy to hard. They keep the learner informed of the nature of his errors and his results; and as the work becomes too difficult and as feelings of failure become too pressing, they ease the pressure and the solutions. Tensions and pressures are necessary, however, because easy successes breed little development. The learner's confidence is built in small blocks through the confirmations allowed by his more precise abstractions. Teachers should exert enough pressure to stimulate development, recognizing that this varies in amount and direction from person to person, from day to day, and from task to task.

Set Models for Emulation

Setting models for emulation is highly supportive for the early uncertain cognitions. The question is how soon after the initial learning can pressure be exerted for other solutions and other uses of the same material. As far as *overlearned* motor or cognitive operations are concerned, the ability to perform operations backward (or in an unusual way) seems most closely related to the ability to perform the same class of operations in a normal manner [337]. Insistence on flexibility too soon disturbs the learner and reverses the development. Unfortunately, the integrity of old perceptual habits limits flexibility; the familiar is so convenient. Soon, but not too soon after a model is imitated, other uses of the experience should be required to avoid stereotyping. Stereotyped possibilities inhibit the search for cues which may lead to the comprehension of relationships. Models for imitation help, provided they do not inhibit the search for significant cues.

Encourage Doing

We learn what we do [Guthrie, 161]. Any direct experience with material is better than no such experience. The student in school learns what he makes himself do and what the school requires him to do. If arithmetic class permits or causes him to add on his fingers, he learns to count on his fingers. As the pupils develop, they may change their set to the abstraction of addition rather than counting. This acquired ability will permit the advance to multiplication and increasingly difficult operations of arithmetic. The person has learned to add in school and now must learn the change of set of his knowledge to the home and the community. This occurs easily if the situation allows the person such participation. Sometimes the home and the community have to require the young to use their learning outside school, but whether required or voluntary, the person learns what he does in the school, the home, and the community.

The long apprenticeship of directed and redirected trials in the search for cues to comprehension is served through continued activity. People learn what they do, and when they stop working with materials, comprehensions cannot mature to cognition. It is work with materials under one's own direction and following the directions of others that makes cognition possible.

Arrange and Rearrange the Field

When teachers arrange and rearrange the field, they set the stage for learning many of the possible relationships. They group, arrange, and organize the perceptual field available to the learner to emphasize the relationships. True, this is the emphasis as the teacher sees it, but he arranges it while the learner works with it. The learner will grasp and identify various aspects of the field, some in familiar ways and some in novel ways. The teacher tells him where to begin, directs his trials, and appreciates each success to foster continued directed search for understanding. The teacher modifies the field organization, while the pupil tries to avoid the dictates of partial understandings based on a particular organization rather than on all possibilities.

Mature knowledge comes only after the learner gets the sense of reordering experience and gratification from that effort. Cognitive attitude is a general disposition of personality that guides responses in a great variety of situations [186]. Teachers foster cognitive attitudes when they take the necessary time, provide a background of relevant experience, build confidence little by little, set models for emulation, encourage activity, and arrange and rearrange the perceptual field while the learner performs. Persons mature as they learn and are taught under the influence of reinforcement and cognition [421].

Perception and Cognition

The paraphrased material in this section is technical. It is presented here because of its intrinsic merit and because it is always provocative for both thought and discussion.[2]

The phenomena with which we are here concerned have been variously designated by the terms "cognition," "perception," "abstraction," and "conceptualization." All these terms designate forms of interaction between the organism and its environment, in which responses are *not governed exclusively by the energy properties of the stimulus or stimulus pattern.* These terms all refer to behavior in which the organism brings to bear resources of its own (both inborn and experiential) in reacting to the pattern of stimuli. It is convenient, although somewhat arbitrary, to distinguish between two groups of factors: (1) those which are directly related to the properties of the stimulus pattern and (2) those which are related to properties within the organism itself. Included in the second group are the needs, motives, values, and previous experiences of the organism insofar as they operate in a particular situation. These factors taken together form the basis of his contact with reality.

In many discussions of these phenomena, two levels of such contact are distinguished: the perceptual and the conceptual or cognitive. This distinction usually refers to the degree to which properties of the stimulus field determine the response. In perception, the contact is immediate ("This blanket is pink"), with a relatively greater opportunity for a feedback from the stimulus field (reality), which serves as a check on the accuracy or appropriateness of the perception. In cognition (or conceptualization) there is a relatively greater opportunity for the operation of interpretive or inferential factors ("This pink blanket would fit in the color scheme of our bedroom").

. . . . . .

Psychologically, conceptualizing is not a qualitatively different kind of mental activity, as the terms "intellectual," "reasoning," and "thinking" seem to imply. Whatever point is chosen for analysis, whether a relatively direct and immediate perception of the external world or a highly generalized construct, the assumption is of an organism striving to achieve order and stability. *Cognition, at whatever level, is a structuring activity in which the organism seeks to establish a relatively stable environment in which to act.* Within certain limits (sometimes exceedingly wide), the structures are patterns which the organism imposes on the environ-

[2] The material from F. Fearing in *Language and Culture*, H. Hoijer (ed.), Copyright 1954 by Robert Redfield, is presented with permission of the University of Chicago Press.

ment. They reflect an organization of force within the organism itself and its need to maintain a frame of reference within which it may come to terms with the external world.

. . . . .

The problem of the development of perception, or rather, the problem of the emergence of different levels of cognitive functioning, has been discussed in several recent papers.

Murphy and Hochberg (1951) have proposed a series of hypotheses regarding the development of perception. Perception is "a form of continuous adjustment to environmental requirements, involving not simply a 'sensorium' or seat of cognitive functions, but the whole organism" which "in coping with its environment, progressively alters its modes of perception and develops more and more complex ones that serve it better." The hypotheses that relate most directly follow:

(1) A primordial aspect of the structure of the percept is differentiation between figure and ground. Figure consists in "shaped regions" against a relatively unshaped ground. The differentiation between figure and ground exhibits varying degrees of sharpness. As Koffka says (1935), we see *things* and not the holes between them. In looking at the landscape, we see the shape of things and not the sky—unless we have that particular orientation.

(2) Structure depends genetically upon two processes: (a) differentiation within a more-or-less homogeneous matrix, and (b) integrations of the differentiated phases. Werner and others have noted that the child's earliest percepts are diffuse and lack differentiation. Progression from (a) *homogeneous* through (b) *differentiated* to (c) *integrated* levels is characteristic in principle, not only of the stages through which the perceptual development of the maturing child passes, but also of the course of every perceptual process regardless of age.

(3) All the sense modalities enter on an equal footing, but not always with equal weight, into the dynamics of perception. These modalities include the receptors that are stimulated by energies external to the organism (exteroceptors), those that respond to stimuli within the organism, especially in the visceral organs (interoceptors), and the receptors in the muscles and tendons (proprioceptors). Traditionally, perceiving has been limited to the exteroceptive fields, especially sight and hearing—as the sole mediators of external reality. Murphy and Hochberg regard the proprioceptive (kinesthetic) components as especially important. Visual information must be pooled with proprioceptive information as to the position and motion of the receptor surfaces if effective contact with the outside world is to be maintained.

(4) It is meaningless to separate the cognitive, affective, and cona-

tive aspects of perception. In other words cognition, affection, and cona-
tion are regarded as independent only in the context of scientific analysis
and abstraction.

(5) Perception develops through experience as well as through neural
maturation. In perception there is both a "systematic perceptual growth
dependent upon a general developmental principle of differentiation and
integration" and the results of experience. It is noted that members of
different cultures perceive as they have learned to perceive. Environments
differ in the extent to which they force one to perceive in certain ways
[118, pp. 60-64].

Reinforcement and Cognition

Learning and teaching are subject to both reinforcement and
cognition. Satisfaction follows a ready response. One may respond
to the reinforcement of others, to his own reinforcement, or, what
amounts to the same thing, may rely on comprehension to direct his
behavior. Behavior is shaped by successive approximations, instead
of through the appearance of the final complete response [359]. For
instance, the initial learning in a motor task was found to be related
to the relative correctness of the information supplied to the subjects, and the subjects adapted quickly to a knowledge of results
[42]. Others can direct a person's learning through the careful use
of reinforcement, and reinforcement may lead him to cognition;
but no matter what the device, learning will occur if he "gets the
notion" [377]. One may learn without awareness of the principles
involved, but when he grasps the principles, he learns more rapidly
and more fully [297]. Limited ability to apply known principles
is partly a function of the extent to which previously learned ideas
have been inhibited or blocked; that is, reactions to reinforcement
and cognition are individual [352]. Although flashes of insight
occur, understanding can be built through reinforced experiences
rather than relying on innate capacities or on the flash of quality
called "insight."

The terms "reinforcement" and "cognition" are used to cate-
gorize learning theories on the basis of their major emphasis and,

as such, are usually placed in opposition to each other. However, Birch has pointed out that they are neither antagonistic nor methodological alternatives [44]. Rather than entering into the argument, it is preferable to consider the operations represented by both reinforcement and cognition.

Summary: Cognition

Cognition is understanding and comprehension. As the background of experience is enriched, as the learner is aware of more relationships, and as there is willingness to venture and explore, more cognitions of good quality develop.

High native capacity supports mature cognition. This is not at all static. It is constantly refined as the learner is aware of the adequacy of his trial results.

There is no way to cause the learner to understand, but teachers help to bring about understanding when they provide a background of experience, set models for the pupil to follow, grade tasks in order of difficulty, and organize the perceptual field to emphasize the important relationships. It is possible to reinforce any response that the learner makes, but it is not possible to induce directly the desired cognitions. Teachers strive to awaken understanding in their pupils by providing relationships from experience and opportunities for organization, but they should not be surprised if understanding does not always develop.

The learner learns what he does, what he is caused to do, and in the sets and contexts in which he must work. Thinking through his cognitions helps, but translating thought into communication and other actions is the doing that is impressed and available for use. Further, the response that others make to a person is based on what he does. Doing shapes self-awareness.

Persons come to learning with sets that determine what they are prepared to pay attention to. The activity itself modifies their perception of the situation, usually in the direction of self-adjustment and self-development. Preparation for learning is managed through reinforced associations that lead to comprehension, but learning which is self-directed reflects superior development and maturity. Parents and teachers can assist in this process through arranging (structuring) the situation and through reinforcing desired behavior.

14

motor learning

CHARACTER AND ORGANIZATION OF SKILLS

REHEARSAL

ATTENTION

ERRORS

CONTEXT AND SETTING

FORM, SPEED, ACCURACY, RHYTHM, AND TIMING

IN THE CLASSROOM

SUMMARY: MOTOR LEARNING

tO SAY THAT the full motor development of the individual is essential for unhampered self-expression focuses attention on motor learning in its proper perspective. The hundreds of studies on skill learning which pay no attention to the development of the person are as unjustifiable as the studies which take no account of motor skill as self-expression.

Motor skill is an expression of level of development. As people learn to read and write, to run and jump, to think and talk, they are relying on the coordinated development of the body. Where motor ability stops and other abilities take over in activities like a golf-swing or typewriting or creative writing is not determinable, yet the motor components of each act are essential for full self-expression.

"Motor learning" is used here to include the learning of physical actions along with the concomitant developments frequently referred to as psychomotor and sensorimotor. "Skill" is used to refer to the degree of the development.

Skill is developed by practicing particular techniques. The learner's attention must be directed to the following components: character and organization of the task as a whole, rehearsal, sufficient attention, the avoidance of errors, set, and individual considerations such as the role of form, accuracy, rhythm, timing, and speed.

Character and Organization of Skills

The first requirement in motor learning is a picture of the character and organization of the whole skill to be acquired. The learner needs to know what the motor performance looks like and observe its effective functioning. For instance, when children are taught to print or write, the teacher must show them how people print and write, and the teacher is well aware of how fruitless it is to show them these skills until they want to learn them. In motor learning, as in all other learning, maturation and readiness produce awareness. The need for a conception of the skill as a whole, when the learner is ready, is equally evident in teaching a swimming stroke, flat dive from a springboard, shorthand and typing, or dance steps. If the teacher cannot demonstrate, he can have others demonstrate or use models, movies, still pictures—anything which will show the total performance and thus provide a picture of the character and organization of the skill as a unit.

When possible, it is better to learn the skill as an entity. When a person learns the parts of a skill and then attempts to integrate them into a smooth performance, he usually has to relearn the total as a unit, and the prior part-learning often interferes. In some situations, however, one must take the skill apart, rehearse its components, and then struggle with relearning the total skill. To illustrate, one can teach a dance step such as a waltz step (slow, quick, slow) as a unit. Even third and fourth graders can integrate waltz steps with their walking and running steps. Code typing and touch typing learned as a unit were found superior to learning each item separately and then attempting to integrate them [89]. But hand positions on the frets of a banjo or guitar and the plucking and strumming of the strings with the other hand may defy a total-skills approach. The learning of one or two hand positions interferes with learning other hand positions, and the separate learning of each position interferes with the integration of all hand movements. There are skills which are too complex to yield benefits from attempting them as total units, e.g., boxing, playing a musical instrument, or judo; but there are others, such as fielding a ball, which benefit from a total approach. In most cases it is possible to work on the parts after some facility has been acquired with the total skill, e.g., footwork, ball handling, and moving to the left in fielding a ball. For those activities in which it is possible, learning the total skill is generally superior, even though later analysis and practice of the components may yield considerable improvement in the entire performance [252].

Rehearsal

Almost everyone accepts the fact that practice develops and maintains skill, but the values of mental rehearsal and verbalizing are not so generally recognized.

While mental rehearsal helps motor learning, practice of the skill itself is essential to capitalize on the cerebration [400]. Here again, the use of the term "mental rehearsal" should not be interpreted as implying a separate and nonintegrated treatment of a part of behavior. No motor act occurs without the assistance of some thought. Mental rehearsal refers to the learner's thinking through the motor act both before and after performance. Thinking about past performances and possible future performances provides thought models by which to modify present performance [53]. A thought model guides performance, but is not a substitute for actual practice.

A similar aid in acquiring motor skills is verbalization. A person's ability to tell himself what he is to do and to describe his motor acts helps greatly in learning and refining motor skills. Generally, verbalizing is not a satisfactory substitute for actual practice, with the possible exception of such sensorimotor habits as spelling, where verbalization is a large part of the learning and performance [205]. Even in spelling, however, most people resort to writing a word out (a further motor act) when there is a question about its spelling.

Skills improve with careful practice, particularly if it is varied. Both mental rehearsal and verbalization help, but neither is a substitute for actual performance.

Attention

While practicing, a person should attend closely to his own reactions in order to detect and eliminate errors, but in motor learning it is possible to overdo such self-examination. In one study where the dominant habit was correct, an increase in drive produced better performance, but another study found that, when the dominant habit was incorrect, an increase in drive caused a speedup and resulted in poorer performance [70]. Enough attention is needed so that one is aware of his errors. Beyond that level, heightened attention produces only tenseness and incoordination. The degree of attention sufficient for good performance is not peculiar to motor learning, but it is more significant there, since tenseness and poor coordination are more readily observable in motor acts.

Errors

Errors of commission and omission plague every learner's performances. In avoiding or correcting errors, it would seem to be possible to rely on understanding, insight and personal involvement; but in practice none of these is wholly satisfactory, unless one also devises ways to avoid making the errors. To illustrate, a clerk's understanding of the kinds and uses of files in the office and her personal involvement whenever she obviously misuses or misplaces something should be sufficient to cause her to correct the faulty procedures. But reliance on understanding, insight, and involvement does not work nearly as well as files of different sizes, or files which are fitted to given spaces, or files which are color-coded so that filing errors are prevented or made so obvious as to approach impossibility. Of course, some will say that this physical illustration of filing is too easy and the principle is not broadly applicable, but any illustration involving thought processes immediately involves memory, and it is unnecessary to elaborate on the devices which are essential for persons to remember what they need to know at a given time. It is regrettable that one's behavior regarding errors does not yield directly to the quality of intellect alone, but it seems to be necessary to use intellect to devise efficient ways of avoiding the errors.

Another interesting fact about errors is that persons correct their effortful errors themselves, but the effortless errors (such as "between him and I") persist almost endlessly, chiefly because they are not often penalized and are not corrected steadily enough and long enough to be eliminated. Effortful movements are more obvious in motor skills than in cerebration. That is why it is simpler to deal with the notion of errors in motor learning, but what is said here applies fully to all learning.

More effortful erroneous movements tend to drop out more rapidly than less effortful ones [11]. People generally make the least possible effort. Any difficult task requires so much of a person that he pays close attention to its nature, its fruitfulness, and its correctness. Thus he detects and eliminates errors adequately. The effortless errors, on the other hand, continue to weaken performance for a long time. The amount of energy and attention required to eliminate slight errors seems scarcely worth the trouble, but the effortful errors tend to eliminate themselves because of the demands they make on one's time and energy.

Because the easy errors are so hard to detect and eliminate, it is preferable for parents and teachers to prevent them from developing, particularly during the early stages of learning. Careless, vague directions, such as, "Do what you can with it," encourage the acquisition of numerous small errors. Careful directions and good models which have been demonstrated, explained, and practiced under supervision, may prevent the majority of simple errors.

Context and Setting

Learning a skill in the setting where it will be used results in greater learning. Practice on a cardboard keyboard to learn finger positions for the piano or typewriter yields little gain in the final performance. The change in writing skill from pencil to pen usually involves some relearning. If the child is to read well in many different situations, he needs practice in a variety of situations.

Practice of the skill in a setting similar to the one in which it will be used is essential for efficient motor performance. The ball player finds each park to be different. The pianist finds differences between similar pianos, or even between the same piano in different rooms. Pupils who sing well in the classroom may do badly in the assembly hall or gymnasium. The prudent teacher arranges for rehearsal of the skill in the setting where it will be used.

Form, Speed, Accuracy, Rhythm, and Timing

In motor learning, several matters deserve special attention: form, speed, accuracy, rhythm, and timing. Which of these aspects one should start with, and which should subsequently be stressed, varies according to the individual nature of each motor task and each learner. Usually, benefit is derived from paying attention to the form first. The rhythm of motor performance supports accuracy and speed, although these two characteristics are often independent. Speed and accuracy are frequently not compatible in motor skills; the slower performances are usually more accurate. Rhythm helps timing, as do form, accuracy, and speed; but the essence of motor skill lies in the timing itself. A baseball swing in good form has a well-defined rhythm, but without timing the bat does not meet the ball with maximum power. A dance step in good form and with appropriate rhythm but lacking timing is clumsy. Typing in good form with rhythm and accuracy can never develop speed without the timing. Speedy typing without timing jams the platen with keys. Usually, attention to form, followed by attention to accuracy, speed, and rhythm, will enable motor learning to develop the timing necessary for skill. However, this varies so with the task and the learner that such a generalization is dangerous. It is probably preferable to have the learner begin with the aspect of the total task which is comfortable for him, after he has a picture of the whole performance. Further demonstration and explanation of a motor task to be learned should direct attention to form, speed, accuracy, rhythm, and timing in adequate proportions for good performance. The level of performance described as skill follows from carefully supervised practice of all aspects of related motor developments, as well as the specifics of a given situation. Skill means "integrated total performance at a high level." Motor learning involves struggling with form, accuracy, speed, rhythm, and timing; motor skill integrates all these aspects in a total performance of high quality.

In the Classroom

It is difficult, if not impossible, to assess either the total or the specific, particular role of motor skill in the classroom, but there is no doubt that the lack of certain skills greatly hampers classroom performance. For instance, at present the usual criteria for advancement or retardation in school are reading and spelling [185]. It is fruitless to try to estimate the part which motor learning contributes to these skills. They are sensorimotor acts that are critical for educational welfare. No subject has received the exhaustive remedial treatment that reading has had and will have, because achievers in school are readers with good work habits and good study habits (rehearsed motor acts) [75].

The development of motor skill allows a person to express and enjoy his capabilities in much the same way as verbal skill and quick wit enhance his personality. Good things tend to go together, so that those who enjoy superior intellectual, educational, social, emotional, and physical development, commonly have at least adequate motor ability. Usually this superiority develops into satisfactory motor skills.

Summary: Motor Learning

Development is based in part on many motor learnings, each of which involves the performing person in some degree; full motor development is essential for unhampered self-expression. When one is concerned with motor learning, attention to particular developments and techniques yields motor skill as part of the individual's expressiveness. The following considerations promote motor development to the point where it results in skill:

To begin a motor learning, one should have a picture of the character and organization of the skill as a whole.

When possible, it is preferable to learn the whole skill as a unit. The part approach is inferior because of the relearning which is necessary to integrate the parts into a total pattern.

Almost all learnings respond to practice of various kinds; mental rehearsal is a kind of practice, although not a substitute for motor practice.

Enough attention must be paid to a performance for full awareness, but not so much as to produce tension and incoordination.

Effortful errors tend to eliminate themselves because of the demand they make on one's time and energy, but the effortless errors may persist endlessly, chiefly because they are so easy.

Whenever one can learn and rehearse a skill in the setting where it will be used, he performs more adequately.

Basic motor learning involves struggling with form, accuracy, speed, rhythm, and timing in keeping with individual differences and task differences. As skill develops, the role of each of these aspects of motor learning is integrated into a unified performance.

Motor learning does not require the degree of comprehension that ideational or verbal learning benefit from, but superior motor development usually accompanies superior abilities in other respects. Adequate motor expression is essential for fullest self-development, while motor skill permits the achievement of such expression.

15

serial learning

MUCH LEARNING CONSISTS of mastering a series of items arranged in a list, such as the names of the presidents of the United States, countries in Europe, or the materials of the earth's crust. In a broader usage, however, list learning refers to the acquisition of ideas, words, or information linked together in sequences or some other arrangement. Unfortunately, a list or series is hard to remember, simply because it is a list. It is not possible to avoid these learning tasks, because a great many of the items to be learned, both tangible and ideational, become lists. Lest anyone be apprehensive over reducing understanding to lists, let it be noted that one does not prepare for comprehension by chance. Full perception comes from a logical, stepwise development, whether the time involved is weeks, hours, or seconds; *and*, as the pieces of the "life-puzzle" fall into place, they have often fallen into a series or list.

The Length of the Series

The longer a list is, the more difficult it is to learn and remember. If there were 14 rather than seven basic colors in the spectrum, they would be harder to learn and remember. It is more difficult to have a car with 27 grease fittings adequately greased than one with 14 fittings, simply because the longer series allows for more confusion and error. One can readily remember the sequence of four playing cards. The sequential dependencies of 13 cards become quite involved, and the order of 52 playing cards is extremely difficult to recall. Almost all things to be learned may be viewed as a series, and the longer the list, the more it taxes ability to learn and to remember.

Serial Position, and the Ease and Rate of Learning

Other things being equal, the position of an item in a series determines the ease and rate of learning that item. The items in the middle of a series and just past the middle take longer to learn because they are in that position. To illustrate, in a four link chain, the easiest link is that between the first and the second items, and the hardest link is between the third and the fourth. This is shown diagramatically in Figure XIII. As is usually the case, the illustration cannot be isolated from the intrusion of factors other than those we wish to make clear. The diagram illustrates the difficulties associated with position, but also includes the notions of word frequency and the association value of a word.

1	2	3	4
orange	green	indigo	violet
easiest		hardest	

FIGURE XIII

Position Difficulty in Serial Learning

The difficulty of learning indigo-violet can be demonstrated with students of any age; e.g., allow a time-lapse between any degree of learning of the list in Figure XIII and then test recall of the names of the four colors. (Note: There are three connections involved after the recall of the first word—one to two, two to three, and three to four.) There will be more errors in the recall of indigo-violet, and more prerecall thought around indigo-violet, to verify that serial position is the determinant of ease and rate of learning, other things being equal.

In the illustration of Figure XIII, there are two other factors which obviously intrude on serial position to determine ease and rate of learning. These are word frequency and the association value of a word. In the illustration, there is an assumption that the four color-names are equally easy to learn and remember. On the basis of frequency of word usage alone [Teachers' Word Book, 389], not to mention the association value of the word [140], "indigo" is harder to learn and remember. Words which are used more frequently are easier to learn and to remember, and "indigo" has low frequency in common vocabulary. The association value of this word is also low, that is, by comparison with words like "black" and "green," "indigo" does not call to mind any ready response such as "black-and-white," or "red-and-green." Leaving aside the greater difficulty present in the word "indigo" because of its low frequency of usage and low association value, its position in the series make it harder to learn. Of course, someone is bound to remember "indigo" because it is different, but usually low frequency in common vocabulary indicates the item is harder rather than easier to recall.

There is also a serial position effect for errors, with more errors occurring later in a series [178].

Two sources of error produce the classical serial-position curve. Intralist intrusions form a distribution about the middle of the list which is almost symmetrical; that is, parts of the list are recalled in places where they do not belong and this erroneous place-recollection is grouped quite smoothly around the center of the list. Second, failure-of-response errors are low at the beginning of the list and reach a somewhat variable peak during the second half of the list [96, pp. 199-202].

In a list of seven things to be learned, items four, five, and six are the hardest to remember because of the influence of errors.

To illustrate the combined influence of difficulty from position and from errors, consider the seven colors of the rainbow. Red and violet are established immediately because of their position as first and last. Colors around the middle of the list are often recalled in error and the earlier colors (red, orange, and yellow) intrude frequently in the last half of the list as the learner endeavors to remember green, blue, and indigo in their proper sequence. Thus the errors pile up just after the middle of the list to produce the serial-position curve of Figure XIV.

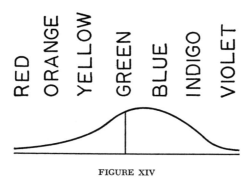

FIGURE XIV

Classical Serial Position Curve

The joint role of anticipation and perseveration (the persistent intrusion of prior learning in the present situation) can also be used to explain the shape of the classical serial-position curve. Learners anticipate items and recall items before their place in the list, and the anticipation and recall naturally cluster around and just after the middle. One starts a list quite easily, and it is not until after a few items that intrusions from anticipation occur. Similarly, some items persist in intruding after their place in the list, so that the errors from perseveration also intrude around the middle and just after the middle of the list. Both perseveration and anticipation produce the recall of items in list learning at inappropriate places, and these errors group themselves around and just past the center of the series in the shape of the classical serial-position curve.

The hypothesis that the serial-position curve is in part a function of one's organization of the material during learning has also been tested [420]. The study confirmed that organization produced by instructions or by the objective nature of the material in the list would yield the serial-position curve for learning.

One approach to defeating the effects of the serial-position curve is adjusted learning [420]. As soon as the first correct anticipation of an item in a list occurs, the item is removed from the list and the person continues with the shortened version, the adjusted list. This procedure makes the learning of the items easier but destroys the sequential dependencies in the list. In effect, each time an item is dropped a new list is formed. In spite of the fact that there is at-tention-getting value in structural changes, adjusted learning is of questionable assistance in serial learning [157].

An interesting study of the relationship of position and ease and rate of learning was concerned with memory for items on a five-by-five matrix [14], i.e., if we let each number represent an item or event, then a five-by-five matrix is arranged as in Figure XV.

1	2	3	4	5
6	7	8	9	10
11	12	13	14	15
16	17	18	19	20
21	22	23	24	25

FIGURE XV

A Matrix

From work with Navy men aged 17 to 21 years, and using matrices of letters, numbers, symbols, geometric figures, and words, the upper left-hand corner, position one, was found to be the favored position. Regardless of the content of the matrix, the first row, positions one to five was favored on the first few trials. With the ex-ception of symbols, the number of correct responses was a decreas-ing function of the order of the row; that is, most of the first row, positions one to five, was correct, and the least correct was the last row, positions 20 to 25. Anderson and Ross explained their findings of memory for items on a five by five matrix through reference to learning habits, rather than through the position or the content of the matrix. People generally start with item one, row one, and work across and down, learning the first row, the second row, etc. In each practice session they proceed in the same order again. If an experimenter were working with Chinese orthography, Anderson and Ross feel that the positional preferences would be different [14, p. 603].

While a matrix cannot be described as a simple series or list because of the first-row, second-row, and third-row influence, matrices are further evidence of the influence of the position of an item on the ease of learning it. If items are of equal difficulty in themselves, the position of the item in a series determines its ease of learning.

An interesting combination, that combines aspects of the matrix, (first row, second row, etc.) and a true list, is found in the names of the Presidents. Washington, Adams, Jefferson, Madison, Monroe, Adams, Jackson, Van Buren, Harrison, Tyler, Polk, Taylor, Fillmore, Pierce, Buchanan, Lincoln, Johnson, Grant, Hayes, Garfield, Arthur, Cleveland, Harrison, Cleveland, McKinley, Roosevelt, Taft, Wilson, Harding, Coolidge, Hoover, Roosevelt, Truman, Eisenhower, and Kennedy.

A list arranged Washington,
                    Adams,
                    Jefferson,
                    Madison, etc., avoids the effect of first row, second row, etc., but most material is not in such pure-list form. The majority of printed and duplicated materials appear in a combination of list and matrix form, and cause added difficulty.

The Content of the Series

In serial verbal learning, meaning decreases the difficulty and increases the rate [288]. College students learned three lists of 12 words which differed in average meaningfulness as defined by an association frequency method [140]. The more meaningful words were learned in fewer trials with fewer errors, but, in spite of differences in the ease of learning and error scores, all the learnings showed the serial-position error curve as illustrated in Figure XIV.

When the rainbow is understood as the three primary colors, red, yellow, and blue, and the intervening colors as complementary combinations of the primary ones, the series is easier to remember. Contextual dependencies extending over five or six words permit positive transfer. The three primary colors bind the series together. It is these familiar dependencies, rather than the meaning itself (the meaning in each word), which facilitate learning. When the short-range contextual dependencies to include five or six words are preserved in nonsense material ("'Twas brillig, and the slithy toves did gyre and gimble . . ."), the nonsense is as readily recalled as is the meaningful material [271]. Meaningfulness in serial verbal learning, as expressed in the meaning of the contextual dependencies, decreases the difficulty of list learning.

Deese and Kaufman found that for lists of words in which there is no sequential association, the last items are recalled most frequently, the first items less frequently, and the middle items least frequently [96]. For connected discourse, they found the order of recall to be that in which the material was presented. Thus, careful consideration must be given to meaning, sequential association, and dependency. For instance, Kimble and Dufort found that the ease of learning the middle word in a list of highly meaningful words varied inversely with the meaningfulness of that term [214]. For college students, least meaning in the middle word made the contextual dependencies of this central term easier than if the word had high meaningfulness in itself. Another interpretation of least meaningfulness of the middle term is possible: if the middle term in a group of meaningful terms is not meaningful, its isolation from meaning makes it stand out. Isolation in any kind of learning leads to vivid impressions, e.g., one red-haired girl among 31 brunettes impresses the viewer more than 11 redheads with 10 blondes and 10 brunettes. One meaningless word in a group of meaningful words is more impressive than four meaningless and four meaningful words. Isolation, rather than contextual dependencies, could make a middle term easier to learn and recall.

Another interesting study summarizes meaning, intraserial dependencies and interferences, the length of the series, the amount of practice, and the intention to learn [306]. The results were consistent with the view that incidental learning establishes fewer correct associations and is subject to less intraserial interference than intentional learning. Therefore, incidental learners benefit less from repeated presentations of the material than intentional learners, but also are less adversely affected by increases in the length of the list. Incidental learners are not involved in the learning.

Distributed Practice in List Learning

In serial learning, the influence of distributed practice is high. Some distribution as compared with massed practice aids in any learning, but especially where items are arranged in a series and the annoyance of having to work at learning a whole series builds up. Being made to work at a series without rest generates annoyance (reactive inhibition). Rest, which is provided by distributed practice, allows reactive inhibition to dissipate.

As stated previously in Chapter 8, the usual high school day provides for distributed practice. Students work for 40 to 60 minutes, leave to go to another class, return to the material as homework, and start with the material again the next day. This convenient and efficient distribution of practice provides for the dissipation of the annoyance (reactive inhibition) that is generated by work, work, work without rest. When there is respect for the mental health and attitude of the learner, some distribution of practice is essential.

Reactive, Proactive, and Retroactive Inhibition[1]

Reactive, proactive, and retroactive inhibition are sources of difficulty in all serial learning. Reactive inhibition is the inhibiting

---

[1] See also Chapter 9.

annoyance generated by being caused to do a task. The more tasks, the more inhibition; so the longer the series, the greater the inhibition. Proactive inhibition is the inhibiting influence of present learning on something which is to be learned and remembered, the inhibiting of present remembering by past learning. This works throughout a series, i.e., Item one inhibits the learning of Item two, which inhibits the learning of Item three, and so on. Retroactive inhibition is the inhibiting influence of present learning on past learning and remembering. This also works throughout a series, i.e., learning Item two disturbs the memory of Item one, and learning Item three disturbs the memory of Item two, and so on. As shown in Figure XVI, reactive inhibition is present in each task; proactive inhibition works forward to inhibit learning (Figure XVII); and retroactive inhibition works back to inhibit memory (Figure XVIII). Let the numbers in Figures XVI, XVII, and XVIII represent any series of seven items. Reactive inhibition is present in each learning item in Figure XVI, increasing at each step. The task arouses annoyance merely because it needs to be done. In Figure XVII, proactive inhibition works forward to inhibit the learning and remembering of four after three, and five after four, etc. In Figure XVIII, retroactive inhibition works back to inhibit the memory of

FIGURE XVI
Reactive Inhibition

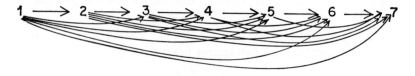

FIGURE XVII
Proactive Inhibition

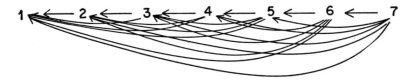

FIGURE XVIII
Retroactive Inhibition

five by six, and four by five. The workings of these three inhibitions explain why any series is difficult to learn and why most learning reduces itself to a series.

Summary: Serial Learning

Many things to be learned consist of a series or become lists to be learned; serial learning cannot be considered as a separate species. The longer a list, the harder it is to master. The ease and rate of learning of a particular item depends on its place in the series, provided that the item is not emotion-provoking, or so unusual as to be especially vivid. Items in the middle of a series and just past the middle are harder to learn because they are in that position. The content of a series, as a determinant of ease or difficulty, is not as influential as the sequential dependencies which develop in the content. Distributed practice is essential for learning lists. The difficulties in serial learning are the product of reactive, proactive, and retroactive inhibition. The longer the list, the more difficult it is; and some list positions are harder than others, but the compounded inhibitions of any series also determine its learning difficulty.

16

problem-solving

IN THE COURSE OF A DAY, we are all confronted by many problems. They are of all degrees of complexity and range from the concrete to the abstract. Some of the ordinary problems of living reach the schoolroom, but most classroom problems are closed (the answer is already known to someone), like this arithmetic problem:

(1) If six men can finish a job in six days, how many men will be needed to finish it in half of a day?

Here are other closed problems. To make the explanation clear, the reader is asked to solve these before going on.

(2) On the A-side of the river are three wives (W1, W2, W3) and their husbands (H1, H2, H3). All of the men can and will row. None of the women will row. Get both the men and the women across to the B-side of the river by means of a boat carrying only three at one time. No man will allow his wife to be in the presence of another man unless he is there also.

(3) A dependent son wrote an appeal for more money to an indulgent father, as follows,

S E N D

M O R E
_____

M O N E Y

The father realized that this was a code and that each letter stood for a digit. If each letter represents only one digit, how much money did the son ask for? Whether problems are closed (like the arithmetic, the husbands and wives, and the son who needed money—answers on page 231) or open (that is, unique, with no fixed answer), some will normally pique interest and lead to involvement, and others are uninteresting and remote. More problems could be offered as illustrations of involvement or lack of it, with the most obvious illustration being the rejection of many closed problems as tricks and games. Games require much the same sort of reasoning and analysis as real-life problems do, which is why the best games have endured so long. Games also have two advantages over problems taken from life, namely, a specific set of rules to be followed and the absence of annoyingly complicated details. Whether in play or in earnest, a person's success with problem-solving depends largely upon the extent to which he is involved in using his abilities. An independent judgment or an innovation is evidence of involvement.

An Individual Ability

Differences in problem-solving have moved psychologists to attempt to classify types of problem-solvers, but without implying that such types are mutually exclusive.

Cyril Burt refers to two kinds of problem solvers. The characteristic procedure of the former group is explicit or analytic reasoning, depending on a succession of logical steps; of the latter, an implicit or synthetic apperception of what later psychologists have called Gestalten or configurations, depending on an intuitive insight which embraces the component aspects almost simultaneously [59, p. 192].

This quotation from *The Structure of the Mind* is suggestive of powers or faculties in the mental processes, but not as causal entities or as elementary or basic capacities. Problem-solving is the product of an integrated development.

Facility in problem-solving means the ability to combine, integrate, and synthesize from one's store of knowledge and skill. A person can solve problems if he has the necessary understanding and skill. It is both the absence of knowledge and skill and the difficulty in combining what is known which makes problem-solving difficult. Of course, there are differences in the quality of solutions, as measured by the gratification which the answers bring the solver and others. It is in the adequacy of the solutions which one will accept that self-development is evident. Some people accept the solutions that others have developed, but usually the uniqueness of human behavior influences persons to try their own ways, even with things which are well-known and understood. Facility in problem-solving is a superior skill characterized by an integration of abilities.

One study compared social climates for subjects of high intelligence and average intelligence [62]. Subjects of high levels of intelligence did better in a permissive social climate; subjects of only average intelligence were considerably handicapped under permissive conditions. The implication for education is obvious. The majority of school children apparently are not ready for problem-solving by open situations which permit wide originality, experimentation, initiative, and invention. Most do better with relatively closed situations that are concerned with acquiring a body of knowledge, memorizing facts, and finding answers to problems—all of which are already known to someone else.

Everything said regarding problem-solving must be interpreted in a context of relativity. For instance, by definition, an open system is characterized by uniqueness in perception and thinking, and thus it is also a closed system (it is known that the answer must be unique); yet it is much less closed than a system which is only concerned with what has already been discovered and agreed upon. Problem-solving is a matter of degree and involvement, as in the following practical situation.

The Conditions Conducive to Problem-Solving

The school board, in a community which has been inundated by a housing development with a consequent great increase in the school population, must provide educational facilities. This is seen as a self-evident problem—no one needs to call it to the attention of the board members. The pressure is also strong to change the existing arrangements in some fashion, such as building more schools and consequently raising the taxes. This is the conventional solution to such a problem, and the board of education may simply go right ahead with this procedure without considering any other alternatives.

In another community, however, the pressure against the raising of tax rates may be so strong that other solutions must be sought. This may give rise to such unconventional notions as the quarter-system, with the existing school buildings in use for the entire year, but with one quarter of the students on vacation at any given time. This adds greatly to the usefulness of the existing schools, although it certainly causes many other difficulties.

Three characteristics which are conducive to problem-solving are evident here: a recognition of the existence of a problem, feeling pressure to change the existing arrangements, and sufficient freedom of choice so that more than one arrangement is possible.

Problem-solving behavior is evoked when the individual is aware of a problem, will act on it, and is not prepared to accept or act on existing solutions. Those who are inclined to contend with the world around them are more aware of adequacy and inadequacy, and are more aware of possible solutions; as a result they feel more pressure to seek better solutions. However, when an individual feels pressure to become more adequate and only a limited number of possibilities exist, he may experience frustration rather than the push to be ingenious. When a person believes that he can contend with his environment, freedom to explore and attempt is essential to promote development. If there is a single most important factor, it is preoccupation with the problem and its solution [299].

An interesting technique for stimulating the generation of ideas and facilitating their expression is "brainstorming" [88] or "buzz sessions" [408]. These consist of group meetings designed to push the persons present into new ideas and creativity, in spite of the accepted fact that majority decisions are not different from those made by average individuals and are inferior to those made by the best member of the group [28]. Although the technique has been made-light-of, there are several commendable aspects. Adverse criticism is banned and "freewheeling" is welcomed. A combination and improvement of ideas is sought. A quantity of ideas is derived. While there is documentation of the fact that a multiplicity of perceptions are conducive to creative solutions [187], it is necessary to point out that another study found no relationship between the rate of hypothesis-formation and problem-solving achievement [320]. In other words, many perceptions are helpful, but the speed of the development of ideas is not a factor. The amount of change from a "buzz session" depends upon participation and individual set for the discussion [408].

Experience

Experience provides the set or frame of reference from which the learner operates—the richer background of experience being considered more fruitful. Unfortunately, a rich background tends to provide solutions from imitation rather than stimulating original thinking. The experienced tend to look to someone who knows the answer rather than to strive for themselves. Novel solutions are as frequent from those whose background is limited as from those who are well-versed. This is not a recommendation for ignorance, but rather an example of the limiting influence of past experience expressed in set or frame of reference. In a study of 132 sixth-grade children in three groups, the middle group learned and transferred as many or more principles than the groups receiving minimum and maximum direction. Further, the middle group retained better [216]. The directions concerned the discovery of principles, the organization of materials, information regarding the organization, and statements of the underlying relationships. With different directions, one would expect different emphases; but the minimum group did not have enough background, and the maximum group had too much to venture and explore. The middle ground is the most fertile.

In the light of the study just cited, which is the best book to use as a text for tenth grade science? On the basis of personal orientation and previous experience, some will say that no book should be designated as a text, but rather that a group of books should be used. These people have become so well-versed in the use of books that they see no problem. At the other end of the scale are those who do not know enough to express a preference, and they are also likely to use books rather than a book. Those whose experience lies between these extremes are the ones who are likely to treat the selection of a textbook as a problem to be solved.

Training

A person's experience is not independent of the training he has received, and training in problem-solving is a two-pronged operation: the development of thought processes and the building of competency in the skills involved [60]. The thought processes are not independent of the skills; thought and action are concomitant in the highest levels of development. The interrelation and interdependence of these factors is illustrated in one study of problem-solving involving airmen. One group solved an equipment problem which resembled a search for malfunction, by actually proceeding directly to the equipment. The second group was not allowed to touch the apparatus until they had explained to the experimenter what they were going to do. The second group made fewer repetitive errors and required fewer trials than did the purely manipulative solvers [313]. Of course, there are great differences in pre-problem verbal responses and postproblem responses, but this does not obviate the necessity for both thought and action [367]. Whenever action is converted into verbal (thought) equivalents, the learner is making better use of his abilities. Take a few minutes to solve this problem: using six wooden matches of equal length, construct four but not more than four equilateral triangles.

Problem-solving appears to be influenced by verbal instructions, even by such general statements as telling the subjects that the problem is solvable [194], or that the problem can be solved by the discovery of the principle involved [102]. However, the range and variety of problems to which such training is likely to carry over has been found to be limited. A group of airmen trained on repeated presentations of the same problem was more proficient in solving problems of the same class than a group trained on a number of different problems [4]. The conclusion drawn was that learning to solve readily a new problem of a specified class was a function of learning set and that learning changes of set is a most complex and demanding function. (Even so, from this study of the training of airmen, there is a suspicion of smooth transitions to new problems as a result of multiple training.) To further document the dubious benefit of training in problem solving, although this smacks of a denial of the benefits of training, Lorge et al [242, 243] found the superiority of groups over individuals in problem-solving to depend not only on the kind of group but also on the kind of problem to be solved. In addition, the diversity of transfer of training for groups and for individuals needs to be considered. To train the learner in many classes of problems, or even to recognize distinctions between classes of problems, is difficult and not above the suspicion that training cannot transcend the individual and group problems involved.

Personal Orientation

The obscure processes leading to problem-solving are peculiarly individual and personal. The problem solution is tangible and finished, but the processes are often unverbalized by the person him-self, and as a result are not stated for others. If stated in retrospect, the excitement and verve of the moment of revelation is seldom fixed with words.

Past experience is often a closed system, a set of questions and answers known to someone. The solved problems exist in the closed past, yet the person-to-person interaction sometimes permits people to stimulate others, to go beyond themselves, and at the same time to be themselves in interacting. In certain situations people are stimulated and feel more free to be themselves—the idea of an attractive conflict [176]. The creativity of problem-solving exists only at the moment. The products of creativity exist only in the past, and *there* is the trap. A knowledge of the past is essential for problem-solving in the present, yet the cue to present creativity may be stifled by the burden of prior solutions.

One other aspect of personal orientation is worthy of mention—personal bias often distorts possible interpretations to limit or pre-vent solutions. Experience, motivation, and set are subject to prej-udice, to personal perceptions and interpretations. The chief effect of bias is to dictate the conclusions to be drawn from the data. Different conclusions can logically arise from the same data as original solutions and novel interpretations are derived. Prejudice causes a person to add extraneous items to the data rather than interpreting the data more objectively. Problem-solving is a high level of human ability in which one establishes answers which others can observe and verify. When others cannot observe and verify the interpretations of the data, it is often personal bias which has influenced the solution reached. Most persons need the verification which the interpretations of others provide in order to feel secure in their interpretations.

· · ·

THE SOLUTIONS TO THE PROBLEMS ON PAGES 224-225. (1) Question: If six men in six days, how many in half a day? Answer: 72 men. (2) The husbands, wives, boat. Answer:

A SIDE	IN BOAT	B SIDE
H1 W1 H2 W2 H3 W3		
H2 W2 H3 W3 ⟶	H1 W1	
H2 W2 H3 W3 ⟵	H1	W1
H3 W3 ⟶	H1 H2 W2	W1
H3 W3 ⟵	H1 H2	W1 W2
H2 ⟶	H1 H3 W3	W1 W2
H2 ⟵	H1 H3	W1 W2 W3
⟶	H1 H2 H3	W1 W2 W3

(3)

```
        S E N D
        9 5 6 7
        M O R E
        1 0 8 5
       ─────────
      M O N E Y
    $ 1 0 6 . 5 2
```

Solution to the problem on page 230.
Construct a three-dimensional figure, like a three-sided pyramid.
Analyze the way you tried to solve this problem. Did you merely

push the matches into various patterns in the expectation that the solution might emerge from these manipulations? Or did you apply what you had just read, by verbalizing as you went along? One does not put the matches down in separate triangles △ △ because it is self-evident that this will not work. Various combinations are tried, however, in which one match is used for a side of two triangles, as in △\. If a person were asked to restate the nature of the difficulty at this point, he might more readily see that every match must be used as a side for two triangles, and that this is impossible in any two-dimensional solution. The individual who proceeds only by manipulation, instead of combining this with verbalization, is likely to solve the problem by accident, if at all.

Summary: Problem-Solving

Problem-solving depends in large measure upon individual capability and is considered to be an expression of superior abilities. Situations which evoke problem-solving in one person are treated as routine events by another person. This difference cannot be fully accounted for, because, although problem-solving is not difficult, particularly if one has the knowledge and skill germane to the problem, there is a limitation in providing a rich background and relevant training. Previous experience and training tend to direct the learner away from both the recognition of problems and novel solutions. Although novel solutions are preferred, there are many situations where the only novelty possible is the arrival of the learner at a solution already known to others. This is a novel solution for an individual, but obviously this makes little if any contribution to knowledge. Problem-solving at its ultimate produces new knowledge, and, in this, many persons find their fullest self-expression.

17

communication

EARNING RESULTS FROM the activity of the organism. The nature, direction, and extent of this activity is the result of stimulations from within and without. While meanings arise from many sources, the place of other people in ascribing significance to one's experience is central. Communication, then, becomes a major factor in adjustment and learning.

The teaching-learning process is essentially a matter of interpersonal relationships. Even when the learner reads a book, looks at a work of art, observes the products of civilization, or watches people at work or play, there are relationships, implicit though they may be, between two or more persons. We live in a social medium, and the lifeline is communication. Learning is part of this life process; to understand it and to increase its effectiveness teachers must comprehend the processes of communication. There are many forms of communication; but, in the transmission of a complex civilization, language has become the principal means of influencing others [57].

Learning and Communication

Everyone concerned with learning is concerned with communication, since all persons both learn from others and enable others to learn. Most people are engaged in receiving and imparting learning stimulation, regardless of whether they consider themselves to be learners or teachers. Even those who tend to keep their ideas to themselves, those who avoid social contacts, depend on others for communications, such as letters, newspapers, magazines, books, radio, and television, from which they can gather meaning. In this sense, learning and communication are so closely interrelated as to be often indistinguishable. Failure to learn may be caused by a failure of communication, and failure to comprehend is quite likely without good communication. Learning and communication are the concern of all persons who are interested in self-betterment and in the betterment of others.

The Rationale

The notion of education as communication is elaborated by Kelley: perception comes from within, not from one's surroundings. The perceiver decides what an object is and where it is. He makes it what he chooses to make it and can make it, in the light of his unique experience and purpose, his own interpretation of what impinges upon him from his environment. Each individual is therefore the center of his unique universe. He shares this universe with others through communication, but only in part, because those with whom he attempts to communicate must interpret what he offers in accordance with their own backgrounds. Thus learning promotes uniqueness rather than diminishing it. Learning, because experience is individually interpreted, increases dissimilarity.

The most important element in anyone's environment is other people. They provide what is needed for development. We help fashion those who fashion us. Since we build others and are built by them, the quality of the psychological self depends on the quality of the people out of whom it is constructed. . . . A rich environment is equivalent to growing up with many good people, with whom one has many transactions for his personal development. Good relationships are indispensable for satisfactory development. We are our brother's keeper, and it behooves us to do the job well; for he is the stuff out of which *we* are fashioned, and our quality depends upon his. Our perceptions come from us, not merely from our surroundings, and this turns the world around . . . the organism perceiving the stimulus is important.

Teachers never start fresh with a child. If the learner does not see it as the teacher does, the authoritarian corrects and blames him. It is better to place the learner in the important position and strive to communicate, because what is really significant is what the learner makes of what he is told, not what the teacher intended. New understandings are necessarily subjective knowledge. Something new is incorporated into the learner in the only possible way, that is, through his unique perceptive process. Since man is what he does, he builds a structure, a form of knowledge, attitude, and habit [210, pp. 250-251].

Each person creates his own world. As such, he is the center of a world not common to anyone else. He shares this world with others through communication. Education is communicated to others in the teacher's way, and sharing his experience with others builds him and them. Sharing with others is the root of self-development.

In teaching, the person who *receives* the communication is the focus. What he makes of what he is told is what he builds into his knowledge, his attitudes, and his habits. His learning is the product of what he does with what he has the experience and the purpose to perceive. Thus the conditions for effective communication are the conditions for learning and for teaching, and teaching is the stimulation of the learner in the light of his background and goals.

Education

Knowledge cannot be literally transmitted. Words cannot directly convey an idea from one person to another, but they may stimulate memories and associations, which in turn may stimulate the development of ideas. Knowledge exists and is developed anew within each individual from infancy on, as a result of his perception of the experiences to which he is exposed. For the development of knowledge, experience is required, both direct and vicarious, plus the ability to see the interrelationships of the items. Vicarious experiences (such as reading) are usually fruitful in proportion to the combined influences of direct experience and the perception of relationships. Reading develops a person's knowledge when he has experiences of sufficient quantity and variety to bring to the book. In the final analysis, there is only learning; there is no such thing as teaching, no conveying of knowledge and information, except through the activity of a learner.

Learning is dependent upon previous learning, so that the development of abstract abilities is based upon observations of basic realities and the building of a structure of graduated concepts to match reality *as one perceives it to be*. These words are italicized to stress the limitations included: the limitations of one's perceptive powers, sensory organs, and background experiences. It is obvious that what a person looks at is not what he sees, and that his memories are faulty and need to be checked by recording his observations carefully. A person's concepts about himself and the world around him are usually ordered and arranged, again within his limitations, to enable him to become more self-sufficient, more self-propelling, more the master of his destiny, and less the victim of circumstances or environment. On this basis, the school, from kindergarten to college, is a place where people come together so that the teacher may provide some of the experiences needed to develop an orderly body of concepts about themselves and the world around them. In this interpretation the word "teacher" applies to everyone who assists another to become more self-sufficient, more capable of coping with reality. Similarly, an educational institution is any place where the development of organized and structured concepts about the self and the environment can be confirmed or denied. Education for the benefit of the individual and society is self-development in keeping with a person's knowledge of himself and the world around him.

Purpose and Empathy

Because the learner perceives what experience and purpose prepare him to perceive, the modes of communication are necessarily as individual as the modes of perception. Perceptions are a function of the perceiver's ways of organizing and interpreting what he experiences, and he experiences what his underlying attitudes permit. These attitudes can be changed through expression of the feelings and prejudices which influence perception. Thus education as communication is the key to individual development. If communication is to flourish, it needs to be fostered by empathy —a social process in which one deliberately identifies with others while developing self-insight. As a person is able to empathize, he promotes education, his own development, and that of others; and this development is unique.

The desire to communicate is expressed in behavior which makes knowledge and experience available to others. The experiences that promote understanding require the desire to communicate and to learn, and the media for doing so. Thus the purposes of communication and of learning, whether from the point of view of the culture or of the individual, are similar, namely, perpetuation and development; and the highest levels of ability follow from the acquisition of knowledge and skill, not as a group but as individuals in a group.

If one is to acquire the knowledge of the ages, or even of one's own time, the desire to communicate must be paramount. Communication, broadly speaking, goes on regardless of the wishes of the persons involved. Communication of explicit specific information, however, with a given intention and interpretation, is not possible unless those with whom one wishes to communicate choose to share the experience and understanding. This involves empathy.

Empathy is the direct apprehension of the state of mind and feelings of others. The chief aspect of sympathy is shared attitude, while the chief aspect of empathy is shared understanding. Communication is based on the empathic process wherein one deliberately identifies with another person while specifically expressing the self [372]. In empathy there is self-control, but not control over others. It is in this way that personal freedom to develop is enhanced by participation in empathic relationships. Whenever one manages to communicate, self-control has permeated the relationship with others to the point where the good will of empathy has fostered understanding.

The shared understanding of communication takes place directly through imitation or indirectly through the symbols of words, pictures, and signs; that is, reality includes all that exists in the two realms: physical things, and the world of symbols, ideas and imagination [286]. Cooperation in the use of symbols is essential, because any symbolic system can be interpreted in many ways, and a particular symbol can have many meanings. The individual meaning of the symbols used for communication further emphasizes the purpose of communication as sharing understanding. Consider the following changes in meaning through the use of the arbitrary signs called punctuation.

My friend Ralph has not yet married Celia.
My friend Ralph has not yet married Celia!
My friend Ralph has not yet married Celia?
My friend Ralph has not yet married, Celia?
My friend, Ralph, has not yet married Celia!
My friend, Ralph, has not yet married Celia?
My! Friend Ralph has not yet married Celia.
My! Friend Ralph has not yet married Celia!
My! Friend Ralph has not yet married Celia?
My! Friend Ralph has not yet married, Celia.
My! Friend Ralph has not yet married, Celia!
My! Friend Ralph has not yet married, Celia?
My! Friend Ralph has not yet married. Celia!
My! Friend Ralph has not yet married. Celia?
My! Friend Ralph has not yet married! Celia!

My! Friend Ralph has not yet married! Celia?
My! Friend Ralph has not yet married? Celia!
My! Friend Ralph has not yet married? Celia?
My friend Ralph has not yet married! Celia?
My friend Ralph has not yet married! Celia!
My friend Ralph has not yet married? Celia!
My "friend", Ralph, has not yet married Celia.
My "friend", Ralph, has not yet married, Celia!
My "friend", Ralph, has not yet married Celia?
My friend, Ralph, has not yet married! Celia!
My friend, Ralph, has not yet married! Celia?
"My friend Ralph has not yet married"—Celia.
My friend! Ralph has not yet married! [152]

The art of communication depends on the choice of symbols, e.g., "When that umpire thumbs a man out, there's no doubt about it." To be skillful, one uses symbols which convey the intended meaning. Communication hinges upon developing the meaning in others. The teacher knows how to use a thesaurus; mother knows how to make a cheese soufflé; and a friend knows how to play the ukulele. They give directions in symbols which evoke understanding. If one is able to follow their directions, progress is smoother, to the learner's benefit and the teacher's satisfaction. A person communicates when his choice of symbols is appropriate, that is, when the symbols used evoke the desired interpretation.

Symbols as Tools of Communication

The tools of communication are symbols. One must develop the ability to equate the symbol with the object and then to represent the object with a symbol. The chief symbols are the spoken word, the printed word, signs, and gestures. Each symbol (word, picture, sign, graph, hand motion, facial expression) stands for its basic value plus individual interpretations and associations. A frown is a depressing facial contortion, but it is also symbolic of dissatisfaction. *Happy* has a meaning as a five-letter combination, but its connotation runs far beyond the simple word. It is a symbol of whatever kinds of pleasure, gratification, or state of well-being the user of the word has experienced or desired. It refers to these events, and is therefore said to have referents; each symbol stands for associations in the background of the user. When the symbol stands for the same referents, its meaning for the users is similar. When the symbol stands for different referents, the intention to communicate can only be confused. Therefore, if communication is the intention, identify clearly the referents of the symbols used. As Korzybski says, man's achievements rest on the use of symbols [219].

Words are symbols which represent ideas or things. As practice is given in speaking, listening, writing, and reading the language, the individual gains control over the symbols system and semantic distinctions, and so over the self and the environment. Wendell Johnson explains this point of view:

Any language by reason of its structure tends to determine the aspects of reality which its speakers may recognize, and the relations among them which they may understand; thus, a language may be regarded as a "thinking machine" which imposes its own special organization upon the personalities of those who use it. Individuals differ significantly in the degree to which they exercise control over their own symbolic processes. Yet only through such control is an individual free to regulate the pattern of this personality development.

Children can achieve such control if they are trained to ask two basic questions: What do you mean? How do you know? [201, pp. 29-34].

To broaden Johnson's statement: as one achieves control over his symbolic processes, he acquires freedom to grow and develop. Such control comes from developing basic language skills and using them carefully to denote what is meant. While denotation tends to emphasize the role of language to transmit information, it is necessary to remember that language is also used to induce mood and to promote action [315]. To transmit information, conceptual clarity is essential: to induce mood and to promote action, lack of clarity is no handicap. The required development includes oral-aural skills, reading ability, writing ability, and the meanings of words as symbols.

Oral-Aural Skills

The better a person learns to speak of his experiences and to listen to the experiences of others, the more adequate he can become. Defects in oral-aural skills severely limit development. Speech defects, ranging from slight mispronunciations to severe malfunctioning such as stuttering and aphasia, have the same general effect; namely, the speaker is not as intelligible as he would be without the defects, and he diverts the attention of the listener from the intended meaning to the speech mannerism itself. Similarly, hearing defects and the inability to listen carefully limit development because the listener misses part or all of the intended meaning of the spoken words. Speech retraining, hearing correction, and training in the values of listening are frequently required since the oral-aural skills are so basic to communication.

Reading Ability

Reading ability is basic to communication. There is no object in belaboring the limiting effects of defective reading. More work has been done on the teaching of reading than on the teaching of any other subject, and more work has been done on remedial reading than on remedial instruction in any other subject. Taken together, these comments suggest that either teachers do not know how to teach reading, or they are simply not doing it. Still, the emphasis on reading is there.

Communication depends on the readability of the material. The same content can be pitched at several different levels of difficulty, depending on the words and sentence structure used. Communication is facilitated when the readability level is matched to the reader's level [91, pp. 218-250].

Writing Ability

Although important, writing ability is not as critical as oral-aural skills and reading, because more persons communicate through listening, speaking, and reading than through writing. Writing also profits from the transfer of oral skills, since it is largely a more formal style of speech. Writing skills respond to practice aimed at stating ideas simply and clearly. This is the essence of communication.

Meaningfulness

Assuming adequate skill in listening, speaking, reading, and writing, communication depends upon the individual meanings which are assigned to the words used. The meanings assigned to symbols are the specifics which each symbol is to denote, modified by the context in which the symbol is used and the mood each symbol arouses. Meanings of words develop as a result of experiences and the association of experiences with words. Since different people have different experiences, they are likely to have different meanings for the same words; and the meanings will differ most when the background experiences differ most. The translation problems at the United Nations, for example, have resulted not merely from the use of different languages, but from the different cultures involved. "Democracy," "free elections," and "people's republic" do not mean the same things to the Soviet and United States representatives. This is true also of people with the same general background, but different biases. If two American economists discuss "a planned economy," their use of the term will be markedly different if one favors a planned economy and the other strongly opposes it. Only as a person knows the experiences of people and their reactions to these events, can he have confidence in his understanding of the meanings they have for the words they use. Because he can never know about all the experiences and reactions of others, he can never fully understand what others mean by the words they use. Meanings for the same words will differ least when experiences have been most nearly identical, and especially for those words which are associated with phenomena that can be counted, weighed, and measured. The physical scientists can communicate much more precisely than the social scientists. We have meanings for words, but what others make of the words we use depends on their experiences rather than ours.

To illustrate, the word "study" may mean to read, peruse, con, pour over, wade through, plunge into, burn the midnight oil; the context determines its significance and usefulness. Context refers to the totality of conditions influencing a behavioral event and the patterning of these conditions. Because persons can dependably produce and distinguish only a relatively small number of different letters or speech sounds, they must use these few elements to talk and write about millions of different items and ideas; so they depend upon the context, the serial orders, the patterning for significance and usefulness. In speech and writing, choice of words depends upon training, needs and intentions, the situation, and the audience. The words used reflect this total context; the meanings which others attach to the spoken or written words similarly depend upon *their* training, needs, intention, and situation. As a person can take account of these aspects of context in himself and others, he communicates more effectively. The more specific one can be about the referents of the symbols used and the total context of these symbols, the better he will communicate.

Instructional Devices

Instructional devices are used to support language symbols. These are direct experience, pictorial and manipulative materials, spoken and written directions that illustrate the referents of words.

When direct experience can be provided to support descriptions, pictures, and experimental materials, the referents of the symbols are clearer. In a classroom, the teacher explains that ingredients are processed into bread in a bakery. She describes the steps involved, and may use pictures, charts, diagrams, and manipulative materials such as flour and water. The direct experience of a trip to the bakery after such an introduction makes the symbols richer and more meaningful. When such instructional aids are not used, the words cannot have the precise denotation, nor the richness of connotation. On the other hand, the lesson which does not convert direct experience and the use of manipulative and pictorial materials to the conventional symbol system of words does not capitalize fully on the opportunity to give the learner control over the material. The teacher should explain before the trip, illustrate before the trip, take the trip, illustrate after the trip, and discuss after the trip. The more precisely each symbol is used and illustrated, the better the quality of the control over the symbol system.

Many teachers wrongly assume that there is great value in all kinds of instructional devices. Recent experimental work has led to conclusions which are not in keeping with expectations. For instance, little difference in learning basic electricity was found between a wiring board with components to be manipulated and a chart on which circuits were drawn; that is, pictorial and manipulative materials were found to be at about the same level of abstraction in contributing to the identification of symbol meaning [282]. In another study, it was found that moving pictures were not superior to instruction with a printed text and a static diagram [226]. In work with college students, Underwood found that the more information he gave them about concepts like white, soft, and large, the faster they acquired the concepts [406]. Listening-comprehension was not aided or upset by note-taking, regardless of whether main points only, or as many details as possible, were recorded [250]. Even if one rejects the studies from which conclusions like these are drawn, they raise doubts about the general belief that the use of any instructional device is superior to spoken or written language.

To recapitulate, communication which involves the spoken word emphasizes oral-aural ability, namely, abilities associated with intelligible speech, adequate hearing, and the ability to listen; communication which involves reading emphasizes the basic ability to read and then reading for understanding; communication which involves writing emphasizes adequate writing ability and writing practice. If these skills are present, communication depends upon whether the words as symbols stimulate what is intended in meaning, mood, or action. This is determined by whether the words used have acquired, through real or vicarious experience, the qualities for the receiver which the speaker or writer intended. If they have, communication which facilitates individual and social development occurs. If the words do not generate the meaning, mood, and action the speaker or writer intended, confusion results, individual development is slowed down, and a basis for ineffectual social relationships is implanted.

Language and Communication

As a symbol system, language is so much a part of us and such a common factor in all human activity, that we seldom consider how learning and human relationships are controlled by language. More waking hours are spent in speaking than in writing; in fact, speech is the second impression one makes—the first being his appearance. Speech functions as language when the persons who make the sounds, and the persons who hear the sounds, associate them with similar experiences. Words as sounds are assigned to identify various elements of experience and carry messages. Thus words open up the paths to knowledge. Used in understandable speech patterns or clear writing, words direct and shape experiences such as ideas and emotions. Language becomes the means by which one acquires knowledge and extends his abilities. Intellectual development is intimately related to the degree and quality of language development.

The function of language and its role in thought is well described in *Language and Thought in Action* [174].

Language development is so critical for personal development, that readiness for language development is customarily equated with readiness for all learning. Such readiness allows the learner to convert his exploration and discovery to the words and symbols of language. This experience can be extended through systematic generalization (once again in words) to the control of language (the conventional symbol system). Language development provides a ready tool for all sorts of contingencies.

The Environment for Language Development

A rich environment for language development requires opportunities for all aspects of speaking and listening, written expression, reading and literature, the mass media, language study, and library usage. The scope of this listing emphasizes that the range extends from prekindergarten to postcollege, and that mastery of all subjects, including those that resort to a symbolism of their own (such as mathematics and chemistry), is dependent upon the skillful use of language. The absence of an ability such as listening or speaking is a more obvious handicap than the absence of some of the other abilities, but a deficiency of any kind in these abilities takes a heavy toll from personal potential. In a world where language competence is of increasing value, every child should have an opportunity to attain full language development, from improving basic language skills to a skillful use of creative imagination in several symbol systems.

Throughout school and adult years, interdependent communication skills need to be stressed. Improvement in techniques, at all levels, benefits the whole range of skills and also emphasizes their interdependence, as in the following illustrations. Writing depends upon skill in observing, listening, speaking, and reading, and upon understanding of behavior, which in turn is dependent upon personal and social adjustment. Skills in speaking and reading are dependent upon skills in observing and listening, which in turn are dependent upon an environment which is comfortable, attractive, and stimulating. Reading evolves into one of the most enjoyable and valuable language activities, particularly when it has developed purpose so that a person can skim or read for the central idea, or read for detail. While speaking and reading are used more frequently, ideas are also recorded in writing; and, in order to express ideas clearly and attractively, one must write legibly and punctuate and spell with reasonable accuracy.

The mass media (newspapers, magazines, motion pictures, radio, and television) are potent influences in the environment. The extent of the contact and the variety of the offering reinforce all basic language skills and usually broaden the horizons. Two neglected areas of the environment remain—foreign language study and library usage. Both of these suffer as sources of enrichment for the same reason; namely, foreign languages are often taught for their own sake, and libraries are frequently just places where books are kept. When foreign languages come to be learned to contribute to total language development, and as libraries become a source of support in learning and knowing, both will participate more fully in enriching the environment for language development.

The Role of Concepts

Control and use of the symbol system reaches its highest level in concept formation. A concept is a meaning sufficiently individualized to be directly grasped and readily used, and thus fixed by a word [99].

Serra explained that concepts exist at all levels of complexity. They can be based on one experience with an object or upon a multitude of experiences, and they will increase in complexity with the amount of experience. They can be based on varying degrees of relationships among objects. Concepts of increasing levels of complexity are based on a hierarchy of concepts dealing with objects and their relationships. They are also symbolized and verbalized by the individual, and the symbols or words in themselves become new concepts with a new hierarchy.

Verbalization, however, is not essential to indicate the existence of a concept. It is obvious that the 14-month-old toddler who, having once touched a hot stove, thereafter avoids all stoves, has a well-established concept of hot-stove, but has no way to verbalize his experience.

. . . Failure of a child to acquire a concept through reading may arise from poor choice of expression by the author rather than from weakness in the child.

. . . The question is simply whether a child is aware of, and in accord with, the common agreement concerning each word. Most words have multiple meanings: that is, they symbolize different concepts. All concepts that have been verbalized can be expressed in many ways, through the use of different words and different syntactical devices. There is a distinct tendency for research dealing with concepts to bog down into investigations of word meanings [342, pp. 275-276].

Serra made it clear that concepts exist at all levels of complexity; they may result from a single experience and from combined experiences; and as they become increasingly complex, ideas and their relationships assume a hierarchical order.

Concepts exist at all levels of complexity, as in the two illustrations which follow. Physical line concepts may range from a line to a straight line, to a triangle, to a pyramid, and to a many-faceted star. Concepts of color develop from the primary red to pink or crimson, passing through many shades of pink which most persons cannot distinguish at all.

Concepts evolve from a single experience and from combined experiences. One may form a generalization about a color like magenta from a single experience, but it is much more likely to develop from a variety of experiences in a wide range of combinations.

As concepts evolve, they become increasingly complex; ideas and their relationships assume a hierarchical order in keeping with the degrees of complexity. To illustrate, ideas have content, and those which are characterized by number, size, and color include the interrelationships of these aspects. Applying these interrelated comparisons of content, number, size, and color to three different fields or contexts causes comparative interrelationships to evolve that are based on the ideas; this is at least two steps away from the initial idea. The ideas which take us through levels of relationships arrange themselves in a hierarchy.

The Development of Concepts

To foster concept-building and the development of control over words to represent each concept, a fertile ground must be provided for language development and a wide range of both vicarious and direct experiences. Breadth, rather than intensity of training, is the key to efficient concept formation [383], and the critical process is concentration on one aspect of the situation at a time [25]. These statements about the development of skill and abstract abilities sound positive, rather like "do it this way and you will develop the ability to form concepts," but there is no one way to develop concepts. The very notion of a single approach is unacceptable because of the implied fixity and inflexibility; concept development is inseparable from shifting, changing and maturing development. Positive statements regarding concept-building are the result of studies, but others may arrive at similar or different conclusions after careful study and thought.

In this area of the development of ideas, it is the wide scope rather than the depth of training which is the key; because concept-formation, decision-making, creative thinking, and problem-solving are closely interrelated. The description of the goal of fullest development is confusing because of the need for precision coupled with diversity and flexibility. The use of an object as a symbol in one function inhibits its use in other functions, while training in the use of objects and symbols in diverse functions inhibits functional fixity and inflexibility. Critical thinking, reasoning, creative thinking, decision-making, and concept formation all respond to the diverse stimulation of unstructured "think sessions" where a deliberate effort is made to avoid the fixity of prior usage, action, and thought in favor of the wide-ranging freedom to explore ideas.

There is always a time lag in the development of concepts and thinking [298]. A changing world requires changing concepts, but new phenomena are recognized grudgingly, so that the necessary regrouping of concepts and development of ideas does not follow for a while, and this produces the time lag.

While verbalization is not essential to indicate the existence of a concept, the communication of concepts relies on verbalization. For instance, concepts such as number, size, and color are fixed by the spoken and written word, but the word may not carry the meaning the speaker or writer intended. If one relies on words to carry concepts—and almost all concepts above the object level are managed with words—the semantics require great attention; but the concepts, which are the product of creative thought, are more than the mere semantic distinctions through which one catches a glimpse of the creativity of the speaker or writer. While semantic distinctions are essential to any consideration of concepts, they are only the means and should not be mistaken for the concepts themselves.

The last statement has a semantic connotation of double talk; but without being caught in a semantic trap, it can be stated that creative thought at all levels of complexity is not hampered by words. It is the *communication* of the concepts which is limited by semantic distinctions. This does not deny that as each aspect of the stimulus is delineated and fixed with words, the quality of the concept is improved. Instead, attention is directed to the need for work with the diverse aspects of each stimulus, because concept formation responds to breadth rather than intensity of training.

The critical process in concept formation appears to be concentration on one aspect of the situation at a time.

In an interesting study with university people, concept formation and critical thinking were examined through a card-sorting task. The five dimensions on the 38 cards were: the word "red" or "black" written on each card (content), either once or twice (number), in either capital or lower case letters (size), with either red or black ink (color), either enclosed in a rectangular border or not so enclosed (field).

It was found that in solving this test, the analytic thinker evolves and tests hypotheses by concentrating on one dimension and ignoring others. For instance, in a concealed-figure test, one must concentrate on the embedded figure to the exclusion of distracting lines. The common process in tasks like these seems to be concentration on one aspect of a complex stimulus situation at a time [25, pp. 298 and 304].

For building concepts, whether based on real or vicarious experiences, breadth of training in diverse meanings and the ability to concentrate on one aspect of the situation at a time are paramount. The well-developed use of concepts provides a wealth of vicarious experience to enrich life and to give their user control over the self and the environment.

One of the marks of maturity is the ability to build a thought model which others can follow. This involves the use of concepts in ways with which others agree. Concepts communicated to others through word descriptions which are precise and definitive represent the highest level of abstraction and a fruitful level of vicarious experience. This is the art of the teacher. For instance, children usually do not explain well to each other because they assume that others know what they know, perceive as they do, and are aware of the world as they are. With increasing sensitivity, adolescents and young adults become aware of the need to explain what they know, and to describe their perception and awareness. Since concepts include the selection of phenomena and values from experience, some of the difficulty in explanation and concept formation is historical, the product of the time lag in concept development [298]. The rest of the difficulty lies in word choice and usage, that is, with the actual techniques of communication. Thought models which others can follow indicate superior development.

Summary: Communication

Communication and learning are so intimately interrelated in many situations as to be inseparable. For instance, it is possible to determine the respective weights of communication and learning in the development of mature comprehension, but it is certain that such understanding does not evolve without good communication. Sharing with others through communication is the root of self-development. In teaching, the person who receives the communication is the focus. What he makes of what the teacher tells him is what he builds into his knowledge, his attitudes, and his habits. His learning is the product of what he does with what he has the experience and the purpose to perceive. In this sense the conditions for effective communication are the conditions for learning.

The purpose of communication is to transmit information, to induce mood, and to promote action in those who wish to know and understand. Unless those with whom one wishes to communicate choose to try to follow the meaning, the essential empathy, the sharing of the state of mind and feelings, does not occur. The sharing, whether between individuals or in groups, may take place directly through imitation of reality or indirectly through the symbols of words, ideas, and imagination. Because each symbol can have many meanings, and because symbol systems are so diverse, the goodwill called "empathy" is essential for any and all degrees of understanding.

The ability to equate the symbol with the object is followed by the ability to represent the object with a symbol. In this process, one uses oral-aural skills, reading, writing, and instructional devices in the effort to reach understanding. Emphasis on these skills provides the environment for sufficient language development to support concept formation. It is through concepts carried by words that persons are best able to stimulate and communicate.

18

the measurement and

evaluation of learning

tHE PURPOSE OF THE TESTS the teacher gives is to let the pupils know how well they are doing and to determine how well he himself is doing. To this end, valid and reliable measures are essential. A valid test measures what it is supposed to measure; a reliable test gives consistent results. If the teacher is careful in meeting these conditions, the tests will inform pupils of their progress toward goals. But whose goals? And what goals? The answers to these questions embrace the philosophy of education and the extended studies on curriculum. Suffice it to say here that it is impossible to construct and use (properly) valid and reliable tests unless the goals of the day, the week, and the school term are clear. To illustrate, should the teacher measure product or process, or both? That is, should he measure what the child knows, or how he learned it and the work he did to reach his answers, or both what he knows and how he got there?

The answers to these questions, in terms of measurement and evaluation, are simple, although they may often be difficult to carry out. Measure what the child knows, and to improve understanding of the teaching-learning process, examine how he learned it and the steps he took to get there. The latter is not done directly through test questions, but indirectly through reviews of his answers and conversation with him about them. Tests which seek only the processes are self-defeating because processes do not exist without content. However, the pursuit of facts without an interest in understanding and processes is sterile. Avoid the tendency to focus attention on the outcomes of learning—test the products of learning, and at the same time examine and discuss processes and comprehension.

Testing results in scores. But what is the value of a score? By now, most persons who use tests realize that the score represents only a small part of the educational value to be derived. For both teacher and learner, there is the identification and preparation of the area of content, the setting of the test and test questions, the marking, the explanation and re-explanation of the content and the test questions in relation to the content, and the examination and discussion with individuals which reveal what they know and understand and how well they know it. This individual work may reveal that some pupils who gave right answers were more lucky than well-informed, while others who gave wrong answers may have had higher general comprehension. Had the same questions been asked in a slightly different way, or if slightly different questions had been used, their responses would have been quite different. Of course, there are always those who know and understand and make high scores, and those who make low scores because they do not know or understand. Between these extremes are the majority of persons tested, and with wisdom and care they need not be defeated or feel frustrated by tests and test scores. The score is a numerical value which represents performance on a test. And performance mirrors preparation, knowledge, understanding, and process.

Validity and Reliability

Validity

Does the test measure what it is supposed to measure? For instance, in a spelling test, is spelling alone being measured, or are factors of hearing, listening, vocabulary, and writing or speaking also influencing the results? In order to spell well one must be able to hear, to listen, to understand the use and frequently the meaning of a word, to write, and to speak. When a child is unable to spell, which of these functions is deficient? All of them, or just one or two? The teacher must be very careful regarding the estimates of the validity of a test, because validity is so many-sided. When the teacher claims to have marked the written English of the class, what has he marked? Spelling? Punctuation? Grammar? Word choice and use? If there is a careful definition of exactly the abilities involved and then measurement in terms of the amount of these abilities, the tests may be valid.

Fundamentally, all procedures for determining test validity are concerned with the relationships between performance on the test and other independently observable facts about the behavior characteristics under consideration [13, p. 135]. The specific techniques employed for investigating these relationships are numerous and may be classified as content, predictive, concurrent, and construct validity [13, pp. 135-149]. Apart from these specific techniques, each test is based on four fundamental assumptions. If any of the four assumptions is not realized, the test score is invalid.

The Basic Assumptions

The four basic assumptions upon which all valid and reliable test administrations are based may be elaborated as follows:

(1) *Equivalence of opportunity in the culture.* If for any reason the cultural opportunity has been limited, for reasons such as the place where the subject lives, the language spoken at home, or

economic limitations, the test results are only comparable with the scores of persons who have suffered similar limitations, and it is difficult to judge the degree of limitation imposed by such influences. An obvious cultural limitation is absence from school; this shows up readily when a pupil is tested on work he has missed during a three week absence, if the test is given only a day or two after his return to school. When equivalence of cultural opportunity has obviously not been available, it is preferable to report the evidence of invalidation rather than the score. If obligated to report the score, the teacher should carefully document this evidence.

(2) *Adequate motivation.* Unless the tester can affirm that the performance represents the subject's best effort, the score is unreliable. When there is evidence of inadequate motivation, the score can be reported if accompanied by an explanation of where and how the motivation was inadequate. If the motivation was inadequate for much of the test, the score is invalidated. Group-test administrations do not permit reliable estimates of the student's motivation. Gross evidence on a timed effort, such as a student sitting still or fooling with the materials, will come to the tester's attention. Other behavior that is equally detrimental may pass unnoticed. The undetected inadequacies in motivation are a major source of unreliability in group-test scores.

(3) *Standardized procedure.* Sometimes, in spite of the best possible effort, the precise procedure of the standardization cannot be followed. If the score is reported, the deviations from accepted procedures should be specified. The most common violation of this basic assumption results from ignorance of the standardized procedure, particularly in group-test administrations. Even when the test procedure has not been standardized, the examination should be given with common instructions and under common conditions. Test scores are invalidated by failure to follow the exact procedures of standardized tests and by failure to follow common procedures for each administration of tests which are not standardized.

(4) *Adequate scoring and interpretation.* Clerical errors bedevil all test scores, because even the most precise worker is prone

to such mistakes. The errors occur in scoring, in comparing scores, in converting raw scores to derived scores, and in transposing scores. It is obvious how clerical errors invalidate scores and the subsequent interpretations.

If any of the four assumptions upon which all valid tests are based is violated, the report should list the conditions of testing and the evidence of invalidation along with the scores.

Reliability

Will the test yield approximately the same results on subsequent administrations? While few tests can lay claim to certain validity, most standardized tests are reliable. For instance, it is quite possible to measure geography knowledge in such a way that the scores are comparable from test to test, but there is always a question as to just what is measured. Tests can be quite reliable without being valid, although they cannot be more valid than they are reliable.

If the question is asked in slightly different form, the issue may be clearer. The child has completed his arithmetic problems. How good an estimate is this performance of his subsequent performance with similar problems? If there is about the same performance each time, then there is reliability, although there may not be a clue as to which abilities are being measured.

Common approaches to the determination of reliability are as follows: the relationship between equivalent forms (Form *A* compared with Form *B*), the relationship between a test and a retest, the split-half relationship, and the inter-item consistency [13, pp. 118-123].

It is easy to dismiss the results of all tests on the basis of validity and reliability. Most are to some extent invalid (they do not measure what they claim to), and some are unreliable (they give inconsistent results). But to discard tests entirely because of these limitations would place the full burden for evaluation on the teacher's judgment. Judgments have been shown to be quite unreliable also, and their validity is fully as questionable as that of tests. Further, by working with both tests and judgments, the teacher may upgrade educational practices and understanding.

Ability, Aptitude, and Measurement

If validity and reliability are assumed, the score a child is given for his performance on a test represents his ability at that time. Many persons would like to estimate a pupil's aptitude or potential from his scores, but this is rarely possible with any great accuracy. For instance, the score from a general science test presumably represents his present ability. If his exposure to science is expanded and intensified, his scores on equivalent science tests should rise, but the teacher still would not know the science potential or aptitude. Without exposure to science teaching, performance would probably be poor. With good teaching, performance will improve, but the amount is unpredictable. Those who insist that they measure aptitude must demonstrate that they are working with something other than ability (performance).

The determination of how much is retained is important, because the demands of society are always in terms of developed ability rather than potential. One must know what he can do to have confidence in his ability. His potential is an interesting speculation, but performance is the determinable aspect, and most performance can be ascertained through productive and reproductive memory. To illustrate, whether a person remembers the names of two people to whom he has just been introduced reflects his adequacy. Ability to recall the two names and to recognize the two people is an important social skill. There are also many formal situations, apart from examinations, where one is required to demonstrate ability to remember. If you must know the four basic assumptions upon which all valid tests are based (pp. 256-258), you will be assured if you can remember the four headings, or you may be assured if it takes less time to relearn the four headings and the accompanying explanatory material. The shorter relearning time is evidence of ability to retain and to reproduce the past and the present in order to meet the demands of the future. How much is retained can be determined by measures of recall and recognition. The savings method is also evidence of remembering, although it is not often used in the classroom as a measure of ability.

Recall

Recall is the ability to reproduce knowledge and information without external support. "Name the states that border on the Atlantic Ocean." This requires that the pupil recite the states from memory, from previous learning, without reminders from others, without a written list of names of the states, and without a map of the East Coast, that is, without any external cues. This is recall, a high level skill developed through learning. Using only the cues devised while learning, he must reproduce the knowledge. It is in one way the hardest test of memory, but in another way it is easier than being required to make judgments; e.g., "After you have recalled the names of seven historians, rank them in order of their contributions to history." The judgments involve value systems, and these vary from person to person; but the judgments in themselves are more difficult than recall, although recall is a high level skill.

Recall and Personal Development

Apart from the fact that recall is evidence of memory, a number of aspects of skill in recall shed light on personal development as a person learns and remembers; these in turn dictate the scores he may get on various kinds of tests. For instance, immediate recall is not as sensitive a measure as later recall or relearning. Studies of recall mirror the environment, the personal orientation to the demands made, and ability to respond. The studies which highlight development and personal orientation can be conveniently organized through stating the major proposition of each study, as follows:

(1) The associative clustering in recall highlights dependence on associations.

(2) The associations that are used more frequently are recalled more easily, as indicated by the relationship between word-frequency and recall.

(3) Personal orientation and approach to learning and remembering are evident in the changes and condensations of recall.

(4) Personal orientation and approach to learning and remembering are evident in recall under tension.

(5) Organization in a sufficient number of categories, enough but not too many, supports recall; broadly speaking, some organization, as compared with none or too little, supports all development.

The elaboration of these propositions backs up the statement that skill in recall is a personalized expression of full development. However, in documenting generalizations with the illustrations found in the studies, one is apt to divert attention from practical to theoretical considerations. When the teacher feels that the excursion into experimental design and theory is remote from the practical situation, he should feel free to turn directly to the next proposition or go on to the topic of recognition, p. 265.

(1) Associative clustering during recall highlights the dependence on associations [198]. A person who is asked to repeat the names of the states which border on the Atlantic Ocean tends to recall the names of neighboring states also. The closeness in the physical relationships of the states is apparent in these associations. Associative clustering is chiefly a function of reinforcement; that is, the more times associations have occurred together and been reinforced, the stronger the clusters are [52]. The clustering of associations facilitates recall, provided one can get started on the cluster. If you can remember any part of the four basic assumptions for valid test scores, you are likely to be able to recall some of the material that accompanied it.

(2) There is a relationship between word-frequency and recall; the more frequently words occur in speaking and writing vocabulary, the easier they are to learn and recall. Hall required 227 college students to recall as many words as possible from lists of 20 words of different

frequencies in the language, as shown in Figure XIX. According to the *Teacher's Word Book of 30,000 Words* [389], list A contained words which had a frequency count of one occurrence per million words; list B, 10 per million; list C, 30 per million; and list D, 50-100 per million words.

LIST A	LIST B	LIST C	LIST D
winsome	astound	upright	forward
outcrop	discard	immense	because
saddler	pastime	revenge	destroy
foolery	forlorn	chimney	special
bagpipe	esquire	earnest	against
timbale	pitiful	contact	weather
muffler	luggage	pasture	another
disport	implore	absence	example
angling	storage	majesty	problem
languor	haughty	scratch	quarter
laconic	freeman	confine	instead
diurnal	lowland	doorway	believe
cession	moisten	blanket	declare
swaddle	ecstasy	despite	outside
interim	chemist	missing	passage
redoubt	mariner	heavily	written
emulate	rapture	furnace	silence
missive	valiant	sparkle	morning
impiety	ghastly	violent	teacher
derange	cleanse	harness	attempt

FIGURE XIX

Word Lists by Frequency of Occurrence

Each word from one of the lists was exposed for five seconds, or a total of 100 seconds for each list, but the mechanical presentation extended this to 120 seconds.

A 30-second rest was allowed between each of four presentations, and the college students were given five minutes to write as many of the presented words as they could. Words which appeared with higher frequency in the language were recalled more easily [163, pp. 138-140].

(3) Personal orientation and approach to learning and remembering are evident in the changes and condensations which appear in recall. For purposes of discussion, it is as if people recalling items fall into two classes: the "changers" and the "condensers." When recall material exceeds verbatim memory span, the reproductions show changes or omissions or both, but if the passage is long enough, all subjects omit more than they change.

Gomulicki analyzed the results from 25 men and 25 women, with a median age of 30, but ranging from 18 to 70. They were read 37 passages in individual interviews. Each passage was read once with appropriate expression and at a normal rate. Immediately after, they were to repeat orally as much as they could recall, using the original words if possible, but reproducing all retained ideas as best they could. The results of 10 of the passages, eight narratives, and two descriptions, ranging from 18 to 86 words in length, were analyzed.

When verbatim recall was impossible, some of the subjects tended to change the content, while others tended to omit it, although the subjects were normally distributed with respect to all other measures obtainable by a word count of the reproductions. The two recall types, changers and condensers, were not grouped according to age, sex, or educational level, but they apparently differed in their approach to the memory task and their conception of what was required of them. The aim of the changers was to reproduce as much of the original material as they could, and they recalled more content in their own words than the condensers did. The aim of the condensers was to adhere to verbatim recall at whatever cost to the ideas. They recalled rapidly and with little hesitation the parts they felt confident about and dropped the rest, presumably for fear of introducing error. Their verbatim recall produced less than the changer's recall.

Others had previously obtained similar results. Binet found "describers," who gave detailed descriptions of separate items without attempting to relate them, and "observers," who were interested in the meaning of the whole and who recalled or guessed at details in the light of their interpretations. Bartlett described "visualizers," who relied mainly on visual images, their confidence (but not necessarily their accuracy) depending on the vividness of the images, and found "verbalizers" who classified and interrelated parts of the material functionally, and who were less concerned with accuracy than consistency in recall. Katona's dichotomy, based on the Gestalt theory of memory traces, divides the subjects in terms of reliance mainly on "individual traces" of discrete items, or on "structural traces" of organized idea-systems. Partridge distinguished a "reducing type" with key phrases extracted almost verbatim and only enough rewording to link bits together, and a "recasting type" that rearranges and rewords freely, preserving most of the original content, but expressing it in a new and much more compact way [145, pp. 387-400].

Gomulicki sought to integrate the differences between the two types of recallers. The changer's preference for changes and the condenser's for omissions meant that, when in doubt, the former would resort to guessing, but the latter would not. The guesses were seldom wide of the mark as to meaning and if the idea was recalled, the original wording was often the most natural way of expressing it. The condensers, besides the effect of their reluctant guesses, suffered from their striving for verbatim recall. They concentrated on individual words at the expense of content, grasping highlights but missing most of the subsidiary ideas. The condensers were atomistic, and the changers holistic; nevertheless, the condensers managed to reproduce nearly all the important material. The two types differed in aim and in relative efficiency of attaining it. The deviations were really synonymous expressions or rearrangements that left the meaning unaltered. Memory processes in general are selective and ensure that whatever is remembered includes the most important items from the point of view of each individual, and this was true of both the changers and the condensers.

(4) Personal orientation and approach to learning and remembering are evident in recall under tension. Recall under a kind of induced tension was consistently better than recall under no tension, which is in keeping with the concept of tension as a drive. The recall of paired adjectives was studied under:

> tension for learning, but no tension for recall;
> tension for learning and tension for recall;
> no tension for learning and no tension for recall;
> no tension for learning, but tension for recall.

Tension was induced by having the subjects grip a hand dynamometer (a device which measures strength of grip by squeezing) adjusted to one-third of each person's maximum squeeze. The tension of squeezing this instrument brought forth ready responses, but did not alter habit strength. Whether the *learning* took place under tension or not, recall was no different, provided enough time was allowed for relaxation. *Recall* under tension was consistently better than recall under no tension [49, pp. 418-422]. However, severe emotional distress reduces recall [218]. The tension of squeezing a hand dynamometer does not arouse much emotion, let alone emotional distress. The tension of having something to do during recall apparently made it easier to recall. This may not apply to all instances of recall, but at least in some cases a slight tension aids performance.

(5) Organizing material into some categories, but not too many, is an aid to recall; broadly speaking, some organization, as compared with none or too little, supports all development. Recall is aided if the learner establishes enough, but not too many, categories. Such classification is important in processing information because it permits the organization of remembering. Obviously, individual differences in developed ability dictate that different people can carry different numbers of ideas; the question is how systematic should the approach be. One benefits most from carrying a pattern of the logical interconnections to the situation in which recall is needed. Beginning psychology students did significantly better on tests of recall after they had classified the names of 24 famous people into six categories, rather than into only two or three categories [264]. Too many categories only confuse recall, while too few categories, such as three or four, usually have sublists attached to them. Too many or too few categories inhibit recall, even when a person is dealing with content which is highly meaningful to him. Meaningfulness usually facilitates recall through the simplicity of comprehension, but comprehension does not develop best with very few or very many categories. Recall is aided if the material is sufficiently organized, and all development is supported by an adequate but not overly organized or constrictively rigid structure.

To recapitulate the propositions from the studies, recall is one evidence of memory. It is the ability to produce knowledge and information without external cues, a high-level skill, developed as one learns. Associative clusters develop in memory, so that one item is often sufficient to cue the recall of the whole cluster. Recall is facilitated if the material is couched in familiar, oft-repeated words. People either change or condense content when recalling, but whether they are changers or condensers, they remember what they consider most impotrant. Slight tensions facilitate recall, but stronger tensions often hinder it. Recall is aided when material is sufficiently organized.

Recognition

Recognition is identification, usually in the absence of recall. A person often needs only to recognize correct or preferred items from material which is recalled for him. If he can recall the material, recognition is superfluous, but it is much easier. "From a list of the names of the states, select those which border on the Atlantic Ocean." Such recognition is evidence of memory.

Recognition is quite simple where noticeable differences exist; but slight differences, such as those between shades of a color, or between the qualities of intelligence in the gifted and nongifted, make recognition a measure of keen discrimination. For instance, which of the following deals with the assignment of a cause or reason? *Ethnology, entomology, etymology, etiology,* or *ecology?* Slight variations like these tax the capacities of memory as compared with the differences between *solenoid, hydramatic,* and *generator.* Even obscure and little used differences, such as those between rare or strange words, are not as demanding as small variations. The more similar items are, the more exacting a measure of retention recognition becomes. Also, the more new stimuli introduced into a test of recognition the more difficult the tests become [123]. Even so, recognition is easier than being required to make judgments. A judgment, such as whether one essay is better than another, is more difficult than sizable differences, and usually more difficult than slight ones.

Recognition and recall are not fundamentally distinct evidences of remembering, because they respond to similar kinds of assistance and interference. Both are more accurate when verbalization has been used in the learning process [222]. If a person either says (recites for himself or others) or writes the material while learning, recognition and recall are more accurate than if this practice has not been done. Unlearning occurs in both because of the competition and interference of other responses—particularly retroactive inhibition [302]. The competition between responses means that some occur, but others are inhibited. Those which are inhibited are even less likely to be made in subsequent similar situations and so are unlearned. The workings of retroactive inhibition as interference are explained on pp. 143-147.

Recall requires more practice than does recognition, because it is a higher level skill, and it is a more sensitive measure of previous knowledge [310]. Memories which are not strong enough for recall are susceptible to recognition. "From lists of names of famous people, select the 12 who are famous for their explorations." "From lists of assumptions, select the four which are basic to valid tests." Recognition does not require the degree of skill involved in recalling the 12 people or the four basic assumptions. Recall requires more ability and needs more preparation time.

The Savings Method

The savings method is the difference in time and effort required for relearning as compared with the original learning. It indicates the residue left from prior practice. Material is recognized or recalled with greater ease and requires less time the second, third, and fourth time that it is relearned. This saving in time and effort enables a person to prepare quantities of material for recognition and recall when he must demonstrate what he knows, as on comprehensive examinations which test a wide range of content. If each relearning required as much time and effort as the initial learning, few persons would have the stamina to meet the requirements of extensive recall and recognition. The savings are evidence of the effectiveness of learning.

In the Classroom

In the classroom the teacher uses tests of recall and recognition to:

> stimulate students,
> establish and maintain quality,
> point up the major issues,
> diagnose,
> reteach.

(1) Tests can be used to stimulate students. They serve as an immediate objective, namely, can the student answer these questions now? (2) In all cases, the quality of the class work is directly affected by the quality of the demands made. If, through tests, explicit, specific, and demanding performances are required, classes

of students respond with better performances than if casual and broadly generalized, easy performances are accepted. (3) Tests can be used to point up the major issues of subject matter. (4) They can also be used as diagnostic devices, although it is not always necessary for the teacher to test formally in order to determine what the student does not know. If diagnostic tests are used, there is an obligation to do the remedial work indicated. (5) Tests may be used as a teaching device. The marked paper provides the evidence for, and acts as a guide to the explicit, specific reteaching which will help the student. Whether used as stimulation, as an immediate objective, as a quality indicator, as a device to impress major issues, as a diagnostic device, or as a teaching device, tests are a fruitful educational aid to the classroom teacher.

Tests used in classrooms are psychometric rather than projective. They measure part of the psyche and yield a score. The score should be interpreted as follows: On this test on this day, the student scored this well. Frequently a single test score is used to imply that the student can do no better than this. Even after allowing for some variability in human performance from day to day, no test score should be overinterpreted. A score is the level of performance on a particular item, and efforts to draw conclusions which extend this interpretation are dubious.

Projective tests are those in which a person reveals himself through the manner and quality by which he handles stimulus materials. He projects himself whether he intends to or not, and qualitative judgments can be made about the projection. Persons reveal themselves in everything they do, and the differences that show up provide a basis for judgments, not for the score of the psychometrist.

Almost all human behavior can be classified in an ordered way to provide a series of standardized judgments of projection. One's choice of clothing, hair style, handwriting, placement of writing on a piece of paper, and color preferences could be arranged to provide valid and reliable judgments of some aspect of personality. The fact that reactions to pictures and inkblots are the best standardized techniques for judging projection should not divert attention from the full range of revelations of personality. The work has not yet been done to standardize judgments of many of these. The present state of development of projective techniques does not affect the classroom teacher to any great degree, since he uses the scores from his psychometric devices rather than the judgments from projective tests.

The classroom teacher uses group tests. These are inexpensive, since many pupils can be tested at once, and the cost of the materials and the cost in time per pupil are low. The teacher does not need a high degree of skill or much training in order to administer these. All that is needed is an understanding of the necessity for giving the tests in a uniform manner to all persons in the comparison group, and the necessity for uniform scoring. Unfortunately, the results obtained from group-test administrations are often as meaningless as they are inexpensive. The conclusion to be drawn is that on this test, on this day, the student did this well. Group testing does not permit speculation as to whether the score for a person is his best possible score, a minimum score, or an average score. Group testing yields only a "naked" score for each member of the group tested.

Individual tests are resorted to when the score needs to be clothed with understanding. When estimates are required as to how well the student can perform, the degree of stress involved in a performance, and variability in performances on various kinds of items, one person is tested at a time with tests which are more carefully constructed than group examinations. Individual tests are expensive, since only one pupil at a time can be dealt with, and only a highly trained examiner can administer the test. Individual tests yield scores plus the clinical insight of the tester, but the results are no better than the skill of the tester.

Standardized Tests

Some classroom tests are standardized. This means that such a test has been tried on people like those on whom the teacher plans to use it. It is to be given in a stated way, scored in a certain way, and then the scores can be compared with the established norms.

"Norms" are statements of the achievement of a standardization group. "Other tenth-graders did this well." Norms may be given in terms of grade scores, e.g., 10.4—the fourth month of the tenth grade; or in terms of age scores, e.g., 15.4 — 15 years four months; or in terms of percentiles or deciles. It is thus possible to compare the level of performance of a class or an individual with that of other persons who have taken this test. Whether the comparison is in terms of scores, or the number of years the person has lived, or his number of years of schooling, it is only valid if the norm population and the persons now being tested are of the same "universe." The scores of Iowa children provide a questionable basis of comparison for California or New York City children.

The classroom teacher uses standardized group tests of intelligence and achievement. The nature of intelligence, and the manner of testing it, would require chapters rather than paragraphs of explanation and discussion, and will not be treated here. Those who are interested may consult any good text on measurement, such as Anastasi [13, pp. 187-325].

The classroom teacher uses group tests of achievement. These are group tests, because the teacher usually has neither the training nor the time necessary to administer individual ones. The tests are standardized, that is, they are to be given and marked in a specified way so that comparisons of performance with others of like background are possible. Such standardized achievement tests are widely used as comparative measures of performance in school subjects.

Achievement tests are of three kinds: the survey or general type, the diagnostic, and the instructional or practice type.

The survey or general achievement test covers general knowledge from one or several school subjects. There is not enough work on any one topic to provide a diagnosis of difficulties. This type is primarily useful to supervisors who wish to compare general levels of achievement within a class or between classes, or between schools or between school systems.

The diagnostic achievement test is detailed and specific. It tests a limited area of knowledge and is constructed to point up exactly what the student knows and does not know, such as whether he knows how to "carry" a number when multiplying, or can handle multipliers containing a zero. This kind of test is most useful to the clasroom teacher, but there is little object in using it unless there is time for the remedial work indicated. Frequently the teacher is aware of the deficiencies in subject matter and does not need the diagnostic test to direct his efforts in remedial work.

The instructional or practice type of achievement test is found in work books or at the end of a chapter in a text. No norms are provided. Instead, the directions usually suggest that if the student completes a given number of questions satisfactorily, his command of the content is sufficient, while performances below this level require relearning and practice. The instructional achievement test is of value chiefly to the student.

Teacher-Made Tests

Most classroom tests are constructed by the teacher and may be broadly classified into essay and objective types. The fullest benefit accrues to the student from the use of both kinds.

Essay examinations are of two types: those which require simple reproduction of the material taught (but in essay form), and those which are thought-provoking. The latter require the student to change the set or context of the material at the time of the examination. For instance, the teacher knows that all tests are governed by four fundamental assumptions (pp. 256-258), and from experience he knows of possible ways to invalidate test scores. He comes to the examination with prepared information regarding tests, and at the time of the test is required to reorganize the knowledge and use his understanding to suggest the relative influence of each of the four fundamental assumptions in invalidating scores in individual test administrations. An essay problem which requires a considerable change of set at the time of the examination is a thought-provoking one.

Such essays reward initiative and originality. Ability to write English clearly is revealed. The essay is a projection of the self, and may give insight into methods of work, personality, and depth and breadth of subject matter. Essay-type questions are relatively easy to devise and administer, but they also have major disadvantages which must be considered.

The essay test is time-consuming to write and score, and the scoring is hopelessly unreliable unless the teacher possesses great skill in devising and using scoring criteria. This type of test overweights knowledge of English and writing ability. Further, the sample of knowledge measured is quite limited, since so few topics can be covered. Apart from the unreliable marking, the inadequacy of the sample of knowledge tends to invalidate the essay test as a measure.

Because of these limitations, teachers also need to use objective tests. The name is somewhat misleading, since they are often only partially objective. After the questions have been constructed and the key to the best answers has been devised, the marking itself is simple and straightforward. Thus, every so-called objective test is heavily loaded with personal interpretations, but at least everyone is marked in the same way with respect to these interpretations. Although this is a limitation of this type of test, it is preferable to the highly unreliable scoring of the essay test wherein 10 people may mark an essay differently, and the same 10 people may mark the same essay differently three months later. The essay test is limited in the sample of knowledge that it measures; but the same problem arises with the objective test, unless the questions are distributed representatively throughout the knowledge to be measured. Further, the questions on an objective test need to be carefully worded. If they are so stated as to measure the ability to read rather than the knowledge gained, the test is invalid. The usefulness of essay tests is limited, but objective tests are not free from a number of pitfalls in construction.

The types of questions usually called objective are: simple recall, agree-disagree, multiple choice, completion, matching, and analogies. These may be illustrated as follows:

Simple recall: What is the formula for the circumference of a circle? Which state is bordered by eight other states?

Multiple choice: Select the letter which represents the best answer: 3¼ divided by 2¼ is:

(A) 1 4/9 (B) 1 3/4 (C) 1 3/10 (D) 1 2/5

Completion: The governor of your state is . . . . ?

Matching:

———— 3 times 4	(A) 92.47
———— 24½ minus 13 5/8	(B) 10 3/8
———— 37 divided by 4	(C) 12.00
———— 13¼ times 7 1/8	(D) none of these choices
———— 102.46 minus 11.28	

Analogies: A circle is to a square as an oval is to . . . .?

All of the advantages of essay tests can be listed as disadvantages of objective tests. The latter are difficult and time-consuming to construct, but they do have advantages. Assuming that they are well-constructed, they sample broadly from the knowledge to be measured. The grading is easy, almost mechanical. The discrimination of best answers is like life situations, wherein few things are unequivocally right or wrong. Handwriting and ability to write English do not influence the score, but the ability to read English does. Further, specific errors in knowledge can be corrected, because each objective question is pointed at specific information.

The greatest benefit accrues to the learner when the teacher uses both essay-type and objective-type questions and is aware of the obvious invalidations which destroy each type as a measure of ability.

Low Interrelationships

The interrelationships between measures of school learning are low [391]. Apart from the fact that few students do equally well with all subjects, measured performances in various school subjects do not agree with each other. The relationships among selected language abilities have been found to be highest (a correlation of .40 to .70 [190]). Students have good subjects and poor subjects, but the low-measured interrelationships between subjects raise questions as to the value of test results as predictors of scores in other subjects and of future test scores in the same subject.

Part of the lack of agreement between test scores can be explained by the variable responses which an individual often gives when asked the same questions a few days or weeks apart. Several reasons have been advanced for this variance, such as, variability of the organic processes, the psychosomatic aspects of performance, and the absence of persistence of character [120]. Regardless of the cause of intra-individual response-variability, one end product is lack of agreement between test scores.

Dowd found that whatever factors operated to depress college achievement also operated before the student entered college [105]. The Dowd study raises the whole question of underachievement, which is a subject of great current interest, but underachievement should not divert attention from the fact that the relationships between measures of school learning are low (for whatever reasons). Whenever one attempts to use test scores to predict, he is on thin ice. As for using test scores to indicate that a student can do certain school work—"You have shown that you can do it by your marks in geography, history, and English" —the teacher would be better off spending time and energy teaching the student instead of exhorting him to work harder.

Evaluation

The scores from tests leave much to be desired. How should they be treated as compared with the personal opinions from oral quizzes, ratings, and individual interviews, and how can the weighting of opinions and tests assist us? The desire for reliable and accurate evaluations often outweighs the desire for self-enhancement.

Oral Quiz

Classroom teachers use oral quizzes for evaluation more than any other device; this is unfortunate because the oral quiz, while sometimes a stimulating teaching device, is too unreliable for the evaluation of knowledge. Each student can only be asked a few questions in any class hour, and the questions asked cannot possibly be representative of either the body of knowledge to be evaluated or of the student's command of that knowledge. In spite of the unreliable sampling evident in this recitation technique, teachers still use it more than other kinds of evaluation.

Rating

Rating is a judgment technique, particularly where opinions are to be collected regarding people. Supervisors are asked to pool their opinions on personnel through selecting a number on a scale which indicates a degree of a given characteristic. Teachers are required to rate their students with respect to certain attributes. The ratings are then entered on a cumulative record, for current and future use. Rating is a convenient way of pooling opinions, rather than relying on meetings and discussions between the evaluators.

The nature of rating scales used influences their effectiveness. The breadth of category to be rated is a major determiner of the effectiveness of rating. If a person is asked to rate personality, he will be faced with a far different task than if he is required to rate more limited characteristics such as honesty, attitude toward others, attitude toward authority, appropriateness of dress, appearance, and speech. One may be asked to rate academic effort in general, or some specific aspect of it, such as study habits, class attitude, punctuality, and attention to detail. "Doing as well as can be expected for this child" is a general rating which is not nearly as helpful as specific ratings which refer to reading, spelling, and speech. An over-all rating may be asked for after a number of judgments on narrower categories have been made, but ratings on more limited and better defined characteristics are more valid and more reliable, and therefore more effective.

A rating scale is most meaningful if a sufficient number of steps are included, usually from five to 10 steps. As few as three steps limits the rater to high, medium, and low. As many as 15 steps are confusing, and the middle steps represent such slight degrees of difference as to be meaningless. The steps of a good scale are not too diversified, and each characteristic is accompanied by verbal descriptions suggestive of each level in the scale. A scale of one, two, three, four, and five for judging conduct is not as good as a scale which reads:

One - poor, two - fair, three - good, four - very good, five - excellent. More descriptive material can be included, but often does not enhance the definitiveness of the scale, and may confuse the choices. It is best to make the word descriptions as full as possible, without sacrificing the clarity of carefully-chosen one-word descriptions.

The ability to judge people is based on appropriate norms, chiefly arising from the similarity of background of the judge and the subject. This ability is based on general and social intelligence, on an intuitive judging factor, and especially on motivation (a strong desire to make accurate judgments) [381]. Improvement in the ability to judge follows from the opportunity both to voice one's prejudices and feelings, and to consider one's contribution objectively, so that here, as elsewhere, doing leads to development.

The Individual Interview

The most fruitful device for evaluation is the individual interview. It is friendly, private, and the person being evaluated need not be made to feel insecure if the interviewer is skillful. It is expensive in terms of time, and it is valid and reliable only according to the skill of the interviewer. The personal adjustment of the individual at the time is also a factor which disturbs validity and reliability, but this may be compensated for through the use of several interviews. Ratings and test scores supported by interviews provide for the most adequate evaluation of an individual.

Weighting

The crux of all evaluation is weighting, that is, what values are to be assigned to test scores, the results of oral quizzes, ratings, and individual interviews. Evaluations will be superior if they are based on more than one approach and on more than one administration. More basic than the specific techniques, is the philosophy; that is, what is of value? For the classroom, this question can be answered as it was in the introduction to this chapter, namely, the important thing is to inform the student of progress toward his goals. To this end, it is not possible to weight any one of the techniques as being more suitable, except as it is both valid and reliable.

Tests, although frequently reliable, must be examined carefully for evidence of their validity.

Oral quizzes are known to be quite unreliable.

Ratings are also of questionable reliability.

The individual interview yields evaluations which are as good as the competence of the person who conducts the interview.

A suggestion for pooling weights and evaluations is offered here (it is desirable to combine weighted test scores and evaluations in keeping with individual and group objectives):

Assign one weight to each of several (four or more) tests, one weight to a rating or ratings, and two weights to the opinion from an individual interview.

Evaluations tend to be superior if based on more than one judgment, but just combining test scores, interview results, and ratings, may only pool ignorance. Evaluations are superior when they are verifiable through observable behavior. Although evaluative judgments are usually treated as confidential, their adequacy can usually be verified if the evaluator can present and explain his opinions to the person he is evaluating without personal embarrassment.

Summary: The Measurement and Evaluation of Learning

The purpose of measurement in the classroom is to inform the student and the teacher of progress toward goals. To this end, valid and reliable tests are sought. Each test must meet the requirements of the four basic assumptions, namely, equivalence of opportunity in the culture, adequate motivation, standardized procedures, and adequacy in scoring and interpretation.

The performance of the student is measured through his ability to recall, recognize, and reorganize content on psychometric rather than projective tests, and on group rather than individual tests. Standardized tests are used to compare performances with norms and to diagnose difficulties, but the standardized test plays a limited role in the classroom compared with the essay and objective tests constructed by the teacher.

When a teacher attempts to evaluate the results of tests and to combine the evaluations with ratings and opinions from interviews, it is obvious that he is dealing with estimates rather than firm facts. Even the best efforts to evaluate are not foolproof predictors of the future performance of an individual.

references

1. ABORN, M. "The influence of experimentally induced failure on the retention of material acquired through set and incidental learning." *J. exp. Psychol.*, **45**, 225-231 (1953).

2. ABORN, M., & RUBENSTEIN, H. "Information theory and immediate recall." *J. exp. Psychol.*, **44**, 260-266 (1952).

3. ADAMS, D. R. "Age, race, and responsiveness of level of aspiration to success and failure." *Psychol. Bull.*, **36**, 573, Abstract (1939).

4. ADAMS, J. A. "Multiple versus single problem training in human problem solving." *J. exp. Psychol.*, **48**, 15-18 (1954).

5. ADAMS, J. A., & REYNOLDS, B. "Effect of shift in distribution of practice conditions following interpolated rest." *J. exp. Psychol.*, **47**, 32-36 (1954).

6. ADAMS, PAULINE, & ADAMS, J. K. "Training in confidence-judgments." *Amer. J. Psychol.*, **71**, 747-751 (1958).

7. ADAMSON, R. "Inhibitory set in problem solving as related to reinforcement learning." *J. exp. Psychol.*, **58**, 280-282, October 1959.

8. ADELMAN, H. M., & MAATSCH, J. L. "Resistance to extinction as a function of the type of response elicited by frustration." *J. exp. Psychol.*, **50**, 60-65 (1955).

9. ADLER, D. L. "Estes' analysis of Lewin." *Contemp. Psychol.*, **1**, (1), 8-9 (1956).

10. ALLPORT, F. H. "The influence of the group upon association and thought." *J. exp. Psychol.*, **30**, 159-182 (1920).

11. AMMONS, R. B., AMMONS, CAROL H., & MORGAN, R. L. "Movement analysis of the performance of a simple perceptual-motor task under various conditions." *USAF WADC Tech. Rep.*, No. 54-36 (1954).

12. AMSEL, A., & WARD, J. S. "Motivational properties of frustration: II. Frustration drive stimulus and frustration reduction in selective learning." *J. exp. Psychol.*, **48**, 37-47 (1954).

13. ANASTASI, ANNE. *Psychological testing.* (2nd ed.) New York: Macmillan (1961).

14. ANDERSON, SCARVIA B., & ROSS, S. "Memory for items in a matrix." *Amer. J. Psychol.*, **68**, 595-604 (1955).

15. ARCHER, E. J. "Postrest performance in motor learning as a function of prerest degree of distribution of practice." *J. exp. Psychol.*, **47**, 47-51 (1954).

16. ARCHER, E. J., BOURNE, L. E., JR., & BROWN, F. G. "Concept identification as a function of irrelevant information and instructions." *J. exp. Psychol.*, **49**, 153-164 (1955).

17. ARCHER, E. J., & UNDERWOOD, B. J. "Retroactive inhibition of verbal associations as a multiple function of temporal point of interpolation and degree of interpolated learning." *J. exp. Psychol.*, **42**, 283-290 (1951).

18. ARNOLD, W. J. "Simple reaction chains and their integration: IV. Homogeneous chaining with serial reinforcement." *J. comp. physiol. Psychol.*, **44**, 276-282 (1951).

19. ATKINSON, J. W. (Ed.) *Motives in fantasy, action and society: A method of assessment and study.* Princeton, N. J.: Van Nostrand (1958).

20. ATWATER, S. K. "Proactive inhibition and associative facilitation as affected by degree of prior learning." *J. exp. Psychol.*, **46**, 400-404 (1953).

21. AUBLE, D., & MECH, E. V. "Quantitative studies of verbal reinforcement in classroom situations: I. Differential reinforcement related to the frequency of error and correct responses." *J. exp. Psychol.*, **35**, 307-312 (1953).

22. AUSUBEL, D. P., SCHIFF, H. M., & ZELENY, MARJORIE P. " 'Real-life' measures of academic and vocational aspiration in adolescents: Re-

lation to laboratory measures and to adjustment." *Child Develpm.*, **35**, 307-312 (1953).

23. AXELROD, J. "Group dynamics, non-directive therapy and college teaching." *J. higher Educ.*, **26**, 200-207 (1955).

24. BABRICK, H. P. "Incidental learning at five stages of intentional learning." *J. exp. Psychol.*, **54**, 259-261 (1957).

25. BAGGALEY, A. R. "Concept formation and its relation to cognitive variables." *J. gen. Psychol.*, **52**, 297-306 (1955).

26. BARCH, A. M. "The effect of initial massing of practice on the transfer task in a proactive interference situation." *Proc. Iowa Acad. Sci.*, **59**, 353-358 (1952).

27. BARNETT, G. J., HANDELMAN, I., STEWART, L. H., & SUPER, D. E. "The occupational level scale as a measure of drive." *Psychol. Monogr.*, **66**, No. 10, Whole No. 342 (1952).

28. BARNLUND, D. C. "A comparative study of individual, majority and group judgment." *J. abnorm. soc. Psychol.*, **58**, 55-60 (1959).

29. BARTLETT, F. C. "Incentives." *Brit. J. Psychol.*, **41**, 122-128 (1950).

30. BARTLETT, F. C. *Remembering: A study in experimental and social psychology.* Cambridge, England: The University Press (1932).

31. BASTIN, E. W., & GREEN, J. M. "Some experiments in prerecognition." *J. Parapsychol.*, **17**, 137-143 (1953).

32. BATTIG, W. F. "Transfer from verbal pretraining to motor performance as a function of motor task complexity." *J. exp. Psychol.*, **52**, 371-378 (1956).

33. BAYTON, J. A., & WHYTE, E. "Personality dynamics during success-failure sequences." *J. abnorm. soc. Psychol.*, **45**, 583-591 (1950).

34. BEACH, F. A. "Open the door, Richard." *Nat. Hist.*, **56**, 326-332 (1947).

35. BECKER, H. "Empathy, sympathy, and Scheler." *Int. J. Sociometry*, **1**, 15-22 (1956).

36. BELMONT, L., & BIRCH, H. G. "Re-individualizing the repression hypothesis." *J. abnorm. soc. Psychol.*, **46**, 226-235 (1951).

37. BENDIG, A. W. "The effect of reinforcement on the alternation of guesses." *J. exp. Psychol.*, **41**, 105-107 (1951).

38. BENNETT, W. F., FITTS, P. M., & NOBLE, M. "The learning of sequential dependencies." *J. exp. Psychol.*, **48**, 303-312 (1954).

39. BENSCHETER, REBA P., & CHARLES, D. C. "Retention of classroom and television learning." *J. appl. Psychol.*, **41**, 253-256 (1957).

40. BEVINGTON, W. G. "Effect of age at time of entrance into Grade 1 on subsequent achievement." *Alberta J. educ. Res.,* **4,** 6-16 (1958).

41. BIJOU, S. W. "Patterns of reinforcement and resistance to extinction in young children." *Child Develpm.,* **28,** 47-54 (1957).

42. BILODEAU, E. A. "Speed of acquiring simple motor responses as a function of systematic transformations of knowledge of results." *USAF Hum. Res. Cent., Res. Bull.,* No. 52-53 (1952).

43. BINDRA, D. *Motivation: A systematic reinterpretation.* New York: Ronald (1959).

44. BIRCH, H. G., & BITTERMAN, M. E. "Sensory integration and cognitive theory." *Psychol. Rev.,* **58,** 355-361 (1951).

45. BIRCH, H. G., & KORN, S. J. "Place-learning, cognitive maps, and parsimony." *J. gen. Psychol.,* **58,** 17-35 (1958).

46. BLAKE, E., JR., & AUSUBEL, D. P. "Proactive inhibition in the forgetting of meaningful school materials." *J. educ. Res.,* **52,** 145-149 (1958).

47. BLATZ, W. E. "Competition." *Bull. Inst. Child Stud.,* Toronto, **17,** (1), 1-2 (1955).

48. BLAU, A. A. "A unitary hypothesis of emotion: I. Anxiety, emotions of displeasure, and affective disorders." *Psychoanal. Quart.,* **24,** 75-102 (1955).

49. BOURNE, L. E. "An evaluation of the effect of induced tension on performance." *J. exp. Psychol.,* **49,** 418-422 (1955).

50. BOUSFIELD, W. A., & COHEN, B. H. "The occurrence of clustering in recall of randomly arranged words of different frequencies-of-usage." *J. gen. Psychol.,* **52,** 83-95 (1955).

51. BOYD, G. F. "The levels of aspiration of white and Negro children in a non-segregated elementary school." *J. soc. Psychol.,* **36,** 191-196. (1952).

52. BRAND, H. "A study of temporal changes in the organization of retention." *J. gen. Psychol.,* **54,** 243-254 (1956).

53. BRAUN, H. W., & BENDIG, A. W. "Effect of addition of irrelevant verbal cues on perceptual-motor learning." *J. exp. Psychol.,* **54,** 105-108 (1957).

54. BRIGGS, G. E., & WATERS, L. K. "Training and transfer as a function of component interaction." *J. exp. Psychol.,* **56,** 492-500 (1958).

55. BROWN, J. S. "Problems presented by the concept of acquired drives." In J. S. Brown, et al, *Current theory and research in motivation:* A symposium. Lincoln: Univer. Nebraska Press, pp. 1-19 (1953).

56. BRUNER, E. M., & ROTTER, J. B. "A level of aspiration study among the Ramah Navaho." *J. Pers.*, **21**, 375-385 (1953).

57. BRUNER, J. S., GOODNOW, JACQUELINE J., & AUSTIN, G. A. *A Study of Thinking*. New York: Wiley (1956).

58. BRUNOT, HENRIETTE. *Le rire sur les planches 1952* (Laughter on the stage in 1952). *Psyché*, **7**, 675-683 (1952).

59. BURT, C. "The structure of the mind: A review of the results of factor analysis. II." *Brit. J. Educ. Psychol.*, **19**, 176-199 (1949).

60. BUSWELL, C. T. "Solving problems in arithmetic." *Education*, **79**, 287-290 (1959).

61. CALLANTINE, MARY F., & WARREN, J. M. "Learning sets in human concept formation." *Psychol. Rep.*, **1**, 363-367 (1955).

62. CALVIN, A. D., HOFFMAN, F. K., & HARDEN, E. L. "The effect of intelligence and social atmosphere on group problem behavior." *J. soc. Psychol.*, **46**, 61-74 (1957).

63. CANTOR, G. N. "Effects of three types of pretraining on discrimination learning in preschool children." *J. exp. Psychol.*, **49**, 339-342 (1955).

64. CANTOR, JOAN H. "Amount of pretraining as a factor in stimulus pre-differentiation and performance set." *J. exp. Psychol.*, **50**, 180-194 (1955).

65. CANTOR, N. "Function and focus in the learning process." *J. educ. Res.*, **45**, 225-231 (1951).

66. CAPALDI, E. J. "The effect of different amounts of alternating partial reinforcement on resistance to extinction." *Amer. J. Psychol.*, **70**, 451-452 (1957).

67. CARON, A. J., & WALLACH, M. A. "Recall of interrupted tasks under stress: A phenomenon of memory or of learning?" *J. abnorm. soc. Psychol.*, **55**, 372-381 (1957).

68. CASSEL, R. N. "The relationship of certain factors to the level of aspiration and social distance for forty-four Air Force prisoners." *J. crim. Law Criminol.*, **44**, 604-610 (1954).

69. CASSEL, R. N., & SAUGSTAD, R. G. "Level of aspiration and sociometric distance." *Sociometry*, **15**, 319-325 (1952).

70. CASTANEDA, A., & LIPSITT, L. P. "Relation of stress and differential position habits to performance in motor learning." *J. exp. Psychol.*, **57**, 25-30 (1959).

71. CASTANEDA, A., & PALERMO, D. S. "Psychomotor performance as a function of amount of training and stress." *J. exp. Psychol.*, **50**, 175-179 (1955).

72. CATTELL, R. B., & WINDER, A. E. "Structural rigidity in relation to learning theory and clinical psychology." *Psychol. Rev.*, **59**, 23-29 (1952).

73. CHANCE, JUNE E. "Generalization of expectancies among functionally related behaviors." *J. Pers.*, **27**, 228-238, June 1959.

74. CHAPMAN, D. W., & VOLKMANN, J. A. "A social determinant of the level of aspiration." *J. abnorm. soc. Psychol.*, **34**, 225-238 (1939).

75. CHAPMAN, R. S. "Achievement and under-achievement in English language ten in an Alberta composite high school." *Alberta J. educ. Res.*, **5**, 41-49 (1959).

76. CHILD, I. L., & WHITING, J. W. M. "Determinants of level of aspiration: evidence from everyday life." *J. abnorm. soc. Psychol.*, **44**, 303-314 (1949).

77. CHODORKOFF, B. "Self-perception, perceptual defense, and adjustment." *J. abnorm. soc. Psychol.*, **49**, 508-512 (1954).

78. CHRISTIE, R. "The role of drive discrimination in learning under irrelevant motivation." *J. exp. Psychol.*, **42**, 13-19 (1951).

79. COHEN, A. P., STOTLAND E., & WOLFE, D. M. "An experimental investigation of the need for cognition." *J. abnorm. soc. Psychol.*, **51**, 291-294 (1955).

80. COHEN, J. "The concept of goal gradients: A review of its present status." *J. gen. Psychol.*, **49**, 303-308 (1953).

81. COHEN, L. D. "Level-of-aspiration behavior and feelings of adequacy and self-acceptance." *J. abnorm. soc. Psychol.*, **49**, 84-86 (1954).

82. COLE, L. E. *Human behavior.* New York: Harcourt, Brace & World (1953).

83. COMBS, A. W. "A phenomenological approach to adjustment theory." *J. abnorm. soc. Psychol.*, **44**, 29-35 (1949).

84. COMBS, A. W. "Seeing is behaving." *Educ. Leadership,* **16**, 21-26 (1958).

85. COMBS, A. W., & SNYGG, D. *Individual behavior: A perceptual approach to behavior.* (rev. ed.) New York: Harper (1959).

86. CONWELL, H. R., & AMMONS, R. B. "Joint effects of cyclical practice and rest in rotary pursuit." *J. Psychol.*, **31**, 137-146 (1951).

87. COOK, RUTH C. "Evaluation of two methods of teaching spelling." *Elem. sch. J.*, **7**, 111-118 (1957).

88. COON, A. M. "Brain-storming: A creative problem-solving technique." *J. Communication*, **58**, 21-27 (1957).

89. CRAIG, W. J. "Preliminary report of an experiment in code-typing." *Mot. Skills Res. Exch.*, **2**, 8-10 (1950).

90. CRONBACH, L. J. *Educational psychology.* New York: Harcourt, Brace & World (1954).

91. DALE, E., & CHALL, JEANNE S. "Developing readable materials." *Natl. Soc. Stud. Educ.*, 55th Yearbook, Univer. Chicago Press, pp. 218-250 (1946).

92. DAS, J. P. "Effect of a completely dissimilar interpolated learning on 'retroactive inhibition.'" *Indian J. Psychol.*, **29**, 161-167 (1954).

93. DAVIDSON, W. Z., ANDREWS, T. G., & ROSS, S. "Effects of stress and anxiety on continuous high-speed color naming." *J. exp. Psychol.*, **52**, 13-17 (1956).

94. DEESE, J. "The extinction of a discrimination without performance of the choice response." *J. comp. physiol. Psychol.*, **44**, 362-366 (1951).

95. DEESE, J. *The psychology of learning.* (2nd ed.) New York: McGraw-Hill (1958).

96. DEESE, J., & KAUFMAN, R. A. "Serial effects in recall of unorganized and sequentially organized verbal material." *J. exp. Psychol.*, **54**, 180-187 (1957).

97. DEESE, J., & KRESSE, F. H. "An experimental analysis of the errors in rote serial learning." *J. exp. Psychol.*, **44**, 199-202 (1952).

98. DEMONTMOLLIN, G., & PERLMUTTER, H. V. "*Apprendre en groupe. Une expérience de psychologie sociale* (Learning in a group: A social psychology experiment)." *Enfance*, **4**, 359-376 (1951).

99. DEWEY, J. *How we think.* Boston: Heath (1910).

100. DIETZE, D. "The facilitating effect of words on discrimination and generalization." *J. exp. Psychol.*, **50**, 255-260 (1955).

101. DINNER, JUDITH E., & DUNCAN, C. P. "Warm-up in retention as a function of degree of verbal learning." *J. exp. Psychol.*, **57**, 257-261 (1959).

102. DIVESTA, F., & BLAKE, KATHRYN. "The effects of instrumental 'sets' on learning and transfer." *Amer. J. Psychol.*, **72**, 57-67 (1959).

103. DORSEY, J. M. "Morale." *Amer. Imago.*, **10**, 346-373 (1953).

104. DOCKRELL, W. B. "The relationship between socio-economic status, intelligence and attainment in some Scottish primary schools." *Alberta J. educ. Res.*, **5**, 16-22 (1959).

105. DOWD, R. J. "Underachieving students of high capacity." *J. higher Educ.*, **23**, 327-330 (1952).

106. DUNCAN, C. P. "The action of various after-effects on response repetition." *J. exp. Psychol.*, **40**, 380-389 (1950).

107. DUNCAN, C. P. "Transfer in motor learning as a function of degree of first-task learning and inter-task similarity." *J. exp. Psychol.*, **45**, 1-11 (1953).

108. DUNCAN, C. P., & UNDERWOOD, B. J. "Retention of transfer in motor learning after twenty-four hours and after fourteen months." *J. exp. Psychol.*, **46**, 445-452 (1953).

109. DUNCAN, C. P., & UNDERWOOD, B. J. "Transfer of training after five days of practice with one task or with varied tasks." *USAF WADC Tech. Rep.*, No. 54-533 (1954).

110. ELLIS, W. D. *A source book of gestalt psychology.* New York: Harcourt, Brace & World (1938).

111. EMMONS, W. H., & SIMON, C. W. "The non-recall of material presented during sleep." *Amer. J. Psychol.*, **69**, 76-81 (1956).

112. ENINGER, M. U. "The role of irrelevant drive stimuli in learning theory." *J. exp. Psychol.*, **41**, 446-449 (1951).

113. ESCALONA, SYBILL K. "The effect of success and failure upon the level of aspiration and behavior in manic-depressive psychoses." *Univer. Ia. Stud. Child Welf.*, **16**, No. 3, 199-302 (1940).

114. ESTES, W. K. "An experimental study of punishment." *Psychol. Monogr.*, **57**, No. 263 (1944).

115. ESTES, W. K. "Statistical theory of distributional phenomena in learning." *Psychol. Rev.*, **62**, 369-377 (1955).

116. ESTES, W. K., et al. *Modern learning theory: A critical analysis of five examples.* New York: Appleton-Century-Crofts (1957).

117. FALES, W. *Wisdom and responsibility: An essay on the motivation of thought and action.* Princeton: Princeton Univer. Press (1946).

118. FEARING, F. "An examination of the concepts of Benjamin Whorf in the light of theories of perception and cognition." From *Language in Culture.* Hoijer H. (Ed.) *Amer. Anthrop. Asso. Mem.*, No. 79, part 2, **56**, No. 6, 41-81, December 1954.

119. FERSTER, C. B., & SKINNER, B. F. *Schedules of reinforcement.* New York: Appleton-Century-Crofts (1957).

120. FISKE, D. W., & RICE, L. "Intra-individual response variability." *Psychol. Bull.*, **52**, 217-250 (1955).

121. FITZWATER, M. E. "The relative effect of reinforcement and non-reinforcement in establishing a form discrimination." *J. comp. physiol. Psychol.*, **35**, 476-481 (1952).

122. FLESCHER, J. "Contribution to psychoanalytical study on projection and introjection." *Psychoanal. Rev.*, **38**, 353-360 (1951).

123. FLORÈS, C. "*Étude sur les relations entre le rappel et la reconnaissance* (Study in relations between recall and recognition)." *Année Psychol.*, **58**, 365-376, (1958).

124. FOLEY, D. P. "An experimental analysis of the relationship between inhibition and learning set for logically related materials." *J. gen. Psychol.*, **50**, 261-267 (1954).

125. FOREL, O. L. "*Das ressentiment: Ein hindernis in der umerziehung* (Resentment: A hurdle to re-education)." *Beih. Schweiz. Z. Psychol. Amvend.*, No. 14, 5-37 (1948).

126. FRAISSE, P., & BLOCH, V. "*Sur l'influence des attitudes dans l'efficience, en rapidité ou en précision* (Concerning the influence of attitudes in efficiency, rapidity or accuracy)." *Année psychol.*, **49**, 99-118 (1950).

127. FRANK, J. D. "Individual differences in certain aspects of level of aspiration." *Amer. J. Psychol.*, **47**, 119-128 (1935).

128. FRANK, J. D. "Recent studies of the level of aspiration." *Psychol. Bull.*, **38**, 218-225 (1941).

129. FRANK, L. D. *Individual development.* New York: Doubleday (1955).

130. FRANK, L. K. "The human aspect underlying Air Force Training." *USAF ATC Instructors J.*, **6**, 55-60 (1955).

131. FRENCH, R. S. "The effect of instruction on the length-difficulty relationship for a task involving sequential dependency." *J. exp. Psychol.*, **48**, 89-97 (1954).

132. FREUD, S. *The basic writings of Sigmund Freud.* A. A. Brill (Ed. & trans.) New York: Random House (1938).

133. GAGNÉ, R. M. "The effect of sequence of presentation of similar items on the learning of paired associates." *J. exp. Psychol.*, 40, 61-73 (1950).

134. GAGNÉ, R. M., BAKER, KATHERINE E., & FOSTER, HARRIET. "On the relation between similarity and transfer of training in the learning of discriminative motor tasks." *Psychol. Rev.*, **57**, 67-79 (1950).

135. GARBER, R. B. "Influence of cognitive and affective factors in learning and retaining attitudinal materials." *J. abnorm. soc. Psychol.,* **51**, 384-389 (1955).

136. GARDNER, J. W. "Level of aspiration in response to a prearranged sequence of scores." *J. exp. Psychol.,* **25**, 601-621 (1939).

137. GATES, G. S. "The effect of an audience upon performance." *J. abnorm. soc. Psychol.,* **18**, 334-344 (1924).

138. GEBHARD, M. E. "The effect of success and failure upon the attractiveness of activities as a function of experience, expectation, and need." *J. exp. Psychol.,* **38**, 371-388 (1948).

139. GILMORE, J. L. "Recall of success and failure as a function of subjects' threat interpretations." *J. Psychol.,* **38**, 359-365 (1954).

140. GLAZE, J. A. "The association value of nonsense syllables." *J. gen. Psychol.,* **35**, 255-267 (1928).

141. GLOYE, E. "Learning as a function of context differentiated through antecedent value experience." *J. exp. Psychol.,* **50**, 260-264 (1955).

142. GOLDNER, R. H. "Individual differences in whole-part approach and flexibility-rigidity in problem-solving." *Psychol. Monogr.,* **71**, No. 21, Whole No. 450 (1957).

143. GOLDSTEIN, K. *The organism: A holistic approach to biology derived from pathological data on man.* New York: American Book (1939).

144. GOLDSTEIN, R., & SOLOMON, R. L. "A serial position effect in 'incidental learning.'" *J. genet. Psychol.,* **53**, 293-298 (1955).

145. GOMULICKI, B. R. "Individual differences in recall." *J. Pers.* **24**, 387-400 (1956).

146. GOODNOW, JACQUELINE J., & PETTIGREW, T. F. "Some sources of difficulty in solving simple problems." *J. exp. Psychol.,* **51**, 385-392 (1956).

147. GORDON, I. J. "Developments in human behavior." *Educ. Theory,* **8**, 259-268 (1958).

148. GORDON, I. J., & COMBS, A. "The learner: Self and perception." *Rev. educ. Res.,* **28**, 433-444 (1958).

149. GORDON, W. M., & BERLYNE, D. E. "Drive-level and flexibility in paired-associate nonsense-syllable learning." *Quart. J. exp. Psychol.,* **6**, 181-185 (1945).

150. GOSS, A. E. "Transfer as a function of type and amount of preliminary experience with task stimuli." *J. exp. Psychol.,* **46**, 419-428 (1953).

151. GOSS, A. E., & RABAIOLI, E. J. "Response strength in a modified Thorndikian multiple-choice situation as a function of varying proportions of reinforcement." *J. exp. Psychol.*, **43**, 106-114 (1952).

152. GOULD, J. "Punctuation of a sentence." *New York Times* (1955).

153. GOULD, ROSALIND. "An experimental analysis of level of aspiration." *Genet. Psychol. Monogr.*, **21**, 1-116 (1939).

154. GOULD, ROSALIND. "Some sociological determinants of goal strivings." *J. soc. Psychol.*, **13**, 461-473 (1941).

155. GRACE, H. A. "A teacher-centered theory for education." *Peabody J. Educ.*, **32**, 273-281 (1955).

156. GRAVES, W. A. "Today's college students." *J. Nat. Educ. Ass.*, **47**, 498-500 (1958).

157. GREEN, R. T. "The attention-getting value of structural change." *Brit. J. Psychol.*, **49**, 311-314 (1954).

158. GREENBERG, P. J. "Competition in children." *Amer. J. Psychol.*, **44**, 221-248 (1932).

159. GREENSPOON, J., & FOREMAN, SALLY. "Effect of delay of knowledge of results on learning a motor task." *J. exp. Psychol.*, **51**, 226-228 (1956).

160. GROSSLIGHT, J. H., HALL, J. F., & MURNIN, J. "Patterning effect in partial reinforcement." *J. exp. Psychol.*, **46**, 103-106 (1953).

161. GUTHRIE, E. R. *The psychology of learning.* New York: Harper (1935 and 1952).

162. GUTHRIE, E. R. "Mueller and Schoenfeld's analysis of Guthrie." *Contemp. Psychol.*, **1**, No. 1, 9-10 (1956).

163. HALL, J. F. "Learning as a function of word frequency." *Amer. J. Psychol.*, **67**, 138-140 (1954).

164. HALL, J. F. "Retroactive inhibition in meaningful material." *J. educ. Psychol.*, **46**, 47-52 (1955).

165. HALL, J. F., & UGELOW, A. "Proactive, retroactive and coactive inhibition with meaningful material." *Psychol. Rep.*, **5**, 313-317 (1959).

166. HARKER, G. S. "Delay of reward and performance of an instrumental response." *J. exp. Psychol.*, **51**, 303-310 (1956).

167. HARLEY, S. F. "Comparison of mental practice and physical practice in the learning of physical skill." *USN Spec. Dev. Cent., Tech. Rep.*, SDC, 269-7-27, 11p. (1952).

168. HARLOW, H. F. "The formation of learning sets." *Psychol. Rev.*, **56**, 51-65 (1949).

169. HARLOW, H. F. "Current and future advances in physiological and comparative psychology." *Amer. Psychologist,* 11, No. 6, 272-277 (1956).

170. HARRIS, A. J. *How to increase reading ability.* New York: Longmans, Green (1947).

171. HARRIS, H. I. "Repression as a factor in learning theory." *Psychoanal. Quart.,* 19, 410-411 (1950).

172. HARTMANN, G. W. "The field theory of learning and its educational consequences." *Natl. Soc. Stud. Educ.,* 41st Yearbook, Part II, Univer. Chicago Press, pp. 165-214 (1942).

173. HARVEY, O. J., & SHERIF, M. "Level of aspiration as a case of judgmental activity in which ego-involvements operate as factors." *Sociometry,* 14, 121-147 (1951).

174. HAYAKAWA, S. I. *Language and thought in action.* New York: Harcourt, Brace & World (1949).

175. HEBB, D. O. *The organization of behavior.* New York: Wiley (1949).

176. HEBB, D. O. "Motivation and thought." *Bull. Maritime Psychol. Ass.,* 8, 4-9, April 1959.

177. HENLE, MARY. "Some effects of motivational processes on cognition." *Psychol. Rev.,* 62, 423-432 (1945).

178. HERMAN, D. T., & BROUSSARD, I. G. "A study in the learning of two types of serial order material presented simultaneously." *J. genet. Psychol.,* 73, 55-70 (1951).

179. HILGARD, E. R. "Success in relation to levels of aspiration." *Sch. and Soc.,* 55, 423-428 (1942).

180. HILGARD, E. R. *Theories of learning.* New York: Appleton-Century-Crofts (1948).

181. HILGARD, E. R., JONES, L. V., & KAPLAN, S. J. "Conditioned discrimination as related to anxiety." *J. exp. Psychol.,* 42, 94-99 (1951).

182. HILGARD, E. R., IRVINE, R. P., & WHIPPLE, J. E. "Rote memorization, understanding, and transfer: An extension of Katona's card-trick experiments." *J. exp. Psychol.,* 46, 288-292 (1953).

183. HIVELY, W. "Implications for the classroom of B. F. Skinner's analysis of behavior." *Har. educ. Rev.,* 29, 37-42 (1959).

184. HOLLANDER, E. P., & BLAIR, J. T. "Attitudes toward authority-figures as correlates of motivation among Naval Aviation Cadets." *J. appl. Psychol.,* 38, 21-25 (1954).

185. HOLMES, J. A., & FINLEY, C. J. "Under- and over-age grade-placements and school achievement." *J. educ. Psychol.*, **48**, 447-456 (1957).

186. HOLZMAN, P. S. "The relation of assimilation tendencies in visual, auditory, and kinesthetic time-error to cognitive attitudes of leveling and sharpening." *J. Pers.*, **22**, 375-394 (1954).

187. HOFFMAN, L. R. "Homogeneity of member personality and its effect on group-problem solving." *J. abnorm. soc. Psychol.*, **58**, 27-32 (1959).

188. HORNEY, KAREN. "Inhibitions in work." *Amer. J. Psychoanal.*, **7**, 18-25 (1947).

189. HOUSTON, G. C. "Toward better self-understanding." *Personnel J.*, **34**, 286-291 (1956).

190. HUGHES, V. H. "A study of the relationships among selected language abilities." *J. educ. Res.*, **47**, 97-106 (1953).

191. HULL, C. L. "The conflicting psychologies of learning—a way out." *Psychol. Rev.*, **42**, 491-516 (1935).

192. HULL, C. L. *A behavior system: An introduction to behavior theory concerning the individual organism.* New Haven: Yale Univer. Press (1952).

193. HUSBAND, R. W. "Positive transfer as a factor in memory." *Proc. Iowa Acad. Sci.*, **54**, 235-238 (1947).

194. HYMAN, R., & JENKINS, N. S. "Involvement and set as determinants of behavioral stereotypy." *Psychol. Rep.*, **2**, Monogr. Suppl. 3, 131-146 (1956).

195. IRION, A. L., & WHAM, D. S. "Recovery from retention loss as a function of amount of pre-recall warming-up." *J. exp. Psychol.*, **41**, 242-246 (1951).

196. IVERSON, M. A., & REUTER, M. E. "Ego-involvement as an experimental variable." *Psychol. Rep.*, **2**, Monogr. Suppl. 4, 147-181 (1956).

197. JACKSON, J. "The influence of word analysis upon spelling attainment." *J. educ. Res.*, **47**, 107-115 (1953).

198. JENKINS, J. J. & RUSSELL, W. A. "Associative clustering during recall." *J. abnorm. soc. Psychol.*, **47**, 818-821 (1952).

199. JENSEN, B. T. "What about transfer?" *Peabody J. Educ.*, **34**, 71-77 (1956).

200. JENSEN, B. T., & INSEL, S. A. "Transfer effects in spelling." *Calif. J. educ. Res.*, **6**, 219-223 (1955).

201. JOHNSON, W. "Symbolic processes in personality development." *Etc. Rev. gen. Semant.*, **9**, 29-34 (1951).

202. JOHNSON, W. *People in quandaries.* New York: Harper (1945).

203. JONES, E. I., & BILODEAU, E. A. "Differential transfer of training between motor tasks of different difficulty." *USAF Hum. Resour. Res. Cent. Bull.*, No. 52-35 (1952).

204. JUZAK, TATANIA. "The effects of praise and reproof on the generalization of learned concepts." *J. Psychol.*, **39**, 329-340 (1955).

205. KAKKAR, S. B. "Psychology of spelling." *Shiksha*, **9**(4), 143-146 (1957).

206. KANFER, F. H., & MATARAZZO, J. "Secondary and generalized reinforcement in human learning." *J. exp. Psychol.*, **58**, 400-404, November 1959.

207. KATONA, G. *Organizing and memorizing.* New York: Columbia Univer. Press (1940).

208. KAY, H., & POULTON, E. C. "Anticipation in memorizing." *Brit. J. Psychol.*, **42**, 34-41 (1951).

209. KELLER, F. S., & SCHOENFELD, W. N. *Principles of psychology.* New York: Appleton-Century-Crofts (1950).

210. KELLEY, E. C. "Education is communication." *Etc. Rev. gen. Semant.*, **12**, 248-256 (1955).

211. KIENTZLE, M. J. "Ability patterns under distributed practice." *J. exp. Psychol.*, **39**, 532-537 (1949).

212. KILLIAN, L. M. "Ourselves and society." *Except. Child.*, **20**, 294-298 (1954).

213. KIMBLE, G. A., & HORENSTEIN, B. R. "Reminiscence in motor learning as a function of length of interpolated rest." *J. exp. Psychol.*, **38**, 239-244 (1948).

214. KIMBLE, G. A., & DUFORT, R. H. "Meaningfulness and isolation as factors in verbal learning." *J. exp. Psychol.*, **50**, 361-368 (1955).

215. KING, INEZ B. "Effect of age of entrance into Grade I upon achievement in elementary school." *Elem. Sch. J.*, **55**, 331-336 (1955).

216. KITTELL, J. E. "An experimental study of the effect of external direction during learning on transfer and retention of principles." *J. educ. Psychol.*, **48**, 391-405 (1957).

217. KNUTSON, A. L. "The concept of personal security." *J. soc. Psychol.*, **40**, 219-236 (1954).

218. KOHN, H. "The effect of variations of intensity of experimentally induced stress upon certain aspects of perception and performance." *J. genet. Psychol.*, 85, 289-304 (1954).

219. KORZYBSKI, A. *Science and sanity.* Lakeville, Conn.: International Non-Aristotelian Library (1948).

220. KOTINSKY, RUTH, & COLEMAN, J. V. "Mental health as an educational goal." *Teach. Coll. Rec.*, 56, 267-276 (1955).

221. KRECH, D., & CALVIN, A. "Levels of perceptual organization and cognition." *J. abnorm. soc. Psychol.*, 48, 394-400 (1953).

222. KURTZ, K., & HOVLAND, C. I. "The effect of verbalization during observation of stimulus objects upon accuracy of recognition and recall." *J. exp. Psychol.*, 45, 157-164 (1953).

223. KURTZ, K. H. "Discrimination of complex stimuli: the relationship of training and test stimuli in transfer of discrimination." *J. exp. Psychol.*, 50, 283-292 (1955).

224. LAFAVE, L. "Habit or attitude as the central tree in educational theory." *Educ. Theory*, 8, 172-178 (1958).

225. LAGACHE, D. "Some aspects of identification." *Int. soc. Sci. Bull.*, 7, 35-44 (1955).

226. LANER, S. "Some factors influencing the effectiveness of an instructional film." *Brit. J. Psychol.*, 46, 280-292 (1955).

227. LAZARUS, R. S., DEESE, J., & OSLER, SONIA F. "The effect of psychological stress upon performance." *Psychol. Bull.*, 49, 293-317 (1952).

228. LAZARUS, R. S., DEESE, J., & HAMILTON, R. "Anxiety and stress in learning: The role of intraserial duplication." *J. exp. Psychol.*, 47, 111-114 (1954).

229. LAZARUS, R. S., & ERICKSEN, C. W. "Effects of failure stress upon skilled performance." *J. exp. Psychol.*, 43, 100-105 (1952).

230. LEARY, R. W. "The rewarded, the unrewarded, the chosen and the unchosen." *Psychol. Rep.*, 2, 91-97 (1956).

231. LEVIN, H., & BALDWIN, A. L. "The choice to exhibit." *Child Develpm.*, 29, 373-380, September 1958.

232. LEVINE, S. "The effects of a strong irrelevant drive on learning." *Psychol. Rep.*, 2, 29-33 (1956).

233. LEWIN, K., DEMBO, TAMARA, FESTINGER, L., & SEARS, PAULINE S. "Level of aspiration." *Personality and the behavior disorders.* J. McV. Hunt (Ed.) New York: Ronald, pp. 333-379 (1944).

234. LEWIN, K., LIPPITT, R., & WHITE, R. K. "Patterns of aggressive behavior in experimentally created 'social climates.' " *J. soc. Psychol.*, **10**, 271-299 (1939).

235. LEWIS, D. J. "Partial reinforcement in a gambling situation." *J. exp. Psychol.*, **43**, 447-450 (1952).

236. LEWIS, D. J., & DUNCAN, C. P. "Expectation and resistance to extinction of a lever-pulling response as functions of percentage of reinforcement and amount of reward." *J. exp. Psychol.*, **54**, 115-120 (1957).

237. LIBERMAN, A. M. "The effect of differential extinction on spontaneous recovery." *J. exp. Psychol.*, **38**, 722-733 (1948).

238. LITTLE, SUE W., & COHEN, L. D. "Goal setting behavior of asthmatic children and of their mothers for them." *J. Pers.*, **19**, 376-389 (1951).

239. LITTMAN, R. A., BLAHA, R., & PATTERSON, G. "Residual drive ('hangover') and latent learning." *J. gen. Psychol.*, **48**, 11-19 (1953).

240. LONGENECKER, E. D., KRAUSKOPF, J., & BITTERMAN, M. E. "Extinction following alternating and random partial reinforcement." *Amer. J. Psychol.*, **65**, 580-587 (1952).

241. LORGE, I. "How the psychologist views communication." *Teach. Coll. Rec.*, **57**, 72-79 (1955).

242. LORGE, I., & SOLOMON, H. "Two models of group behavior in the solution of Eureka-type problems." *Psychometrika*, **20**, 139-148 (1955).

243. LORGE, I., TUCKMAN, J., AIKMAN, L., SPIEGEL, J., & MOSS, GILDA. "Problem-solving by teams and by individuals in a field setting." *J. educ. Psychol.*, **46**, 160-166 (1955).

244. LORGE, I., TUCKMAN, J., AIKMAN, L., SPIEGEL, J., & MOSS, GILDA. "The adequacy of written reports in problem-solving by teams and by individuals." *J. soc. Psychol.*, **43**, 65-74 (1956).

245. LUCHINS, A. S., & LUCHINS, EDITH H. "Cooperativeness of task in relation to discovery of contradictory communications." *J. gen. Psychol.*, **56**, 159-178 (1957).

246. MACKAY, R. P. "Memory as a biological function." *Amer. J. Psychiat.*, **109**, 721-728 (1953).

247. MACPHERSON, S. J., DEES, VALERIE, & GRINDLEY, G. C. "The effect of knowledge of results on learning and performance. II. Some characteristics of very simple skills." *Quart. J. exp. Psychol.*, **1**, 68-78 (1948).

248. MACPHERSON, S. J., DEES, VALERIE, & GRINDLEY, G. C. "The effect of knowledge of results on learning and performance. III. The influence of the time interval between trials." *Quart. J. exp. Psychol.*, **1**, 167-174 (1949).

249. MC CLELLAND, D. C., & LIBERMAN, A. M. "The effect of need for achievement on recognition of need-related words." *J. Pers.*, **18**, 236-251 (1949).

250. MC CLENDON, P. I. "An experimental study of the relationship between note-taking practices and listening comprehension of college freshmen during expository lectures." *Speech Monogr.*, **25**, 222-228 (1958).

251. MC FANN, H. H. "Effects of response alternations and different instructions on proactive and retroactive facilitation and interference." *J. exp. Psychol.*, **46**, 405-410 (1953).

252. MC GUIGAN, F. J., & MAC CASLIN, E. F. "Whole and part methods in learning a perceptual motor skill." *Amer. J. Psychol.*, **68**, 658-661 (1955).

253. MADDEN, MARIAN S., ADAMS, J. A., & SPENCE, SHIRLEY A. "Memory-drum versus adjusted-learning techniques in the study of associative interference in learning by paired associates." *Amer. J. Psychol.*, **63**, 186-195 (1950).

254. MAIER, N. R. F. "The premature crystallization of learning theory." *Kentucky Symposium.* New York: Wiley, pp. 54-65 (1954).

255. MALRIEU, PH. "*Le problème de la conscience du passé d'apres les études recentes* (Recent studies concerning the experience of the past)." *J. Psychol. norm. Path.*, 47-51, 91-108 (1954).

256. MARKS, M. R., & JACK, O. "Verbal context and memory span for meaningful material." *Amer. J. Psychol.*, **65**, 298-300 (1952).

257. MARKS, ROSE W. "The effect of probability, desirability, and 'privilege' on the stated expectations of children." *J. Pers.*, **19**, 332-351 (1951).

258. MARQUART, DOROTHY I. "Group problem-solving." *J. soc. Psychol.*, **41**, 103-113 (1955).

259. MARX, M. H. "Spread of effect: A critical review." *Genet. Psychol. Monogr.*, **53**, 119-186 (1956).

260. MASLOW, A. H. "A theory of human motivation." *Psychol. Rev.*, **50**, 370-396 (1943).

261. MASLOW, A. H. "Some theoretical consequences of basic need gratification." *J. Pers.*, **16**, 402-416 (1948).

262. MASLOW, A. H. *Motivation and personality.* New York: Harper (1954).

263. MASON, G. P. "Word discrimination and spelling." *J. educ. Res.,* **50,** 617-621 (1957).

264. MATHEWS, RAVENNA. "Recall as a function of number of classificatory categories." *J. exp. Psychol.,* **47,** 241-247 (1954).

265. MAY, M. A., & DOOB, L. W. *Competition and cooperation.* (Bull. 25) New York: Soc. Sci. Res. Council (1937).

266. MECH, E. V. " 'Resistance to extinction' of the two patterns of verbal reinforcement." *J. exp. Educ.,* **22,** 155-163 (1953).

267. MEDDLETON, I. G. "An experimental investigation into the systematic teaching of number combinations in arithmetic." *Brit. J. educ. Psychol.,* **26,** 117-127 (1956).

268. MEEHL, P. E. "On the circularity of the Law of Effect." *Psychol. Bull.,* **47,** 52-75 (1950).

269. MELTON, A. W. "Learning." *Encyclopedia of Educational Research.* (2nd. ed.) W. S. Monroe (Ed.) New York: Macmillan, pp. 668-690 (1950).

270. MILLER, D. R. "Responses of psychiatric patients to threats of failure." *J. abnorm. soc. Psychol.,* **46,** 378-387 (1951).

271. MILLER, G. A., & SELFRIDGE, JENNIFER A. "Verbal context and the recall of meaningful material." *Amer. J. Psychol.,* **63,** 176-185 (1950).

272. MILLER, N. E. "Comments on multiple-process conceptions of learning." *Psychol. Rev.,* **58,** 375-381 (1951).

273. MONTAGUE, E. K. "The role of anxiety in serial rote learning." *J. exp. Psychol.,* **45,** 91-96 (1953).

274. MONTGOMERY, V. E. "Transfer of training in motor learning as a function of distribution of practice." *J. exp. Psychol.,* **46,** 440-444 (1953).

275. MORROW, ANN E. "Who wants to memorize?" *Education,* **77,** 442-444 (1957).

276. MOURSY, E. M. "The hierarchical organization of cognitive levels." *Brit. J. Psychol. Statist. Sect.,* **5,** 151-180 (1952).

277. MOWRER, O. H. "On the dual nature of learning—a re-interpretation of 'conditioning' and 'problem-solving.' " *Har. Educ. Rev.,* **17,** 102-148 (1947).

278. MOWRER, O. H. "Learning theory: historical review and re-interpretation." *Har. Educ. Rev.*, **24**, 37-58 (1954).

279. MOWRER, O. H. "Ego psychology, cybernetics, and learning." *Kentucky Symposium.* New York: Wiley, pp. 81-90 (1954).

280. MOWRER, O. H. "Two-factor learning theory reconsidered, with special reference to secondary reinforcement and the concept of habit." *Psychol. Rev.*, **63**, 114-128 (1956).

281. MOWRER, O. H. *Learning theory and behavior.* New York: Wiley (1960).

282. MURNIN, J. A., VANDER MEET, A. W., & VRIS, T. "Comparison of training media: Trainee manipulation and observation of functioning electrical systems versus trainee drawing of schematic electrical systems." *USN Spec. Dev. Cent., Tech. Rep.*, No. 269-7-101, 30p. (1954).

283. MURPHY, G. *Personality.* New York: Harper (1947).

284. *Nebraska Symposium of Motivation.* Lincoln, Nebraska: Univer. Nebraska Press, Volumes I-IX (1953-1961).

285. NEIMARK, EDITH, & WALTZMAN, I. J. "Intentional and incidental learning with different rates of stimulus-presentation." *Amer. J. Psychol.*, **66**, 618-621 (1953).

286. NESBIT, R. R. *Language, meaning and reality.* New York: Exposition Press (1955).

287. NEWTON, K. R. "Visual recognition thresholds and learning." *Percept. mot. Skills*, **6**, 81-87 (1956).

288. NOBLE, C. E. "The role of stimulus meaning (m) in serial verbal learning." *J. exp. Psychol.*, **43**, 437-446 (1952).

289. NORCROSS, KATHRYN J. "Effects of discrimination performance of similarity of previously acquired stimulus names." *J. exp. Psychol.*, **56**, 305-309 (1958).

290. NORTH, A. J., & HARRINGTON, J., JR. "Learning response compounds have two critical components." *J. exp. Psychol.*, **47**, 173-178 (1954).

291. OTTERMAN, L. M. "The value of teaching prefixes and word-roots." *J. educ. Res.*, **48**, 611-616 (1955).

292. PARKER, C. A. "Empathy." *Personn. Guid. J.*, **34**, 89-93 (1955).

293. PEMBERTON, CAROL L. "The closure factors related to other cognitive processes." *Psychometrika*, **17**, 267-288 (1952).

294. PEMBERTON, CAROL L. "The closure factors related to temperament." *J. Pers.*, **21**, 159-175 (1952).

295. PERLMUTTER, H. V. "Group memory of meaningful material." *J. Psychol.*, **35**, 361-370 (1953).

296. PETERS, R. S. *The concept of motivation.* New York: Humanities Press (1958).

297. PHILBRICK, EMILY B., & POSTMAN, L. "A further analysis of 'learning without awareness.'" *Amer. J. Psychol.*, **68**, 417-424 (1955).

298. PLANK, R. "Historical illustrations of concept formation." *Etc. Rev. gen. Semant.*, **12**, 96-102 (1955).

299. PALANYI, M. "Problem-solving." *Brit. J. Phil. Sci.*, **8**, 89-103 (1957).

300. PORTER, L. W. "The effect of 'right' in a modified Thorndikian situation." *Amer. J. Psychol.*, **70**, 219-226 (1957).

301. POSTMAN, L. "The generalization gradient in recognition memory." *J. exp. Psychol.*, **42**, 231-235 (1951).

302. POSTMAN, L. "Retroactive inhibition in recall and recognition." *J. exp. Psychol.*, **44**, 165-169 (1952).

303. POSTMAN, L. "Learned principles of organization in memory." *Psychol. Monogr.*, **68**(3), No. 374 (1954).

304. POSTMAN, L., AMES, PAULINE A., & PHILLIPS, LAURA W. "Studies in incidental learning: II. The effects of association value and of the method of testing." *J. exp. Psychol.*, **49**, 1-10 (1955).

305. POSTMAN, L., & ADAMS, PAULINE A. "Studies in incidental learning: VI. Intraserial interference." *J. exp. Psychol.*, **54**, 153-167 (1957).

306. POSTMAN, L., & ADAMS, PAULINE A. "Studies in incidental learning: VII. Effects of frequency of exercise and length of list." *J. exp. Psychol.*, **56**, 86-94 (1958).

307. POSTMAN, L., & JENKINS, W. O. "An experimental analysis of set in rote learning: The interaction of learning instruction and retention performance." *J. exp. Psychol.*, **38**, 683-689 (1948).

308. POSTMAN, L., & RAU, LUCY. "Retention as a function of the method of measurement." *U. Calif. Publ. Psychol.*, **18**, 217-270 (1957).

309. PRONKO, N. H., & LEITH, W. R. "Behavior under stress: A study of its disintegration." *Psychol. Rep.*, Monogr. Suppl. 5, **2**, 205-222 (1956).

310. POULTON, E. C. "Previous knowledge and memory." *Brit. J. Psychol.*, **48**, 259-270 (1957).

311. RAO, K. U. "The effect of interference with certain aspects of goal setting on level of aspiration behavior." *Psychol. Stud.*, Mysore, **1**, 1-10 (1956).

312. RAO, N. C. S. "Experimental study of the effects of psychological stress on rigidity in problem solution." *Indian J. Psychol.*, **29**, 97-102 (1954).

313. RAY, W. S. "Verbal compared with manipulative solution of an apparatus problem." *Amer. J. Psychol.*, **70**, 289-290 (1957).

314. RAZRAN, G. "A note on the use of the terms *conditioning* and *reinforcement*." *Amer. Psychologist*, **10**, 173-174 (1955).

315. REICHENBACH, H. *Elements of symbolic logic.* New York: Macmillan (1947).

316. REICHMAN, FRIEDA FROMM. *Principles of intensive psychotherapy.* Chicago: Univer. Chicago Press (1950).

317. REMMERS, H. H. "Learning—what kind of animal?" *J. educ. Psychol.*, **44**, 44-49 (1953).

318. RESTLE, F. "A theory of discrimination learning." *Psychol. Rev.*, **62**, 11-19 (1955).

319. REYNOLDS, B., & ADAMS, J. A. "Psychomotor performance as a function of initial level of ability." *USAF Hum. Resour. Res. Cent., Res. Bull.* No. 53-39 (1953).

320. RHINE, R. J. "The relation of achievement in problem solving to rate and kind of hypotheses produced." *J. exp. Psychol.*, **57**, 253-256 (1959).

321. RIOPELLE, A. J. "Learning sets from minimum stimuli." *J. exp. Psychol.*, **49**, 28-32 (1955).

322. ROCK, I. "The role of repetition in associative learning." *Amer. J. Psychol.*, **70**, 186-193 (1957).

323. ROCK, I. "Repetition and learning." *Scient. Amer.*, **199**(2), 68-72 (1958).

324. ROGERS, C. R. "Some observations on the organization of personality." *Amer. Psychologist*, **2**, 358-368 (1947).

325. ROGERS, C. R. *Client-centered therapy.* Boston: Houghton-Mifflin (1951).

326. ROSENBERG, S., & HALL, R. L. "The effects of different social feedback conditions upon performance in dyadic teams." *J. abnorm. soc. Psychol.*, **57**, 271-277 (1958).

327. ROSENZWEIG, S. "Preference in the repetition of successful and unsuccessful activities as a function of age and personality." *J. genet. Psychol.*, **42**, 423-441 (1933).

328. ROSSMAN, IRMA L., & GOSS, A. E. "The acquired distinctiveness of cues: The role of discriminative verbal responses in facilitating the acquisition of discriminative motor responses." *J. exp. Psychol.,* **42,** 173-182 (1951).

329. RUBENSTEIN, H., & ABORN, M. "Immediate recall as a function of degree of organization and length of study period." *J. exp. Psychol.,* **48,** 146-152 (1954).

330. SAKODA, J. M. "Individual differences in correlations between clustering and recall of meaningful words." *J. gen. Psychol.,* **54,** 183-190 (1956).

331. SALTZMAN, I. J. "Delay of reward and human verbal learning." *J. exp. Psychol.,* **41,** 437-439 (1951).

332. SALTZMAN, I. J. "Incidental and intentional memory for lifted weights." *Amer. J. Psychol.,* **70,** 253-257 (1957).

333. SALTZMAN, I. J., & ATKINSON, RITA L. "Comparison of incidental and intentional learning after different numbers of stimulus presentations." *Amer. J. Psychol.,* **67,** 521-524 (1954).

334. SAMUELSON, E. E. "A study of the effects of excessive overloads on summer school students." *Educ. Adm. Superv.,* **41,** 90-98 (1955).

335. SARASON, S. B., MANDLER, G., & CRAIGHILL, P. G. "The effect of differential instructions on anxiety and learning." *J. abnorm. soc. Psychol.,* **47,** 561-565 (1952).

336. SCHEERER, M. "Cognitive theory." *Handbook of Social Psychology.* I. G. Lindsey (Ed.) New York: Addison-Wesley, pp. 91-142 (1954).

337. SCHEIER, I. H. "An evaluation of rigidity factors." *Canad. J. Psychol.,* **8,** 157-163 (1954).

338. SCHILLER, P. H. "Innate constituents of complex responses." *Psychol. Rev.,* **59,** 177-191 (1952).

339. SEARS, PAULINE S. "Levels of aspiration in academically successful and unsuccessful children." (Doctoral dissertation) Yale University (1939).

340. SEIGLE, W. F. "Prediction of success in college mathematics at Washburn University." *J. educ. Res.,* **47,** 577-588 (1954).

341. SEMNE, LEILA R. M., & WARREN J. M. "Proactive facilitation of performance on the Wisconsin Card Sorting Test." *Psychol. Rep.,* **1,** 433-436 (1955).

342. SERRA, MARY C. "How to develop concepts and their verbal representations." *Elem. Sch. J.,* **53,** 275-285 (1953).

343. SEWARD, J. P. "Learning theory and identification. II. The role of punishment." *J. genet. Psychol.*, 84, 201-210 (1954).

344. SEWARD, J. P. "Reinforcement and expectancy: Two theories in search of a controversy." *Psychol. Rev.*, 63, 105-113 (1956).

345. SEWARD, J. P. "Drive, incentive and reinforcement." *Psychol. Rev.*, 63, 195-203 (1956).

346. SHEFFIELD, VIRGINIA F. "Resistance to extinction as a function of the distribution of extinction trials." *J. exp. Psychol.*, 40, 305-313 (1950).

347. SHELLEY, H. P. "Level of aspiration phenomena in small groups." *J. soc. Psychol.*, 40, 149-164 (1954).

348. SIDDALL, G. J., & ANDERSON, D. M. "Fatigue during prolonged performance on a simple compensatory tracking task." *Quart. J. exp. Psychol.*, 7, 159-165 (1955).

349. SILVERMAN, R. E. "Anxiety and mode of response." *J. abnorm. soc. Psychol.*, 49, 538-542 (1954).

350. SIMON, C. W., & EMMONS, W. H. "Learning during sleep?" *Psychol. Bull.*, 52, 328-342 (1955).

351. SINHA, SHASHILATA. "Frustration as a determinant of level of aspiration." *J. Educ. & Psychol.*, Baroda, 12, 10-14 (1954).

352. SKINNER, B. F. *The behavior of organisms: an experimental analysis.* New York: Appleton-Century-Crofts (1938).

353. SKINNER, B. F. "Are theories of learning necessary?" *Psychol. Rev.*, 57, 193-216 (1950).

354. SKINNER, B. F. "How to teach animals." *Sci. Amer.*, 185, 26-29 (1951).

355. SKINNER, B. F. *Science and human behavior.* New York: Macmillan (1953).

356. SKINNER, B. F. "Some contributions of an experimental analysis of behavior to psychology as a whole." *Amer. Psychologist*, 8, 69-78 (1953).

357. SKINNER, B. F. "The science of learning and the art of teaching." *Har. Educ. Rev.*, 24, 86-97 (1954).

358. SKINNER, B. F. *Verbal behavior.* New York: Appleton-Century-Crofts (1957).

359. SKINNER, B. F. "Reinforcement today." *Amer. Psychologist*, 13, 94-99 (1958).

360. SKINNER, B. F. "Teaching machines." *Science*, 128, 969-977 (1958).

361. SMITH, D. E. P. "Applicational transfer and inhibition." *J. educ. Psychol.*, **45**, 169-174 (1954).

362. SMOCK, C. D. "The influence of stress on the perception of incongruity." *J. abnorm. soc. Psychol.*, **50**, 354-356 (1955).

363. SOLLEY, C. M., & LONG, J. "When is 'uh-huh' reinforcing?" *Percept. mot. Skills*, **8**, 277 (1958).

364. SPENCE, K. W. "Cognitive versus stimulus-response theories of learning." *Psychol. Rev.*, **57**, 159-172 (1950).

365. SPENCE, K. W. "Learning and performance in eyelid conditioning as a function of intensity of the UCS." *J. exp. Psychol.*, **45**, 57-63 (1953).

366. SPENCE, K. W. *Behavior theory and conditioning*. New Haven, Conn.: Yale Univer. Press (1956).

367. STAATS, A. W. "Verbal and instrumental response-hierarchies and their relationship to problem-solving." *Amer. J. Psychol.*, **70**, 442-446 (1957).

368. STAATS, CAROLYN K., & STAATS, A. W. "Meaning established by classical conditioning." *J. exp. Psychol.*, **54**, 74-80 (1957).

369. STEISEL, I. M., & COHEN, B. D. "The effects of two degrees of failure on level of aspiration and performance." *J. abnorm. soc. Psychol.*, **46**, 79-82 (1951).

370. STEVENSON, H. W., & ISCOE, I. "Anxiety and discriminative learning." *Amer. J. Psychol.*, **69**, 113-114 (1956).

371. STEVENSON, H. W., & MOUSHEGIAN, G. "The effect of instruction and degree of training on shifts of discriminative responses." *Amer. J. Psychol.*, **69**, 281-284 (1956).

372. STEWART, D. A. "Empathy, common ground of ethics and personality theory." *Psychoanal. Rev.*, **42**, 131-141 (1955).

373. STOLUROW, L. M., HODGSON, T. F., & SILVA, J. "Transfer and retroaction effects of 'association reversal' and 'familiarization' training in trouble shooting." *Psychol. Monogr.*, **70**, No. 12, Whole No. 419 (1956).

374. STRAHM, CAROLYN L. "The influence of instruction on performance of a complex perceptual motor task." *Canad. J. Psychol.*, **9**, 168-172 (1955).

375. SUMNER, F. C., & JOHNSON, E. E. "Sex differences in levels of aspiration and in self-estimates of performance in a classroom situation." *J. Psychol.*, **27**, 483-490 (1949).

376. SUTCLIFFE, J. P. "Responsiveness of the level of aspiration to success and failure as a function of task variability." *Aust. J. Psychol.*, **7**, 34-44 (1955).

377. SWANSON, R. A. "The relative effectiveness of training aids designed for use in mobile training detachments." *USAF Pers. Train. Res. Cent., Tech. Rep.*, No. 54-1 (1954).

378. SWEENEY, M. J. J. "The principle of learning." *J. gen. Psychol.*, **47**, 189-194 (1952).

379. SYMONDS, P. M. "What education has to learn from psychology." *Teach. Coll. Rec.*, **56**, 277-285 (1955).

380. SYMONDS, P. M. "What education has to learn from psychology: V. Learning is reacting." *Teach. Coll. Rec.*, **59**, 89-100 (1957).

381. TAFT, R. "The ability to judge people." *Psychol. Bull.*, **52**, 1-23 (1955).

382. TALLAND, G. A. "Criteria in conceptual transposition." *Amer. J. Psychol.*, **70**, 263-267 (1957).

383. TAYLOR, D. W., & MC NEMAR, OLGA W. "Problem-solving and thinking." *Am. Rev. Psychol.*, **6**, 455-477 (1955).

384. TEAHAN, J. E. "Future time perspective, optimism and academic achievement." *J. abnorm. soc. Psychol.*, **57**, 379-380 (1958).

385. TEEL, K., & WEBB, WILSE B. "Response evocation on satiated trials in the T-Maze." *J. exp. Psychol.*, **41**, 148-152 (1951).

386. THOMSON, R. *The psychology of thinking.* Baltimore, Md.: Penguin Books (1959).

387. THORNDIKE, E. L. *The fundamentals of learning.* New York: Teachers College, Columbia Univer. (1932).

388. THORNDIKE, E. L. *The psychology of wants, interests and attitudes.* New York: Appleton-Century-Crofts (1935).

389. THORNDIKE, E. L., & LORGE, I. *The teacher's word book of 30,000 words.* New York: Teachers College, Columbia Univer. (1944).

390. THORNE, F. *Principles of personality counseling; an eclectic viewpoint.* Brandon, Vermont: *J. clin. Psychol.* (1950).

391. TILTON, J. W. "The intercorrelations between measures of school learning." *J. Psychol.*, **35**, 167-179 (1953).

392. *Time*, p. 71, July 2, 1956.

393. TOLMAN, E. C. *Purposive behavior in animals and men.* New York: Appleton-Century-Crofts (1932).

394. TOLMAN, E. C. "There is more than one kind of learning." *Psychol. Rev.*, **56**, 144-155 (1949).

395. TOLMAN, E. C. "The psychology of social learning." *J. soc. Issues*, **5**, supplement No. 3, 5-19 (1949).

396. TOLMAN, E. C. "A psychological model." *Toward a general theory of action.* T. Parsons & E. A. Shils (Eds.) Cambridge, Mass.: Harvard University Press, pp. 279-361 (1951).

397. TOLMAN, E. C., & POSTMAN, L. "Learning." *Ann. Rev. Psychol.*, **5**, 27-56 (1954).

398. TSAO, J. C. "Studies in spaced and massed learning: II. Meaningfulness of material and distribution of practice." *Quart. J. exp. Psychol.*, **1**, 79-83 (1948).

399. TSAO, J. C. "Studies in spaced and massed learning: III. Paired-associate and serial learning." *Quart. J. exp. Psychol.*, **2**, 13-18 (1950).

400. TWINING, W. E. "Mental practice and physical practice in learning a motor skill." *Res. Quart. Amer. Ass. Hlth.*, **20**, 432-435 (1949).

401. UNDERWOOD, B. J. "Studies of distributed practice: IX. Learning and retention of paired adjectives as a function of intralist similarity." *J. exp. Psychol.*, **45**, 143-149 (1953).

402. UNDERWOOD, B. J. "Studies of distributed practice: XV. Verbal concept learning as a function of intralist interference." *J. exp. Psychol.*, **54**, 33-40 (1947).

403. UNDERWOOD, B. J., & ARCHER, E. J. "Studies of distributed practice: XIV. Intralist similarity and presentation rate in verbal-discrimination learning of consonant syllables." *J. exp. Psychol.*, **59**, 120-124 (1955).

404. UNDERWOOD, B. J., & HUGHES, R. H. "Gradients of generalized verbal responses." *Amer. J. Psychol.*, **63**, 422-430 (1951).

405. UNDERWOOD, B. J., & RICHARDSON, J. "Studies of distributed practice: XIII. Interlist interference and retention of serial nonsense lists." *J. exp. Psychol.*, **50**, 39-46 (1955).

406. UNDERWOOD, B. J., & RICHARDSON, J. "Verbal concept learning as a function of instructions and dominance level." *J. exp. Psychol.*, **51**, 229-238 (1956).

407. VANDERPLAS, J. M. "Transfer of training and its relation to perceptual learning and recognition." *Psychol. Rev.*, **65**, 375-385 (1958).

408. VINACKE, W. E. "Some variables in buzz sessions." *J. soc. Psychol.*, **45**, 25-33 (1957).

409. VOEKS, VIRGINIA W. "Postremity, recency, and frequency as bases for prediction in the maze situation." *J. exp. Psychol.*, **38**, 495-510 (1948).

410. VOEKS, VIRGINIA W. "Formalization and clarification of a theory of learning." *J. Psychol.*, **30**, 341-362 (1950).

411. VOEKS, VIRGINIA W. "Gradual strengthening of S-R connection or increasing number of S-R connections." *J. Psychol.*, **39**, 289-299 (1955).

412. WALL, W. D. "The psychology of basic educational techniques." *Current trends in British psychology.* C. A. Mace & P. E. Vernon (Eds.) London, England: Methuen, pp. 59-71, New York: British Book Centre (1953).

413. WEIGAND, G. "Goal aspiration and academic success." *Personnel Guid. J.*, **31**, 458-461 (1953).

414. WEISE, P., & BITTERMAN, M. E. "Response-selection in discriminative learning." *Psychol. Rev.*, **58**, 185-195 (1951).

415. WERTHEIMER, M. *Productive thinking.* New York: Harper (1945).

416. WHEELER, R. H. *The science of psychology.* (2nd ed.) New York: Crowell (1940).

417. WHERRY, R. J., & RETHLINGSHAFER, D. "An experimental verification of the structural nature of set." *J. gen. Psychol.*, **51**, 161-172 (1954).

418. WILLIAMS, M. "Rate of learning as a function of ego-alien material." *J. Pers.*, **19**, 324-331 (1951).

419. WINNICK, W. A., & HUNT, J. MC V. "The effect of an extra stimulus upon strength of response during acquisition and extinction." *J. exp. Psychol.*, **41**, 205-215 (1951).

420. WISHNER, J., SHIPLEY, T. E., JR., & HURVICH, M. S. "The serial-position curve as a function of organization." *Amer. J. Psychol.*, **70**, 258-262 (1957).

421. WOHLWILL, J. F. "The definition and analysis of perceptual learning." *Psychol. Rev.*, **65**, 283-295 (1958).

422. WOODWORTH, R. S. "Review of Hilgard, *Theories of learning.*" *J. abnorm. soc. Psychol.*, **44**, 124-129 (1949).

423. YERKES, R. M. "The mind of a gorilla." *Genet. Psychol. Monogr.*, **2**, 1-193 (1927).

424. YOUNG, R. K. "Retroactive and proactive effects under varying conditions of response similarity." *J. exp. Psychol.*, **50**, 113-119 (1955).

425. YUKER, H. E. "Group atmosphere and memory." *J. abnorm. soc. Psychol.*, **51**, 17-23 (1955).

426. ZIMMERMAN, D. W. "Durable secondary reinforcement: Method and theory." *Psychol. Rev.*, **64**, 373-383 (1957).

index